Sebastian Snow was [illegible] ted at Eton during the [illegible] arly travels included [illegible] nd and a lone overland [illegible] ot, from Istanbul to K [illegible] raq, Iran and Afghani [illegible] th America was as a m [illegible] urvey team exploring [illegible] mazon, and since then he has a [illegible] cities in Ecuador and made the first [illegible] from the source to the mouth of the A [illegible]

The Rucksack Man

SEBASTIAN SNOW

Foreword by Eric Newby

SPHERE BOOKS LIMITED
30/32 Gray's Inn Road, London WC1X 8JL

First published in Great Britain
by Hodder & Stoughton Ltd 1976

First Sphere Books edition 1977

To my father
1890–1975
a man among men

TRADE
MARK

Set in Linotype Baskerville

Printed in Great Britain by
Hazell Watson and Viney Ltd
Aylesbury, Bucks

Acknowledgements

I would like to thank all the participants in this book, without whose help this journey could not have been achieved.

In addition, I would like to thank George Greenfield and Christian Bonington for their staunch encouragement and support and Eric Newby for introducing me to *The Observer* and for writing the preface.

I am indebted to Jeremy Hunt of *The Observer* for his many kindnesses and to Tony Lock for helping with the equipment.

Also I am grateful to Venetia Pollock, Susan Lowndes Marques and Margaret Body of Hodder and Stoughton for their assistance with this book, and last, but by no means least, to Julian Tennant for virtually saving my life.

Contents

Illustrations

Acknowledgements
1 Chris Bonington
2 Wade Davies

Preface

This is the idiosyncratic account of one of the longest uninterrupted walks ever accomplished by one man, a distance of 8,700 miles from Tierra del Fuego to the Panama Canal.

The author, Sebastian Snow, has made numerous other serious attempts to perish, principally while exploring in Central and South America; but so far, what can only be described as a well-merited fate has been capriciously denied him. He came close to success while climbing the 17,496 foot Sangay, one of the world's more active volcanoes, having already climbed the highest active volcano in the world, El Cotopaxi (19,650 feet) thirteen years previously at the age of twenty-four. He also faced peril and privation on his numerous crossings of the sub-continent, among the more ambitious being a 3,505 mile traverse by way of the Amazon which took him ten months; another a bisection of it by inland waterways from the delta of the Orinoco to the estuary of the Rio de la Plata at Buenos Aires.

Few other men could have survived such a walk. It took him one and a half years. Christian Bonington, a conqueror of the Eiger and a personal friend, sent out by *The Observer* to accompany him on part of his journey was, according to Sebastian, reduced to wreckage after a few days. (I had suggested to *The Observer* that they should sign up Sebastian to send them despatches from the field. Henceforth he continued to do this unaided.)

Few would have survived the walk; few would have embarked upon it. The sheer monotony involved in walking all the way BY ROAD from Tierra del Fuego to Alsaka, for this was his original intention, in the age of the motor car, boggles the mind. This is why when I met Sebastian in London before he set off and asked him what sort of compass he would be taking (thinking that he would be fighting his way across the grain of South America through trackless country), I received the reply, 'Do you really think I ought to take one? Surely it's only a matter of keeping on going north?' And this he did, except in the last stages, where he made the crossing of the terrible swamps in the Darien Gap – the description is the best thing in the book – which finally breaks him and brings this chronicle of courageous endurance to a close.

Sebastian sets off from Tierra del Fuego, carrying sixty pounds weight of equipment on his back and a briefcase; what would be an enormous weight for a week on the Pennine Way, let alone traversing the entire American continent from south to north. He describes thirty-seven kilometres a day with this scarcely diminished burden (on page 45 he gives away the compass with which I had capriciously loaded him) as 'easy going'. He drinks what he calls 'the precious fluid' from ruts in the road without noticeably ill effects. What he calls 'a brisk walk' is the sixty-two miles or so from Latacunga to Quito, the world's highest capital, which he covers at an average altitude of 8,500 feet in eighteen hours, ten minutes. In Bolivia he averages over twenty-five miles a day for four days at heights between ten and twelve thousand feet. I stress these feats because otherwise his reasons for embarking on such a journey, apart from the attaining of almost impossible speeds – four and a half miles an hour in Patagonia with a ninety-five miles per hour following wind – are sometimes obscure. At one point, near Machu Picchu in Peru, in addition to his own load, he humps the hold-all of an American writer, eighty pounds in all.

And now he suffers in pursuing his inexorable rhythm, walking for one hour, then five or ten minutes rest, then 'on and on with the same swinging pace, hour after hour'. By the time he reached Medellin in Colombia he had taken eleven million, seven hundred and forty-five thousand paces. And he never accepted a lift. Sometimes it was almost too much for him, as when tottering along the tourist-infested shores of Lake Titicaca, bowed down by his load and an Argentinian money-belt stuffed with enough 'dollars, cheques and greenbacks' to ensure the immediate assassination of anyone but Snow, a walking gold mine, 'like a poor old blinkered Shire horse who has not long to go before he makes his last journey to the knackers' yard'. Blinkered because the contact lenses with which he has modishly equipped himself are choked with dust and cannot be extracted; frantic because sadistic drivers are aiming their vehicles at him so as to graze the off-side sleeve of his anorak.

Sebastian is prone to every kind of accident, some of them ludicrous. Besides having his toes sucked by great vampire bats and being in danger of being consumed by tigers and pumas while literally with his pants down, on one occasion he finds himself zipped inside an unzippable sleeping bag inside an equally unzippable tent which has collapsed on him – he attracts help by blowing a whistle.

What is Sebastian Snow? A strange mixture of naivety, diabolical intelligence, modesty, self-esteem, sentimentality, cynicism and sheer bloody toughness and courage. At times one is reminded of William Boot the anti-hero of Evelyn Waugh's *Scoop* and in fact, until recently, Boot and Snow had much in common, both inhabiting extensive houses in the country largely occupied by bed-ridden domestics who kept their savings under the bolster!

At others he more resembles another West Country traveller, the rumbustious Thomas Coryate of Odcombe in Somerset, who, between May and October, 1608, when he reached London from Venice, covered 1,975 miles, mostly on foot, visiting forty-five cities. On his return he hung up his shoes in Odcombe church. Later he departed for India where he perished from 'the flux'.

Frequent references in his book testify to Sebastian's affection for his old school. This I can substantiate.

In the summer of 1975 I happened to be crossing Dartmoor from north to south with what were at the time little more than the remains of the recently-returned-from-Central-America-Snow, still as blind as a bat with his contact lenses lost somewhere beneath his upper lids, now in nil visibility with wind force 7. Here, somewhere in a trackless morass, we stopped so that he could eat a great, gruesome, squashed pasty, provided by his mother. When he finally hove it from his pack it was found to be wrapped in an Old Etonian tie.

'Sebastian,' I shrieked (the only way to make myself heard above the blast). 'What on earth are you doing in the middle of Dartmoor with an Old Etonian tie?'

'Oh,' says Snow, 'I though we might meet someone.'

ERIC NEWBY

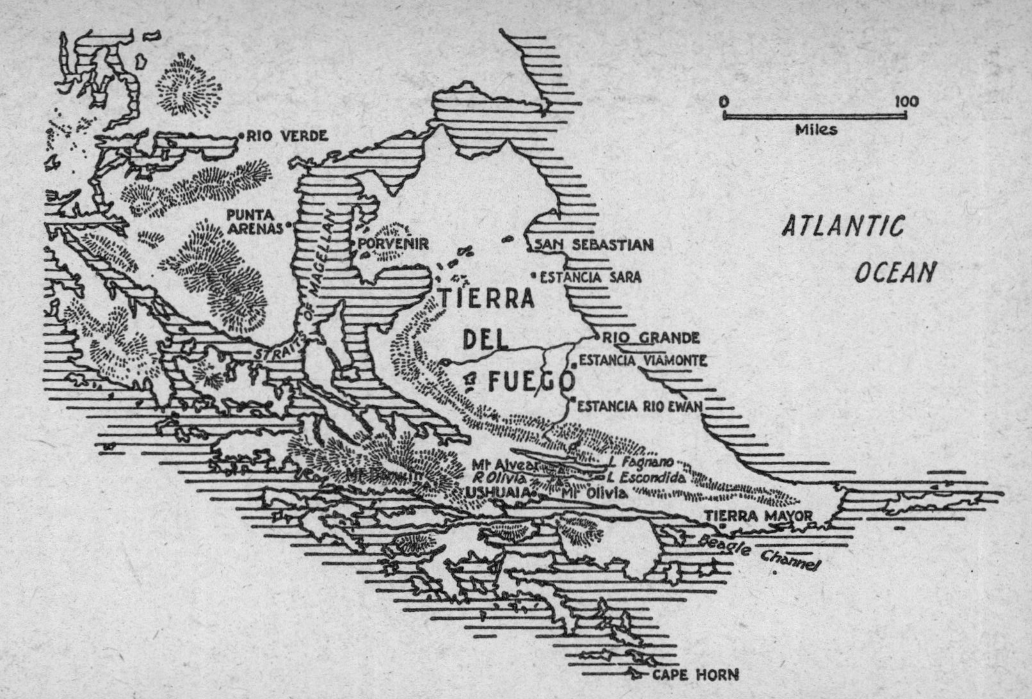
0
100
Miles
RIO VERDE
PUNTA ARENAS
STRAITS OF MAGELLAN
PORVENIR
SAN SEBASTIAN
ESTANCIA SARA
TIERRA DEL FUEGO
RIO GRANDE
ESTANCIA VIAMONTE
ESTANCIA RIO EWAN
ATLANTIC OCEAN
Mt Alvear
R Olivia
USHUAIA
L Fagnano
L Escondida
Mt Olivia
TIERRA MAYOR
Beagle Channel
CAPE HORN

CHAPTER ONE

TIERRA DEL FUEGO

In order to walk the continent of South America from south to north, I had first to reach my starting point, the southern most tip of Tierra del Fuego, which was the city of Ushuaia. Despite missing connections through oversleeping, losing my grandfather's ebony walking stick, suffering a very choppy, sea-sick-making crossing of the Straits of Magellan and mending many punctures on other people's cars, I managed to fly, ferry and hitch-hike from England to my destination by February. This was important as only the autumn and winter months are calm, cool and relatively free from violent winds.

Cape Horn is, of course, the most southerly point of all but it is a bare rock in the midst of the ocean. To get there would mean hiring a boat. As I was on a walking trip, there seemed little point in sailing out to the Horn, touching it, and sailing back again as no walking would be involved, so Ushuaia it would have to be.

Ushuaia was a strange place in which to set foot, the capital of the island, the most southern city in the world, though city was surely only a name for this place, for it was little more than a small town snuggling into the foothills of the southern-most ranges of the Andes. The Yahgan Indians had always used it as a port long before the Argentinians raised their flag there. Now its deep water harbour makes it a most useful naval base.

I wandered its windswept streets looking for somewhere to stay. I tried the police station and the church but found no joy in either. Finally I fetched up in a two dollar a night doss house called rather grandly the Hotel Castellar. The first person I met there was a bespectacled bearded American collecting material for a travel guide, who immediately asked me if I had read a very amusing book called *A Short Walk in the Hindu Kush*: I had indeed; a proud moment for Eric Newby.

Earlier I had encountered a soignée American anthropologist who was endeavouring to preserve the Ona Indian language for posterity. A fight against heavy odds as there appeared to be only about one pure Ona Indian left on the island. Avid for more information, I plied her with questions about the Indians, for I would be living amongst them in days to come and wanted to know what to expect. Evidently there had been four distinct indigenous tribes on Tierra del Fuego, each speaking their own language, and the Onas had been the largest and most important. They hadn't been killed off by the Argentinians but had caught the diseases of the first white men to arrive and had rapidly succumbed to tuberculosis, measles and 'flu.

The Ona had lived on the guanaco, an animal somewhat like the llama which I hoped to encounter the following day when I began my walk.

The Ona, my new acquaintance informed me, had hunted it on foot with bows and arrows and had worn its skin fur-side out for clothing. They appear to have been ferocious people as another Indian tribe, the Yahgan, used to move camp every few days for fear of the Onas and had only dared to venture into the interior once a year to make their heavy sea-going canoes. The Yahgans had been extremely deft with their harpoons and spears, catching seals as well as fish. Their canoes were rowed by the women and the children crouched in the centre round a fire of glowing wood which was always kept on a heap of flat stones at the bottom of the canoe. They had to have fires as their clothing consisted of just a small sealskin and in this way they could carry fire from campsite to campsite. Mounds of mussels all round the beaches of the Beagle Channel marked where they had been.

For dinner that night I had a most delicious *centolla,*

a large orange coloured crab and excellent mussels. Sad to think that there were only five pure Yahgans left alive despite their staple diet of mussels and crab being so plentiful. Still, that was better than the Haush tribe: none of them were left. What about the fourth? I enquired. They were called Alakalufs: they had had sails on their canoes and so had ranged farther afield to more isolated spots. Nobody knew for sure how many of them remained but it was thought that there were more of them than any of the other tribes scattered throughout the islands.

It didn't sound as though I was likely to meet many Indians, which perhaps was just as well. Having satisfied myself on that score I went off to check my rucksack.

I had spent some considerable time wondering what I should take with me. It was an impossibly difficult task, for I would be travelling through snow and desert sand; in rain and at immensely high altitudes; the variations were extreme. Best therefore to simplify the whole and wear what I was used to and stick to what I walked in at home: some Derbyshire tweed knickerbockers, a pair of long Norwegian mountaineering knee socks made out of pure wool, a heavy double ventile anorak and the usual vest, pants, shirt and hand-knitted sweater. I'd need several changes of clothes but they could all be of the same type and the less I took, the less I would have to carry.

Vitally important were several pairs of contact lenses, my spectacles, a Pindisport tent and sleeping bag, a watch and a camera. But most essential of all would be several pairs of footwear. I walked in soft light supple Italian Sella walking-cum-climbing boots made of leather. How long would each pair last? How many should I carry?

Would I need something to read on lonely evenings as I did not speak the language, or would I be so tired I'd fall instantly asleep? In the end I took too many books for they were so very heavy. Medicines, maps, a compass and a torch were a must and also a plastic mug so that I could drink from passing streams. Water would be too heavy and awkward to carry and so would food but I'd have to take something for when I got stuck on the way and had to spend the night camping in the wilds. Otherwise I was determined to eat at local inns. If I travelled light then I would need money; money to pay for food and lodgings for months on end. That and my passport had to be thief proof.

I dithered about, pushing things in and pulling them out. Finally the next day, 5th February 1973, I started walking due north, carrying a sixty-pound pack on my back. It was so heavy that I had the greatest possible difficulty getting out of Ushuaia. Within ten minutes I lost all movement in my arms which had become completely numb, as I had tied the rucksack straps too tight.

Although it was impossible to get lost I enquired of a passerby the road to Kaiken and was told there was only one road and I was on it. As I slowly headed and heaved north I saw the photogenic Mount Olivaia towering four thousand feet to my right and the peaks of the Martial Massif to my left looking like Gothic spires.

The road was not tarmaced. I found the going heavy; sweat poured off my face and eyebrows in rivulets and every time a vehicle passed I was blinded with dust which infiltrated behind my contact lenses causing agony – an agony that I stupidly put up with for nineteen months.

After about nine and a half kilometres of dog-potting through the mountains a Canadian motorcyclist stopped beside me and said, 'Poor soul. Aren't you a famous author?'

'No,' I replied, but he persisted, saying,

'Yes, I've got it – your name is Scott.'

'My name is Snow.'

'Ah, yes, I knew it began with an "S".'

He'd driven from Quebec in exactly three months which sounded good going.

I wondered how long it would take me to reach Panama City and what adventures would befall me on the way. I had walked and climbed before in South America and had always found walking by far the best way of getting to know and understand a country. You are in touch with the land, palpably through the soles of your feet the entire time, not insulated from it by glass or perspex. You see the landscape unfold slowly before you and come to understand something of its rhythm, its harshness or softness, its sense of space. You see a village a long way off, and approach it slowly as the inhabitants do. By the time you have reached it you are getting to know its silhouette well, you have had time to assimilate it, to work out its plan, to think about its people and to wonder what lies ahead.

You can talk to all whom you meet at your leisure and you have some understanding of their lives, their problems and their attitudes for you too are steeped in the landscape, in the contours of the land, in the feeling of the wind and the rain and the force of the elements.

Walking is man's natural pace, his normal speed of progress. At this tempo you have time to think, to reflect and to cogitate on what you see around you. It is lonely but then I've always found it a welcome loneliness. Once a steady rhythm has been established you can let your mind go quite blank or you can be alert, watching for birds or animals. You can amble along in a peaceful relaxing silence or you can indulge in a thought-provoking period, in reflection or private inner argument. Nobody interrupts.

Walking is a delightfully self-reliant activity, no companions to let you down, no animals to contend with, no engine to fail. If you feel lazy, stay another day. If you feel immensely energetic, increase the speed. It's a hobby in which all can indulge, it doesn't need vast equipment, complex training schedules or other people.

The great art is not to worry or fuss, not to bustle or push but to set yourself a task and to muddle through the pressures at your own pace; ignore physical discomfort, remain amused by complications. Just keep going.

Or at least, that was what I'd always found. Would it be the same walking a whole continent?

As I stumbled along that first day I wished that my preparations for the trip had been more thorough. I had wandered the lanes of Devon for a couple of hours each day in order to get fit, but it had clearly been insufficient training. I only managed another three and a quarter kilometres that day which made it the shortest of my whole trip. I stopped exhausted at a hosteria where cakes and soft drinks were served, only too grateful to rest.

At night the hosteria turned into a nightclub. It was called Monte Olivaia and was crowded out with a busload of elderly American tourists who, of all things, had just been to the South Pole. They were all very enterprising, enthusiastic and vociferous, equipped with very expensive cameras that hung – ready for instant action – around their necks, drooping like pendulums over paunchy stomachs. I took my hat off to them. One of them edged up to me and said critically, 'You are from Exeter, England, are you not?' 'Yes,' I answered. 'How on earth did you know?' 'I can read people's minds,' was the enigmatic rejoinder.

A very chic heavy-lidded French dame – rather like Juliette Greco in her younger night-club days – yelled out that I would never make it over the first range of mountains. I made a very rude sign – which she reciprocated with gusto – and passed on.

That night I made my first camp near the hosteria beside a trout stream. I took one and a half hours putting up my tent which a clueless boy scout could have run up in three minutes blindfold in a force ten gale. All I had to do was to slip three clips into five holes. I had no sleep, experiencing bloody awful toothache and squitters – until the tent fell on top of me and I had something else to think about.

On 6th February I left Monte Olivaia late – at ten fifteen a.m. – I couldn't get out of the tent – under a very hot sun tempered by a fresh breeze. The few drivers of the vehicles that passed looked at me as if I was 'loco' for no Argentine walks and he is inclined to despise those who do or thinks they are creatures from another planet – Martians perhaps.

I stumped along the Cabajal Valley red with sphagnum covered swamps on either side of the trail. I noticed the shadow lakes which had sometimes formed and the jagged peaks of the mountains that are the highest in the island. Alvear, an extraordinary dome-shaped mountain loomed ahead of me, but the shapes of the ever more enclosing hills were astonishing, blue and white glaciers glistened in the sun, long after the valley was deep in shadow, turning a rosy red as the sun went slowly down.

That day I covered about twenty-four kilometres laagering in a small beechwood corral between the road and the River Olivaia. The site resembled an Alpine pasture with lush green alfalfa grass and snow capped peaks.

The following day – 7th February – there was much uphill work as the Cabajal Valley narrowed at last into the Valley of the Tierra Mayor. Here the forests begin and it was fascinating to see the workings of the beavers, who make dams all along the many tributaries. The large beaver dams are protected by law and in many cases the dams have disguised the narrow trails along the canyons in the mountains and sheep can and do cross the ice bridges formed by beaver lakes in winter.

At last I reached the 432 metre (1,419 feet) pass called Garibaldi, named, God knows why, after an Ona Indian in the service of the police force. The track up the mountains followed the Rio Hambre but just before reaching the summit of the pass, I had fortunately been told to look out for a hidden waterfall and from there it was easy to reach the top of the mountain above with a marvellous view of almost the whole of the range. Great Andean condors hovered high above.

An extraordinary variety of birds haunt Tierra del Fuego. I was astonished to see flamingoes, humming birds and a huge number of geese and many different breeds of ducks, including the steamer duck which paddles rapidly over the surface of the water, using its wings as it cannot fly. Rare sea birds flew in from the ocean, giant petrels, albatross, blue and white eagles and large hawks hovering for prey.

Once through the pass the road dropped in steep corkscrew to the Escondida Lake, well hidden far below by ubiquitous beech trees. Having made my way down I stopped at the Hosteria Petrel and blessed the man who had thought of placing this rest house in such a splendid position. Strangely enough, but then Tierra del Fuego is a land of surprises, the largest sawmill in the world operates on the far shores of this lake. The local beechwoods are cut and processed for local use and for export.

Next day I was shadowed by two dogs for several kilometres, a sheep dog and a fierce looking Alsatian. However, I plodded on steadily to the next lake, Fagnano, which turned out to be a vast body of water over 100 kilometres long but only about a quarter as wide. No boats to be seen as it is constantly storm swept and has a reputation for turbulence and treachery. The western end of this lake creeps across into Chile but I walked round its eastern Argentinian end under a modest looking mound called Mount Heuhuysen which the superstitious Onas once venerated with awe, believing that the wrath of the gods would come down on anyone attempting to ascend it.

On the low cliff face directly below the mountain was the Kaiken Hosteria which overlooked an 'abandoned' observation station built by the French for tracking satellites, reminding me of one of Don Quixote's windmills.

At Kaiken, which is the Fuegian name for the upland goose, three Argentinian policemen very sportingly transported my rucksack to Estancia Viamonte – the home of the British Consul, Oliver Bridges – two days' march further up the road.

On leaving Kaiken I was again followed by more dogs, three this time, one was soon collected by its owner, but the other two came all the way to Estancia Rio Ewan – over twenty kilometres distant. I walked it in four and a half hours non-stop with a great deal of head wind.

At Estancia Rio Ewan I was bounteously entertained with great hospitality and kindness by the Reynolds family. The Reynolds are cousins of the Bridges, their land is contiguous. The estancia has approximately 17,500 hectares (43,242 acres) carrying 12,000 sheep plus one 'tame' one. With one sheep per hectare (two and a half acres) and one cow per five hectares (twelve and a half acres) it is an expensive form of farming – probably the most expensive form in the world; but it must be borne in mind that land is very cheap by European standards. On average a single field is 1,600 hectares (4,000 acres) in extent and some are as much as 2,828 hectares (7,000 acres). The estancia is beautifully situated in a wide valley through which the small River Ewan flows gently below Antarctic beech covered hills – festooned with lichens – rising some 213 metres (700 feet) above the valley.

On nearing Estancia Ewan one of my dogs caused widespread panic among the Reynolds' sheep (the supreme solecism in this part of the world); I trust we were unobserved, although I'm inclined to think this unlikely. All the same, I was benignly greeted by Moses, the camp cook, with four bumper mugs of delicious hot tea. Then George Reynolds arrived and took me up to the estancia where he introduced me to his mother, Hélène, and his sister Pamela. His mother introduced me to a bath. She flashed a tin of Johnson's Baby Powder at me in an arch kind of way, then frog-marched me to the bathroom in a rather menacing, yet wholly delightful manner – as if introducing me to the block.

I stayed a couple of days with the Reynolds family, mooching round their drawing room feeling slack after recurrent attacks of squitters. One evening Pamela suddenly played 'Whispering' on the gramophone, without knowing that for years it had been my favourite tune.

Resuscitated, the next day I sauntered some twenty kilometres further down the unasphalted and undulating road to Estancia Viamonte, where I was warmly greeted by Betsy Bridges who at once made me feel at home.

The Honorary British Consul, Oliver Bridges, was out fishing for mullet; the rivers are well stocked with brown and rainbow trout, some as big as seventeen and a half pounds.

The Bridges family are the most respected and best known on the island and their knowledge of it is unparalleled. Oliver Bridges' uncle, E. Lucas Bridges wrote the classic *Uttermost Part of the Earth* and Oliver Bridges' grandfather Thomas Bridges and his wife Mary were the first white people to settle permanently in Tierra del Fuego. Thomas Bridges first came to Keppel Island in 1856 at the age of thirteen – and grew up to establish an Anglican mission. In 1886 Thomas Bridges left the mission, became an Argentine citizen and on behalf of the Government was offered land in return for his work among the natives and shipwrecked sailors. Bridges chose Harberton, built in 1890, some fifty kilometres east of Ushuaia on the coast among fjords where he began the very first farm on the island.

In 1902 Thomas Bridges' son Lucas Bridges opened the first road, drove his cattle over the mountains and established himself at Viamonte. Viamonte now has 36,000 hectares (87,956 acres).

The day after I arrived, Oliver went out fishing again and Betsy became very worried when he did not return at the stipulated time. A rescue expedition was sent and then a further rescue expedition to rescue the rescue expedition. Oliver had had a bad heart attack last year; however, he returned in great good humour with a goodly haul of mullet in the back of his Land Rover. As he came in he said with a grin in a conspiratorial aside to me, 'I expect I shall get scolded for this.'

During one of the six days I spent with the Bridges, Betsy and I had a very giggly time trying to get my camera back in its case. It took us over two hours just to make it fit, which it didn't.

On my last day at Viamonte, we went to the Reynolds' for an *'asado'* or barbecue. We arrived punctually, *el hora Ingles* being observed, but unfortunately twenty-four hours too soon! We bolted down a Martini proffered by the Reynolds' butler and fled!

I asked Oliver, who was a mine of information, what animals were indigenous and he said the guanaco and the Fuegian red fox. The latter is large with a superb pelt. As they kill sheep whenever they have a chance, a high price is paid for their skins which make excellent rugs, but they are in no danger of being exterminated as there are vast expanses inland where they can breed in peace, for these parts of the island are seldom penetrated by man. There is also a small rodent, the cururu or tucu-tucu, which lives in shallow burrows and a small lizard with yellow stripes on its brown skin. Unfortunately rabbits were introduced into the island and have become, as elsewhere, the greatest pest, many formerly rich sheep farms now being reduced to a few animals because all the pastures have been eaten or fouled by rabbits. The most original importation however was that of reindeer from Scandinavia, which might well have become naturalised, with who knows what results, but all traces of these animals have disappeared.

Each day I was at Viamonte I went for a brisk walk to keep in training; one day I took Pandora, Betsy's thirteen-year-old poodle (ninety-one years old in a dog's life span) – she went along on her leash like a whizz-bang. I couldn't keep up with her – the only time I was out-walked.

When I came to leave Viamonte, Betsy furnished me with introductions from Bariloche to Panama City. Until one has experienced it, one has no idea of the lengths these people go to help strangers; they seemed to me then, and now, very courteous, very civilised and very cosmopolitan people.

I strolled into Rio Grande, about thirty-one kilometres from Viamonte, passing El Frigorifico Freezer en route where between one hundred and fifty thousand and two hundred thousand sheep and lambs are slaughtered and frozen annually. Rio Grande – population 5,000 – is very much like a Wild West town, Laramie perhaps, as one enters from the south. I stayed a couple of nights there, putting up my tent in an unoccupied plot in the centre. I purchased food from the supermarket for the remainder of my journey across the island. At dinner on my last evening in Rio Grande I heard an English voice just behind me in an unpretentious restaurant – his name was Jack Comben of *The Express* – a real journalist. All the world is a tent – especially when he said, 'I know you, you are old Sibby Snow'.

Actually we had never met, although of course, I had heard of him by repute. He had covered the Latin American scene for over twenty years. What he was doing in Rio Grande, Tierra del Fuego, I do not recall – but I do remember he asked me the most pertinent question anyone ever asked throughout my entire walk. Quite simply, 'What do you think about when you are walking?' At that very early stage I was stumped for a reply.

A few miles north of Rio Grande are oil rigs and there is a big camp built by the Tennessee Argentina Company but now completely state owned. Here I received a great welcome at the club for employees. Not far away was a Salesian agricultural school and farm for boys. It had started as a mission to the Indians but when the Indians gradually faded away the Salesian Fathers sensibly turned the place into a technical training school with a local museum attached. I wandered round this museum and found it full of local Indian remains and artefacts.

Gradually the terrain changed completely. Here in the northern part of the island, the rainfall was much lower and the land less rugged. The sea was deep blue and beside it were mile upon mile of grassy salt flats, a haven for sheep. It was here, on this salty herbage, that I got my first really good view of a guanaco and first heard its strange laughing cry. I was even more astonished than I expected to be by this llama-like animal's strange proportions, for it looked as if it had been drawn by a clever child. They usually spend most of their time up in the mountains where miles of wild bog and close scrub protect them from hunters.

Two days later I arrived at the Estancia Sara, the biggest one on the whole island of Tierra del Fuego, 60,000 hectares (145,260 acres) with 70,000 sheep. Despite various land reform legislation passed by different governments, not all the sheep ranches have been divided up. About fourteen kilometres away was the world famous Maria Behety Estancia which has the largest sheep shearing shed in the world, big enough for forty shearers to work inside at once.

The Sara's manager was a Scot Falkland Islander who most kindly entertained me to dinner and provided me with quarters. He told me that most of the unskilled labourers on all the estancias came originally from the southern island of Chiloe. Work is hardest at lambing time in October, then in November the sheep's ears are marked, their tails cut off and they are castrated. In late December shearing starts and continues into January.

When all is done the wool is graded, baled and trucked to the nearest port. In February all the sheep are dipped completely, in March the castrated ones are sold. In April and August the sheep are sheared round their eyes which is known as wigging; in no time at all it is round to lambing again.

The great estancias are largely self-supporting, growing most of their own food and having on their pay rolls carpenters, electricians, blacksmiths, painters and stonemasons. Essential non-local supplies come once a year in summer from Buenos Aires when the owners too come for their annual visit. Many do not live on their properties because there are no schools for their children and their wives find it rather bleak, lonely and remote.

However I was in luck in more ways than one at the Sara for one of the owners dropped in for a drink with his wife and kindly offered to take my rucksack to the Argentine border post for me whilst I walked.

I had a further slice of luck at San Sebastian, the Chilean frontier post. Ordinarily, tourists, such as myself, have to spend ten dollars (or four pounds) a day excluding bed and board during their stay in Chile under the present regime. I was 'exempted' for twenty-five days as I was walking, a very charitable gesture, but I had to keep walking . . . that was the rule and the rub.

From the frontier I made the final 144 kilometres to the end of the island in four and a half days, slow going, but I encountered very strong headwinds which I could practically lean against without falling over. If these were light autumn winds, I was glad I was going to be off Tierra del Fuego before March brought stronger gales.

Two nights before I reached Porvenir my tent blew out of my hands as I was struggling to put it up. Eventually I caught up with it a full quarter of a mile down the road towards San Sebastian. When I finally got it up, it fell on top of me at midnight.

I reached Porvenir on Wednesday, 28th February in

good time to sail on the *Melinka* at seven p.m. She was a World War II D Day landing craft that plied twice a day across the Straits of Magellan, a distance at this point of about twenty miles which she managed in just over three hours. The crossing was choppy and many were sick, some deliberately so – over me. No facilities for being sick so everywhere was sick. I saw a good number of birds circling round the boat, cormorants, black gulls, terns and ducks. I had hoped to see dolphins but was out of luck; quite a few albatross wheeling overhead though.

Arriving at Tres Puentes, I walked the final five and a half kilometres into the heart of Punta Arenas in forty-five minutes and very nearly disappeared forever down a manhole en route. Although I had only covered a paltry 300 kilometres I was beginning to get into my stride.

CHAPTER TWO

CHILE

Punta Arenas, on the mainland of South America, turned out to be a much bigger town than I had expected with over eighty thousand inhabitants, a mixed bunch of Spanish, Chilean, German and Yugoslav. The conversation of the latter increased its similarity to an Adriatic town. Once of international importance, the opening of the Panama Canal had left it with only local significance. The British club, founded in 1899, was rather forlorn and lonely but I drank whiskey with the warm-hearted British Consul and talked cricket.

During my stay I wandered round the town, gazed at the imposing bronze monument to Ferdinand Magellan, first man through the Straits in 1520 and wondered what had happened to him. Had he been eaten by cannibals in the Moluccas? I could not remember. Wasn't it he, though, who had christened Tierra del Fuego, Fireland, because as he passed through the Straits he saw the camp fires of the Ona Indians burning busily?

I stocked up with the bare necessities of life such as a tin of Nescafé, two kilos of raisins, twenty bars of milk chocolate and a rude, foot long stick of salami – gratis – like a policeman's truncheon. With the connivance of a local Englishman I tried to purchase porridge but failed. Eric Shipton had left Punta Arenas the previous day to climb Mount Burney and he had denuded the town of porridge.

There was a great shortage of domestic essentials in the city such as lavatory paper (paperback books came in handy), toothpaste, biscuits, tinned milk, soups, vegetables, rice, sugar, cocoa and coffee. Complaints were levelled against the regime although Punta Arenas was alleged to have been ninety per cent in favour of Allende. Whilst I was there, there was an election in progress for deputies and senators to the Chilean Congress and clearly trouble was expected for there were large numbers of troops with sub-machine guns in evidence but nothing occurred. I felt let down.

As I crept out of Punta Arenas at early dawn and headed northwards past the airport, the country graduated from an almost treeless pampa or steppe to rolling, rounded undulating hills and valleys dotted and pockmarked with pine and cypress coppices carpeted with lush fields of dandelions where vast flocks of sheep and lambs grazed, together with herds of cows that stared at me with large red rheumy eyes, plus horses who snorted and whinnied and cantered beside the roadside fence as I passed, tails flying in the wind.

On occasion I saw herdsmen in sheepskin jackets and 'chaps', long leggings made from sheepskin, with their dogs, herding sheep across the dirt road. Once I thought I saw a small ostrich. I did. In fact I saw many small ostriches wisely trying to bury their heads, but not succeeding.

As things worked out I need not have brought any food at all. I need not have stocked up with all that Nescafé, chocolate and salami nor need I have humped a fifty pound pack along on my back, for everywhere people were extremely hospitable and generous.

Averaging between twenty-four and thirty-two kilometres a day I stayed at estancias belonging to the state, co-operative estancias, roadmen's small yellow wooden houses and a road construction camp.

Approximately sixty per cent of the estancias in Chile belong to the state, twenty-five per cent are co-operatives and the rest are still privately owned, but the latter are dwindling every day and they are all, in Argentinian terms, 'small' – the largest being about 5,000 hectares (12,355 acres).

There are two large state-owned estancias between

Punta Arenas and Puerto Natales, one is 120,000 hectares (296,520 acres), called Laguna Blanca, and the other, where I stayed in some luxury, is Estancia Tranquillo of 40,000 hectares (98,840 acres), employing 150 men carrying 30,000 sheep and 10,000 head of cattle. It was administered by a charming man, whose father was Yugoslav, who gave me a great deal of assistance. A friend of President Allende came to dinner and stayed the night.

The co-operative farms are rather different. The one I stayed at called Tehuelche has 20,000 hectares (49,420 acres) and 21,000 sheep. A group of twenty workers run it, each having his own share of 1,000 hectares (2,471 acres): there is no boss, but an agricultural technician. Some of the fields are 7,000 acres in extent, rather like England before enclosure.

Puerto Natales turned out to be in the district of Ultima Esperanza meaning Last Hope but it teemed with life, positively vibrated. Last year even a ship came in, magic of magics.

I was moving slowly up the map; I would have liked to have continued due north through Chile but there was an ice cap in the way so I had to cross over into the Argentine.

Puerto Natales
13th March 1973

Dear J.,
I have lost my Olympus camera. I am greatly annoyed as the scenery is becoming increasingly compelling. Have asked my parents to send another (Olympus) to the Bank of London and South America Ltd., Av. San Martin 1498, Mendoza, Argentina. Mendoza is miles north, but there is no place in between of any consequence.

My khaki shirt has turned white and I haven't taken off my climbing breeches since I began, otherwise I am very fit and in excellent spirits. I am running out of shoe (boot) leather. Could you *very* kindly ask 'Pindisports' Holborn (there is a man called Tony Lack or Ray Garratt whom I had dealings with re: equipment), to send two pairs of 'Sella' boots, size nine to the Bank of London, Mendoza, Argentina.

I think Tony Lack or Ray Garratt have a record of the size of my boots.

Yours ever,
Sebastian.

P.S. Please have the bill sent to my parents who have my power of attorney.
P.P.S. Could you ask Pindisports to put on the parcel *'TO AWAIT ARRIVAL'*.

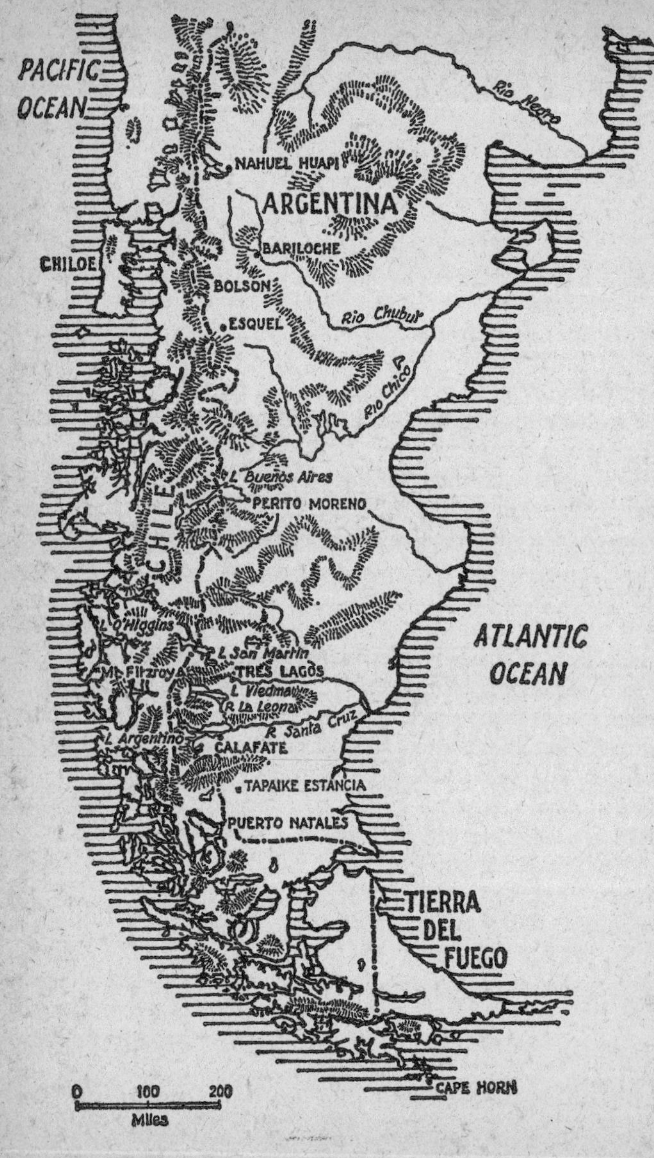
PACIFIC
OCEAN
NAHUEL HUAPI
ARGENTINA
Rio Negro
BARILOCHE
CHILOE
BOLSON
ESQUEL
Rio Chubut
Rio Chico
L. Buenos Aires
PERITO MORENO
CHILE
L. O'Higgins
L. San Martin
Mt. Fitzroy
TRES LAGOS
L. Viedma
R. La Leona
R. Santa Cruz
L. Argentino
CALAFATE
TAPAIKE ESTANCIA
PUERTO NATALES
ATLANTIC
OCEAN
TIERRA
DEL
FUEGO
CAPE HORN
0
100
200
Miles

CHAPTER THREE

PATAGONIA

At the Argentinian frontier post I was greeted by the local frontier police who asked me if I was a poet as my hair had grown so long.

Then rain set in. It rained like hell in the very early morning and I thought I would have to stay in my tent all day, but around eight a.m. the weather cleared and I managed to make my way to a local pub called the Fuentes del Coyle. Thirty-four kilometres in six hours due to the most ferocious following wind I have ever encountered in my travels. Really formidable 200 kilometre gusts that often changed direction and I would be thrown bodily across the dirt road to lie in an undignified heap in the opposite ditch. This occurred no less than four times on the way.

With such a wind, the mind becomes woolly and completely benumbed: it was only through a conscious act of will that I managed to remember where I was heading. I have never taken such a beating. I was given a friendly greeting at a lonely pub and paid only about tenpence for a large dinner and a night's stay.

'You have only stayed the night, have you not, Senor?' asked the owner with a wink. I lied and replied 'Yes.'

'You have only had two cups of coffee, haven't you?' he prompted again.

Such is Patagonian hospitality.

The following day I reached the estancia of Tapi-aike which was a large farm of 60,000 hectares (148,265 acres) carrying 26,000 Corriedale sheep. This is a breed created in New Zealand from a cross between a merino and Romney Marsh, a Lincoln and a merino. The owner was of Spanish descent and told me how his great-grandfather had sailed from Asturia to the Argentine in 1865 and had come to own over a million hectares of land. He had been the husband of Maria Behety of the-largest-sheep-shearing-shed-in-the-world fame, that I had already heard about in Tierra del Fuego. Evidently this old boy in his prime had possessed over four hundred thousand sheep. He'd died in 1918 and then his son (grandfather of the man to whom I was talking) had enlarged the family holding until he owned three or four million hectares (7,413,000 or 9,884,000 acres) including thirty or forty farms in Argentina, more in Chile, others on Tierra del Fuego, the whole island of Chiloe and Aconcagua, the highest mountain in South America. I've always wanted to own a mountain ever since I met the owner of the source of the River Amazon and its surrounding cirque of lakes.

The grandfather died in 1952 leaving a vast family of about one hundred and thirty descendants of fourth and fifth generation Argentinians who averaged some seven thousand sheep apiece.

From this estancia I walked over some waterless pampa of the pre-cordillera which was bare, windy, undulating steppe. They had warned me at the farm to take another bottle of water along with strict instructions to harbour the 'precious fluid' but on the contrary I found no difficulty in finding the odd stream or spring.

I was also told there was a shepherd's hut thirty kilometres away which had water in abundance. It is customary in these parts to enter the huts and drink one's fill whether the shepherd is there or not. But I did not stop and after about forty kilometres I camped in a large valley with a delicious pellucid stream running through it and high lush green alfalfa-like grass. Whenever there is verdant, succulent grass there are nearly always sheep grazing and horses gambolling – tails outstretched, like pennants in the wind.

En route I met but one vehicle – belonging to an

American schoolteacher and his wife who took an entire roll of film of me, before I could say 'Cut'.

Next day (21st March – Wednesday) I fetched up at an isolated Police Puesto where a youngish policeman in plain clothes and his wire-haired terrier scrutinised my passport and gave me an early luncheon of mutton and vegetables together with endless cups of Nescafé.

I reached the unpaved main road at a lonely pub called El Cerrito having passed through the flat open waterless scrub country after leaving the Police Puesto. El Cerrito is not exactly a four-star joint and one would not find it in Egon Ronay's good food guide, but the manager and his attractive wife were very courteous and made me feel at home. At the bar there was a very charming gentleman completely drunk, highly convivial and sublimely boring.

The next day I endeavoured to reach a similar kind of pub at a place called Rio Bote – fifty kilometres distant – but failed, due to a really hellish headwind relentlessly singing around my ears that rendered me sightless in a cataclysmic cloudburst. I was forced to camp on the high, bare arid windswept plateau of the pre-cordillera near a lake, where, I was later told, someone had once camped and had not survived the night. I took two hours to erect my tent, which normally efficient people would do in three or four minutes, because of the really bloody awful tempest that beset me and inflated the tent like a barrage balloon. Three times the tent blew into the lake 270 metres away before I was able to peg it into some loose chalk shale. I couldn't have chosen a more exposed or inhospitable camp site if I had tried – and I did try. Sleep was out of the question and twice the tent blew down on top of me: I had a fearful time in the freezing cold and total darkness erecting it again. It was even too cold to die. I was away at eight o'clock next day. It was utter hell packing my rucksack, my fingers burnt with the cold – even with three pairs of gloves on. It was four hours before any feeling whatever returned to them.

Down in the valley the local people took one horrified look at me and kept repeating, 'What a sacrifice, Senor!'

'What a record!'

'What courage!'

'What patriotism!'

I was destined to hear the same epithets repeated many, many times on my long march.

At the bottom of the valley I dined at the Hotel Bote and camped outside it in a pig and chicken run. I had a comfortable night; two birds came and roosted in the 'foyer' of my tent – and one had the courtesy to lay an egg for my breakfast.

The proprietor of the hotel had said unequivocably at dinner that I would not be able to go any further, because a river called the Centinela was utterly unfordable; the bridge had broken down and been demolished by flood. However, when I arrived at this 'terrible' torrent I just waded across it; the water only came up to my knees. I did not even trouble to take my boots off, I didn't have the time or the inclination.

My goal in this part of the world was Mrs. Atkinson's estancia in the midst of a national park full of glaciers. Once I had arrived at the Estancia Lago Roca I would have covered 700 kilometres (455 miles) from Ushuaia which would look quite a respectable distance even on a small scale school atlas.

Mrs. Atkinson turned out to be the acme of warmth and generosity. With her two brothers she farms over nine thousand hectares (22,240 acres) at the head of Lake Argentino not far from the famous Moreno glacier. The glaciers extended over enormous areas in Pleistocene times and the present ones were formed over thirty thousand years ago. The great Moreno has been advancing slowly for years and each time it does so Mrs. Atkinson's farm gets inundated. In the past they tried bombing it in order to try to break it up but with no success. This year, for some unknown reason, it started advancing, then broke open and began to recede.

There is an estancia nearby simply called Quien Sabe – who knows – it was given its name by Mrs. Atkinson's husband when the owner, also an Englishman, asked Mr. Atkinson what he thought about it. 'Quien Sabe' was the wise reply.

The trees sheltering Estancia Lago Roca are both attractive and utilitarian – Lombardy poplars, willows and pine. Speaking of trees, the Yerba tree is only found in the Argentine province of Missiones; it is a sort of bush. Put the Yerba in a small gourd and – when it is made – you have Maté. Maté is imbibed at all hours of the day, especially in the early morning, through silver, or possibly pewter, tubes and passed from hand to hand, frequently replenished by hot water. Both men and women imbibe; it was the gaucho's only vegetable. I, personally, don't like it for it is very bitter.

I asked Mrs. Atkinson why the inhabitants of Puerto Natales had had an Eskimo look. Her theory was that a Japanese junk had once long ago been wrecked on the nearby island of Chiloe and that this accounted for their Asiatic features.

Rupert Clarke, with whom I had stayed in Puerto Natales, had been of the opinion that their Mongolian countenances derived from the Ona Indians. Possibly the Onas themselves derived originally from the Mongols.

The last night I was at Mrs. Atkinson's estancia the electric generator failed and Mrs. Atkinson, her two brothers and myself all dined by the light of candles which were stuck in two vermouth bottles, one gin bottle and an antique brass candlestick. George I silver decorated the table which made it somewhat bizarre in the so-called back of beyond.

On Wednesday, 28th March, I regretfully left Estancia Lago Roca and walked back to Calafate. Mrs. Atkinson very kindly transported my rucksack forty kilometres by car.

In Calafate I purchased an energising diet consisting

of two packets of glucose, one packet of porridge, a lot of chocolate, one pot of honey and some raisins for my journey across the Meseta de la Muerte (the Plateau of Death) – a stretch of high ground of approximately seventy kilometres over which no dirt road could possibly be dug. The actual Meseta de la Muerte itself is about twelve kilometres long, 1,829 metres (6,000 feet) high; more funnel-like than a plateau, down which the wind whistled keenly indeed.

Some twenty-five kilometres east of Calafate I stayed at Estancia Bonn Accord owned by Mrs. Horton de Dickie; she was not there, but I spoke to her over the radio in Rio Gallegos. At Estancia Bonn Accord I was informed categorically that the Meseta de la Muerte (the very name fascinates me) was absolutely impassable so late in the year. I did my best to look convinced – but was not. I was also told that many years ago two tourists had been frozen to death at Laguna Escarchados (Frozen Lake) where I had just been camping before coming to Calafate. A shepherd looking for frozen sheep under the snow had found frozen tourists instead.

From Bonn Accord I made my way northwards across two rivers, El Santa Cruz and La Leona, by metal raft to the south-easterly corner of Lake Viedma, staying en route at Estancia Irene, where in a fit of impeachable generosity I gave all my supplies for the Meseta de la Muerte to a small child.

Further on towards Lake Viedma I was given fruit and money at an estancia called the Divine Light. I tried to refuse the latter, Not Very Hard, but found it impossible.

At the small 'pub' in the south-east corner of the lake I met a New Zealander, Peter Redcliffe. Peter had been the photographer on Eric Shipton's expedition that had successfully climbed Mount Burney. He is a really nice guy, great company and the living image of a younger Rolf Harris. He was on his way to join some fellow Kiwis climbing in the Cuzco area of Peru.

From the lake the great peaks of Cerro Torre and Fitzroy looked most impressive in the early morning light as I set out for the *pueblo* of Tres Lagos, a staging post on my way towards the Meseta de la Muerte.

Here I experienced one helluva of a time with the wind which threw everything at me head on, dust, pebbles and even stones. I tried to pitch my tent fairly early in the afternoon in order to take cover, but it blew out of my hands and bustled off back in the direction of Lake Viedma. I walked on, stumbling about like a drunken marionette. I could see nothing ahead of me as my contact lenses gave me extreme agony and I could not get them out of my eyes; in fact they were still there in my head, high up under my lids some place – two pairs of them, at the last urbane count, probably more – for a long time afterwards.

At Tres Lagos the Chief of Police, called Domingo Suarez told me it was much too late in the year to attempt the Meseta de la Muerte. There was too much wind and too much snow; it would be very dangerous. He backed up his unequivocal statement by showing me some photographs of an abortive attempt he had made with horses floundering up to their necks in snow and panic-stricken men trying to coax them. Instead, he suggested another very long roundabout route that would take me half-way across Patagonia, right over to the South Atlantic coast in the direction of San Julian, where Francis Drake hanged Thomas Doughty after they had breakfasted amicably together on his circumnavigation of the globe in the *Golden Hind* between 1574 and 1577.

But I still remained unconvinced and stuck to my guns and said I was going anyhow. Seeing that I remained resolute in my folly he conscripted a guide who knew the way. His name was Mario Arredondo, he had a Basque father and an English mother and was a fine man, forty-nine, with very steady wide apart eyes. I trusted him instantly, I never asked for a reference.

On Thursday, 5th March we left for the Estancia Federica which was some ninety kilometres north-west near the shores of Lake San Martin or as the Chileans call it, Lago O'Higgins.

I had been given an introduction to the patron of Estancia Federica by Mrs. Atkinson. He turned out to be a charming man called Marcelino Diaz, who had a cook who resembled Charles Laughton. During the night I was at Estancia Federica it rained like bloody hell and Senor Diaz asked if I would like his pick-up truck to cross the river that flowed into the lake. Diaz claimed that after so much rain, it would be up to my waist. I indicated I would take my trousers down and wade. I think he thought I was bonkers; in fact the 'terrible' river hardly wetted my ankles.

From Federica, Mario Arredondo, his three dogs Morocho, Talero and Turco (Turco was my favourite) and I made our way to a shepherd's hut or *puesto*. Although it was only some thirteen or fourteen kilometres distant the wind doubled me up until I was virtually crawling along on all fours. Mario mounted, leading a packhorse, had a rough time too.

The hut was occupied by a Chilean called Ventura Rain, with strongly marked Auracanian features.

Looking across the arm of the lake I saw another estancia and enquired who lived in such a lonely spot – 'Meester Arry' was the reply. I was intrigued and thought he might be an Old Etonian gone native.

The following day, Mario and I moved up to another shepherd's hut which was a real log cabin, a real Abe Lincoln job. The shepherd was not 'at home' when we fetched up, so we helped ourselves to everything we could lay our hands on which is the accepted custom.

We decided to cross the Meseta de la Muerte on the morrow, Mario mounted, I on foot, but it was rained off – by hail, snow and high wind; in fact a complete white out. The weather then improved so the next day the assault was on. I experienced no difficulty on the Meseta except for driving wind and very deep snow. I was forced to cross a number of small, fast-flowing torrents; instead of taking my boots and socks off, I waded across without ceremony. I later heard that three people, two French and a Dane, had got lost on the Meseta de la Muerte for three days only a couple of weeks beforehand.

Once arrived at Estancia Tucu-tucu with my mission impossible accomplished, Mario, his two horses and three dogs headed home to Tres Lagos. Mario and I had become firm friends so I gave him my Swedish compass. He was the last man in the world to need such an instrument as his bump for locality was twice as accurate as any instrument, but I never had known what to do with it despite a Major General, a Major and a Flight Lieutenant all trying to teach me.

I continued north alone, averaging approximately thirty-seven kilometres per day, for it was easy going, except for complete lack of water. This is always something of a problem to the walker crossing miles and miles of dry pampa. All I could carry was a canteen that held a litre of the precious fluid which I endeavoured to keep topped up. It was, I must admit, very lonely in this limitless pre-cordillera pampa; the dirt road stretched straight, flat and boring until it lost itself in the horizon; a dog would have been a wonderful companion. The loneliness became so depressing that if I had fifteen minutes of pleasure out of any twenty-four hours, I felt surprised.

I saw very few vehicles, perhaps two or three in a good day. Sometimes they stopped to ask if I wanted a lift. I would answer 'No, thank you very much,' and point to my head indicating that I had a screw loose. They would feign commiseration whilst stepping hard on the accelerator. Argentinians, I had been warned, do not generally pick up people, fearful of rape, robbery or murder.

As I journeyed through the low scrub punctuated with tussocks of long needle sharp coarse grass and sandy soil, it mercifully started to rain and I did not hesitate to fill my canteen from the innumerable ruts in the dirt road without compunction. Who in the hell would be so stupid as to employ Halizone tablets in these latitudes? I would have if I'd had some – which I hadn't.

In the small town or big village Perito Moreno I made for the little, cheap Hotel Belgrano. I was so tired when I arrived after trudging through deep cloying mud in rain against a head wind that I could have slept in a cemetery. I wish I had. I need not have got up in this incarnation. The hotel was named after a General Belgrano who created the Argentinian flag, for the Argentine is a very military country and bank notes, railway lines, towns, villages and streets are frequently named after some great general. As I staggered into the hotel soaked to the skin I spotted a youngish man drinking tea alone.

He was Australian and his first words, as I shoved myself and rucksack through the door, were 'Thank God, somebody is not a softie'.

The Australian and I got on very well. He had just been in Chile and was very interesting about the problems the poor Chileans have had to face. For instance after President Allende came to power, he at once expropriated twenty-one farms. Formerly Chile had had the second highest standard of living on the sub-continent of South America, only superseded by Argentina, but rampant inflation had soon taken hold and costs had soared, telephone charges in Chile were doubled overnight and such miscellaneous objects as a brand-new horse plough cost forty-five dollars on the black market and potato crisps were five dollars a packet. A kilo of mouse-trap cheese cost four dollars fifty cents and it took two dollars to buy a bottle of rot-gut wine. Cameras were virtually unobtainable. The Australian told me that as a result of this financial chaos, 15,000 Chileans had left the country permanently. I remembered that on my way to Ushuaia I had to stop at Santiago and the air hostess had positively beamed with excitement because she had managed to purchase a tube of toothpaste for the equivalent of about five pounds sterling: it had been a bargain.

I was sorry for the Chileans at large for they have great charm, a kind of tranquil serenity that is most un-Latin. Their scenery is second to none and I felt sad that I had not been able to walk more of the way up their side of the Andes, but once the ice cap had forced me over to the Argentinian side of the mountain range, glaciers and towering peaks stopped me crossing back. It seemed best to stick to the Argentinian side all the way to Bolivia now. Up to this moment I had covered approximately nine hundred and eighty-five kilometres and by the time I had reached the Bolivian frontier I would have accomplished nearly half of my journey. What a vast expanse Argentina was.

My progress may have seemed slow and snail-like – it was: but this is a long, long country. I have crossed a large slice, 125 kilometres, of Pampa Seco in three days without water. *Three days* without water. I arrived in Tecka dog tired; for the final hour I was literally staggering about the dirt road like a dispirited drunk.

The following day I had every intention of rolling on towards Esquel but while breakfasting I decided to give myself a break. It was fortunate I did, otherwise I would not have met James Brand, an Anglo-Argentine, in the local general store where I was purchasing provisions of chocolate, apples, bananas and biscuits for the way ahead.

It seemed almost to be pre-destined that I should meet Anglo-Argentines or English speaking persons in unlikely places just at the right moment. Pure co-incidence?

Brand kindly furnished me with an introduction to Ben Cooke in Esquel and other introductions in Bolson and Bariloche. I was getting passed along the 'Gringo' grapevine like a hot potato, like an escape from Colditz.

I reached Esquel (population 15,000) on 11th May. It is very attractively situated, surrounded by mountain and hill and laid out in the typical Spanish grid system.

The town had originally been founded in 1908 by someone called Morelli – not Marconi – as a telegraph post. However, my first impression was that it was very dusty – every passing vehicle threw clouds of dirt that billowed into my face and eyes.

On arrival I went straight to the tourist office where no one spoke English and all the brochures were in Spanish; I would have thought that the brochures should have been translated for the benefit of the English-speaking world and thereby promoted more tourism. However, one of the girls at the office, a buxom lady, told me the boss, who was not present, spoke perfect English; she could not pronounce his name very well and I came away with the impression it was either 'Penguin', 'Bedouin' or 'Berwyn' – something Welsh anyway.

I soon found Ben Cooke to whom I had been given an introduction and together we ran Senor Berwyn to earth. Ben Cooke had once been an estancia administrator but now he was selling veterinary equipment. He looked exactly like Arthur Lowe in 'Dad's Army' and was the soul of kindness. Senor Berwyn did indeed turn out to be Welsh for there are quite a number of third and fourth generation Welsh scattered around the district. Their forebears had emigrated to the Argentine in the last century after religious dissensions in Wales. Just as the Irish had fled to America after the great potato famine so many of the Welsh had fled under attack to this part of the world where they could carry on their old occupation of sheep farming in hilly country.

Senor Berwyn was a young live-wire who suggested that the quickest way for me to reach Bolson and Bariloche was to go straight due north across the Condon de Esquel which rises to a height of 914 metres (3,000 feet), instead of going around in a semi-circle, and thereby save myself at least fifty kilometres. I thought this a very good wheeze. Cooke and Berwyn both said I could not possibly lose myself as there was only one track, traversing some forty-five kilometres of hill country. I replied that they did not know my infinite capacity for getting lost. So Ben Cooke showed me the track, told me 'to keep right on to the end of the road' and stick closely to the Percy, the left bank of a river of that name, but on no account cross it. I kept so close to it that I fell in it from a height of about twenty metres: it was like sliding down the banisters at home, rather exciting.

Soon after that little episode in which I could have very easily drowned in an infantile kind of way, I lost the one and only track altogether and nosed around multifarious sheep runs like a ewe on heat. I was diligently looking for any sign of bullock shit as I had been told that the occasional bullock cart went this way carrying firewood to Esquel, for lighting fires, I suppose. Droves of sheep and cattle were also meant to come this way so there should have been a good wide path somewhere around.

Finally I picked up some aged cow shit and reached a very lonely estancia where the head man told me I was on course, but that I must cross the mountains before reaching my destination and that I could not possibly lose my way, there being only one track. Of course, I lost my way immediately and crossed the wrong range of mountains, found a stream, followed it and fetched up at a far-flung estancia completely off course – in the direction of where I came – Esquel. I may have saved fifty kilometres, but I lost more than two days in doing so.

When I finally struck a main turnpike, I walked along it, not at all sure whether I was travelling north or south. Curiously it didn't seem to matter much. Finally I pitched my tent near a small concrete bridge by a gurgling brook. A cow lowed to its friend a bull across the stream all night. I was awakened around dawn, which is 8.15 a.m. in winter time down here, by the tent falling on top of me. The lovesick old cow had tripped over the front guy rope. This absurd situation turned out to be ludicrous for I could not find my torch to zip open the inner lining of the tent, my sleeping bag zip jammed as it often does, and I could not get an essential part of my anatomy out of a plastic bottle (always a tight fit – must remember to purchase a bigger bottle) which I always keep handy – like in the bag. Fortunately I had my little red whistle in the bosom pocket of a filthy Austin Reed bush shirt; got out the whistle and blew like hell every time a vehicle passed twenty or thirty yards away. Hardly any vehicles did pass and those that did passed me by very quickly. Finally one did stop and a Good Samaritan rescued me from a tight corner – and I did the rest. He fled. I don't know why. Perhaps he'd seen everything.

As I laboriously struck camp I took careful stock of myself and my possessions, for as a seasoned air hostess once told me, it doesn't matter losing a few passengers here and there and everywhere, but on NO account lose their baggage.

Healthwise, as the Americans would say, I was in good shape; a bit thin but 'lean and hungry' fit. My clothes were not in good condition. For instance, my Norwegian mountaineering stockings (four pairs) all had gaping holes in either toe or heel and were beyond patching. Fortunately the soles of my feet were so hard and my soft leathered Italian walking cum climbing boots were, like Johnny Walker, still going strong, but became very heavy when wet, causing me to move almost as slowly and as deliberately as an astronaut over lunar landscape, in slow motion. Every down step became an individual act of will.

I had one pair of contact lenses left (I started out with four pairs); at least two pairs were high up under my eyelids and ungetatable. I had one pair of glasses remaining (I started out with three). I had some books, but never managed to read them, the dénouement was inevitable; kind of attrition of the utilitarian variety.

It was really quite extraordinary how absentminded I had become, especially as I checked all goods and chattels every day, like a pilot before take off. I scrupulously checked and fumbled for everything, even for parts of the body here and there; you can't be too careful – they might not be there in the morning. Luckily I was expecting a 'drop' of the bare necessities of life in Mendoza which I arranged to be sent out from London before I left.

Despite losing my camera, I maintained a firm grip over the essentials, the possessions which really matter: passport, watch and money; my body-belt never left my waist night or day. I marched by my watch at approximately four and a quarter miles per hour with a 95 m.p.h. following wind on a gradient of one in three precisely.

As I struggled to pack up all my gear, I carefully scrutinised all my belongings, two by two like Noah's Ark, with my torch and its 'never ready' batteries, for it's pretty dark in the mornings and no one got up much before nine a.m. except myself. As the Southern Hemiphere gets near mid-winter the days shorten by two minutes every twenty-four hours until 21st June. At last all was collected and I could continue on my way.

At Bolson the first person I met was an Irishman, a charming man called Richard Mulhall, who had been educated in England at Beaumont and Trinity College, Cambridge. He has not been back to Europe for forty years and had, actually, travelled out to South America on the same ship as Peter Fleming in 1933, when the latter was the leading exponent on an expedition to find legendary Colonel Fawcett.

Mulhall and I had two things in common; he wore contact lenses and so did I and just as his great aunt was the first white woman to go up the Amazon my great aunt on my paternal side was the first white woman to cross the Rockies in a snowstorm on a mule with her maid, one Lark, riding pillion.

On my way to Bolson I had been interested in the forestation and the patches of superbly succulent lush lucerne grass; subconsciously the words 'How Green was My Valley' kept cropping up as I plodded along in the rain. I had never read Richard Llewellyn's best-seller, but over dinner that evening in Bolson, Richard Mulhall told me that Llewellyn had been out here many years ago.

I set out for Bariloche manana, where I had two different introductions from two different places – which by remarkable co-incidence were contiguous: namely Moreno 19 and Moreno 20.

It was said here at Bolson that there are lots of Nazis at Bariloche. I wondered if Bormann was of their number. Gosh, how exciting!

ANTOFAGASTA
PACIFIC OCEAN
SAN SALVADOR DE JUJUY
SALTA
SANTA MARIA
LONDRES
CHILE
CHILECITO
JACHAL
CORDOBA
SAN JUAN
ARGENTINA
MENDOZA
VALPARAISO
SANTIAGO
SAN RAPHALL
GRAN ALVEAR
Rio Salado
0 100 200
Miles
CONCEPCION
Rio Colorado
Rio Negro
NEUQUEN
NAHUEL HUAPI
BARILOCHE
ATLANTIC OCEAN

CHAPTER FOUR

ARGENTINA

All the way from Bolson to Bariloche is forested. The principal trees being Cohiue, Lenga, Nire and Cipress, all indigenous, all Araucanian names or derivatives, all generically related to conifera. Bariloche means the people from beyond the lake and it is situated in the middle of a national park. Some forty kilometres short of the town I stopped at a forest ranger's house to find out something about this Nahuel Huapi Park. Evidently it is the largest and oldest of all Argentinian National Parks and was created in 1922 by a certain Exequiel Bustillo, who, as it happend, died the day before I arrived in Bariloche.

The Park covers 730,000 hectares. If a hectare is taken as about two and a half acres the park is over a million acres in extent, well over, in fact nearer two million than one. And all this is rigorously preserved for the conservation of nature and is absolutely independent, indeed autonomous, from the province of Rio Negro within which it lies and from the town of Bariloche, even to the extent of having its own mayor. If, for example, the provincial government wants to construct a road or bridge it must have its plans approved by the Park first.

No hunting is allowed for it is a sanctuary for animals all of which are indigenous. There are two kinds of hornless deer, one called *pudu pudu,* the other *huemul;* the puma, or American lion, the red fox, and there are also birds, especially eagles, condors and hawks. Fishing for brown, rainbow and salmon trout and for salmon is only permitted in summer between November and April. Permission is also needed for camping and then only on special sites. The whole place had the look of Switzerland before man got cracking; remote, wild, and without any of the fantasy, yet.

Unfortunately I did not find any Nazis, let alone Bormann, but the only Old Etonian living here tells me there are some. When Germany was winning the war they were Germans, when losing, they were Swiss.

San Carlos de Bariloche sits on the southern shore of Lake Nahuel Huapi which means Tiger Island in Araucanian – if you have a working knowledge of Araucanian. It is a new city of some twenty-five thousand people, excluding a permanent floating population who home in from all quarters of the compass for the town is entirely tethered to tourism, like some polarised juggernaut, blindly disposed.

I am not a good tourist, I never have been and never will be. Moreover I arrived in the rain and left in the rain; never have I witnessed such a penetrating and protracted downpour in my life. In addition to Rain! Rain! Rain! a whiplash wind cracked through the streets rising off the turbulent lake with its on-coming white horses.

The place abounded in genteel tea shops: choosing one at random I sought secluded comfort from the wind and rain. Sitting by the window I could not help ogling young sinuous svelte ladies girt with gamps of many shapes and colours, 'taking off' like dear Mary Poppins, their skirts strictly observing the Queensberry Rules, ballooning, billowing and blustering well above their belts, or in naval terms, their Plimsoll lines. I sat mesmerised, digging my teeth even deeper into delicious crumpet, swiss roll, and gateau, getting them stuck up my nose like a naughty schoolboy.

I had missed the official tourist season for the ski-ing season chimes in on 9th July with the regularity of a cuckcoo clock, the only applicable epithet, in an area where a preponderance of Germans and Swiss were observing strict Teutonic punctilio. The ski-ing is said to be excellent, attracting people from all over the world, in the main Brazilians who, of course, have never seen snow. The ski runs are long, with all the latest Alpine concomitants, such as six double chair lifts, ski lifts and ski schools. Built in the traditional architectural style of a very overgrown Alpine village it is a 'with it' and 'trendy' place, despite being founded as long ago as 1895, by a certain gentleman called Carlos Wiederhold.

I wandered along the three Main Streets of Mitre, Moreno and 12 de Octobre. Bartolome Mitre seemed to me to be the smartest, the epicentre, aptly named after the first President of the United Argentine. All three streets seemed to be selling the same wares, tea, cake, crumpet and sympathy, all the shops being run with marshal efficiency by Germans or Swiss. Boutiques, bric à brac and curio shops all sold the same things, but not in vain: a tourist's paradise.

Through the Gringo grapevine I had an introduction to an Argentinian called George Kennard. His wife lavished copious draughts of tea upon me and found me quarters at a cheap pension or 'Hotel Residencial' as it is called, which means that it provided bed and breakfast only but it cost me just twelve dollars for five days. It was run by an elderly genial German who sang 'Waltzing Matilda' and 'She's coming round the mountain when she comes' all day and gave me treble helpings at breakfast.

George Kennard was magnificent, he went out of his way to help smooth my path in every direction. He provided the very best Shell maps and introduced me to the Jefe or Head of the Immigracion Departamento who sorted out my passport dilemma.

Before leaving the United Kingdom I did not know that journalists could get special visas from the Argentine Consulate and writing home to *The Observer* certainly qualified me. I was travelling on an ordinary tourist visa which only runs for ninety days, then has to be renewed for a further ninety days. But, as I was walking, ninety days was not nearly long enough for only certain towns had offices where I could get renewals and I might not reach one before my time ran out. Here in Bariloche, with Kennard's help, I was very charitably given a further ninety days dated from 17th June plus a note to the Jefe's counterpart in Salta, some five hundred kilometres south of the Bolivian border.

I met a man from Mendoza, a Rumanian by origin, who not only gave me a note to his sister, a big noise on television, but mapped me out a route which saved over two hundred kilometres of boot leather. He also told me that from now on, for the next few hundred kilometres, water would again be something of a problem. Only a minor one, I hoped.

Following the Mendozan man's advice I slowly made my way through the province of Nequen until at long last I hobbled into Piedra del Aquila on 4th June, just after dark, having covered nearly sixty kilometres in ten hours, which brought my total score to something over two thousand eight hundred kilometres.

Although just beginning to get into my stride I decided, like a good old Etonian which I occasionally try to be, to take the day off in deference to Founder's Day, so that I could compose a suitable telegram giving my longitude and latitude, in Greek, Latin or Chinese. It has always been the custom of far-flung Etonians in unlikely latitudes to send pithy cables which they hope will be pinned to the school notice board. As I was not conversant with Greek, or Chinese or my longitude or latitude *'Floreat Etona'*, had to suffice. In my time Chinese was not an obligatory subject, and presumably still isn't, but my thoughts ran across the globe to Shanghai where the legendary 'Long Arm Sutton' used to prop up the Long Bar and claim – allegedly – to be the only old Etonian to be a Chinese General under Chiang-Kai-shek, in sole command of the Immobile Latrine Unit.

Here at Piedra del Aquila I was informed, categorically, that there would be no water for many a league. I was told to carry an extra eight litres which would have been a helluva burden; but I was sure there would be ochre coloured stagnant rainwater in abundance lying in every dyke and ditch, literally 'lakes' of the stuff. Stagnant water is delicious; I was developing a palate for water.

Also at Piedra del Aquila I was formally introduced to a thoroughbred Argentine dog: it was bred from a Bull Terrier, Bulldog, Great Dane, Boxer, Mastin de los Piranaos, Perro del Pelea Cordobes, Irish Greyhound, Pointer, Dogo de Bordeaux and Mastin. It is the first all Argentine dog – Argentine Dogo; bred and evolved in 1947. A very simpatico animal – with a pronounced Boxer's cum Doberman's countenance.

On the roads dead dogs and shattered windscreens were prevalent. It was very distressing to see the dogs left in the middle of the highway; I always carried them to the verge; some had eyes glazed and frightened; some with teeth and gums bared defiantly in their final mortal agony; while others lay in gentle and tender repose, as if in sleep, their worldly problems over; the latter's death touched the heart.

Shattered windscreens were a very common sight; shattered by stones on the bridle path on the periphery of the turnpike. Many people exerted prudence and had double windscreens or cages super-imposed.

Four years ago I was in a car in the Pampas, driven by a friend, when his windscreen broke into kaleidoscopic pieces. While trying to clear it up he put his wallet containing 500 pounds momentarily on the roof. A bus driver and passengers came to the rescue, but he never saw his wallet again. If I am to be 'picked off' I am sure it will be on the roads where there is no latitude for error. For instance when I was very tired I absent-mindedly wandered across the asphalt; a cat it is alleged has nine lives, I must have well exceeded that. But I had to spend much of my time on the tarmac roads as they took the shortest distance between the towns and have been surveyed and laid down because they follow the straightest possible course with the best use of gradient. If I had not taken the most direct route, I should have been blundering about South America for years.

Day after day I toiled through unending waterless expanse, a sea of low scrub bushes in greens and browns that apparently flourish in the sandy salt soil. For hundreds of kilometres there was nothing to distract or divert the eye, except for the very few vehicles that passed in a cloud of dust. Many of the drivers of these vehicles came to know me and always waved or hooted a greeting. I was known by the country people as El Muchillero or the rucksack carrier.

Whilst walking I involuntarily, through the course of the long day, assumed sub-consciously, widely disparate roles, exacerbated by my degree of tiredness. For instance in the morning, when I was feeling bright-eyed and bushy-tailed and the day exuded promise, I figuratively put on my seven league boots like Tom Thumb. At other times I slipped, chameleon like, into the role of dear Don Quixote de la Mancha when he was feeling bonkers and chivalrous, charging at imaginary windmills (indeed there are windmills in this area used for drawing water) all for the sake of the lady he named Dulcinea del Toboso. Curiously enough El Hombre de la Mancha was currently appearing there on the silver screen.

When feeling jaunty aimlessly walking down a dead straight dirt road for league after league I assumed the mantle of the immortal Charlie Chaplin, duck feet, baggy trousers, big boots; only the moustache, bowler and cane were missing.

When feeling ebullient and optimistic, not even the cynical Voltaire could refute Candide's philosophy 'that all is for the best in this the best of all possible worlds' dinned into him by his tutor, Dr. Pangloss, who caught a nasty bout of syphilis while philandering with a chambermaid; thus demonstrating there is no cause without effect or vice versa.

When clouded with melancholy I felt like a poor old

harlequin long past his prime, 'over the hill' and he knows it. A pathetic parody of his palmy days; there is nothing much sadder than that, the applause derisive and mocking.

Much of the Pampa Seco is compounded of salt flats and pellucid ponds rippling in the breeze inviting the weary wayfarer to slake his thirst but woe betide he who does; for those limpid lagoons are as salt as sea-water. In fact I never touched any kind of beverage on the march – not even during the heat of noon when 'to move at all is seldom ever done'. Intake of liquid made me heavy and weakened the will.

In the Pampa Seco there are isolated *boliche* or small general stores, where I stopped to buy numerous bars of sustaining white chocolate and small packets of sweet biscuits and jujubes. At such times, at the end of the long day, I drank literally litres of tea, dosed with very liberal soup spoons of sugar which had the effect both of revival and the rejuvenation of my natural resilience. For example by the time I fetched up at one of these *boliches*, so far apart for the plodding pedestrian, every step had long since become an act of will, but after a 'bumper' jug of tea all my ebullience returned, flowing through my body like elixir.

Up until 21st June (mid Winter's Day) I had spent almost fourteen hours a night under canvas, so short were the days; but then perceptibly every day was lengthening out by two minutes. The nights were cold, especially between the hours of five, six and seven a.m. when the temperature often dropped to ten degrees below zero (Centigrade) – real brass monkey weather.

I had some odd dreams at that time; for instance I awoke and wondered not only what bed I was in or in what town – it even took a couple of minutes to register what country I was in.

The only constructive criticism I had, is that in the remoter parts of the country there was often a paucity of lavatory paper, sink plugs and towels. How many times had I been caught with my trousers down with no place to 'go'.

Nearing Mendoza I was charmed to see horses and traps clip-clopping along with the driver's dog keeping pace, maintaining station, between the high wheels; thus avoiding both the traffic and the torrid mid-day sun. I was reminded of the Algarve – The Land of Beyond – where the same custom is observed.

I received many spontaneous kindnesses such as the man who cut my hotel bill by twenty per cent. A boy and two girls of university age who seeing me staggering about the road in the darkness, beyond normal fatigue, dazzled by the lights of oncoming traffic outside Neuquen (I had walked over sixty-five kilometres that day) rushed off in their car and returned with manna in the form of a thermos full of delicious piping hot coffee and an unlimited amount of fresh bread. The very old man cloaked in an equally old poncho, near Mendoza, who came up to me at dawn, just as the sun was struggling out of bed, and gave me three sweets; a touching gesture. The little boy who saved my life by plucking me on the arm just as a fast Torino car skimmed past. The innumerable people who proffered me tea, coffee, bread and biscuits without asking for payment.

The roadmen, too, need an especial mention for I have found them to be the most courteous and gracious of men; their refuges modern and well equipped, spotlessly clean aluminium caravans laagered round by heavy machinery and bulldozers. On numerous occasions they have provided me with a bunk and a board gratis. Kind hardworking men wearing leather balaclavas, redolent of Mongolia or Tartary with only their pets for company: puppies, little ostriches or tame deer, they always welcomed me with gusto, asking innumerable questions as they made for the gas or primus stove where they would brew up soup before I could say knife. I owe them a great debt. I also found that the Automobil Club Argentino petrol stations were extremely helpful, effective and efficient; they were the best in all South America.

Just before I reached Mendoza the weather had the last word for I encountered the worst sand and windstorm I ever hope to meet. My tent collapsed on top of me, five tent pegs lost, spectacles broken, watchface smashed, dog bite and of course not a second of sleep.

The day I entered Mendoza (July 3rd) a town of over three hundred and fifty thousand people, some hundred kilometres from the frontier with Chile, I went direct to the Banco de Londres y Sud America and caused a minor sensation by appearing – *deus ex machina* – unshaven, filthy and stinking, but all the staff especially Michael Garton were charming and overlooked my loathsome appearance.

Whilst staying in Mendoza, I appeared on local television. Naturally the first question asked was the motive for my journey: why was I walking? If I remember rightly, the general gist of my reply was that I felt that by walking I was in touch, palpably, down to the tap roots with the people whose country I was passing through. An entente, a rapport was established which could not possibly be achieved travelling by car or aeroplane. Moreover it gave me time, time to assimilate, to retain, to reflect upon every detail of the most mundane contingencies, which often I had hardly been aware of before. Walking taught me to accept and to live with loneliness for the alleged loneliness of the long distance runner pales before that of the long distance walker. It teaches self-sufficiency too, even a kind of Heath Robinson philosophy that nothing in this world is so bad, or so good, as one first thought it: it is an extremely long endurance test of will-power.

Well, I certainly needed all the philosophy, endurance and will-power I could summon up the next day, for a few kilometres after quitting Mendoza my rucksack broke irrevocably, or at least the aluminium frame did, and I had to lug the remains of the pregnantly heavy sack all the 176 kilometres to San Juan slung around my bottom, very arduous. On the final day before striking San Juan I covered sixty-three kilometres (nearly forty miles) with the incubus on my back. As I tottered into the city centre I espied a kiosk bearing the legend 'Helados Alaska' (Alaskan Ice-Cream). I asked for one, but was told, 'The wrong *epoca,* Senor!' *Epoca* such an expressive word, fraught with significance: it certainly felt like the wrong time of year for me.

The entire district of San Juan Province is geared for sportsmen fond of angling, drinking and hunting: the South American lion or puma, which is in reality a big cat, can be found nearby in the high cordillera as well as foxes, hares, partridges, guanacas and vicunas: trout and perch abound in the San Juan River and of course it is a centre of intensive viniculture. There seems to be a great deal of internecine rivalry where the best Argentine wine comes from, San Raphael, Mendoza, San Juan or Salta. Argentinians remind me of Texans, they seem to have, or imagine they have, the biggest and best of everything. They are a very proud people, yet at the same time very, very kindly. San Juan is a city of some four hundred thousand inhabitants, a fine example of modern urbanisation with wide clean boulevards and tree-lined avenues. The architecture is modern as most of the town was destroyed by an appalling earthquake in 1944 which killed over twenty-five thousand people and shattered all the old colonial buildings. Although not so interesting as Mendoza, it has the same vigorous, champagne-like climate that makes even the most comatose citizen feel buoyant and ebullient. San Juan's pride and joy is the museum where Domingo Faustino Sarmiento was born, inside is kept everything which testifies to the great teacher's protracted struggle for liberty and civilisation. Indeed, Sarmiento did become one of Argentine's very best presidents.

I spent the last of my three days in San Juan with a Scots engineers and his Argentinian wife, whom I met quite fortuitously. He was one of the three Britons resident in the town. He told me San Juan had one of the greatest natural race-track Formula I circuits in the world. A natural amphitheatre, it had been opened in June 1970 with some international drivers competing but since then there apparently has been no racing of any consequence. The Argentine Grand Prix is held in Buenos Aires. He also informed me that San Juan had one of the best architecturally designed music auditoriums in all the Americas, similar to the concert hall of the Lincoln Centre in New York but, alas, no famous orchestra has ever visited it. In a way it is rather analogous to the Grand Opera House in Manaus, 1,000 miles up the Amazon, built during the hey-day of the rubber boom barons, where Anna Pavlova once danced but which is now empty.

As an aside, the Scotsman gently mentioned that an elderly British matron had walked across America, from San Francisco to New York, at a steady hundred miles a day; wilting newspaper men could not keep up with her; I can't imagine why not.

From San Juan I continued walking northwards for several days for about one hundred and forty kilometres to a small but important, town called San José de Jachal, of 18,000 inhabitants, *plagued all the way* by the worst attacks of squitters I had had so far. Very debilitating; it seemed to get worse every time I drank coffee. I suppose the cure was not to drink coffee. I like coffee.

San José de Jachal (pronounced Hachal) is famed for its onions, the biggest and the best anyone has ever seen: 40,000 tons of onions a year; the neighbourhood also yields 300,000 tons of calcium carbonates and dolomites (whatever they are); 30,000 tons of tomatoes and 5,000 tons of something else, which I have mercifully forgotten as I am sure no one is in the least interested in bald figures. At Jachal I met a very nice gentleman who invited me to come and see his fabulous onions some sixteen kilometres distant. I said I would have to go on foot and that as I had already been over four thousand kilometres on foot would he please bring an onion to me. I also met a charming Italian lawyer who had fought in the desert in the war: he esteemed Rommel highly but at the same time stated that Alexander was just as good and as quick: Monty not so good. Later he had joined the Italian partisans. Now he knew South America well and so was very interested in my walk, telling me to be careful of Southern Colombia as there had been a great deal of guerilla activity there during the past three years. Which side shall I join? The police by day and the guerillas by night perhaps?

From San José I made an arduous haul to a little place called Chilecito entirely surrounded by mountains. Arduous because of a little adventure I had at the top of the Miranda Pass. My second rucksack broke exactly on the very crest of the pass, 2,020 metres (13,218 feet) above the sea. It split down the bloody middle and I had to carry it like a babe-in-arms for fifteen kilometres before I found a house where I could get it temporarily sewn up with twine. Despite my ire I did have time to notice that the pass was an impressive feat of engineering and later I discovered that it has taken ten years to construct and contained over two hundred dangerous curves.

Chilecito was so christened by Chilean miners who came over the Andes in search of gold and stayed to turn the place into a diminutive Chilean homeland for themselves. It was a delightful spot full of smiling people, encompassed by hills and vineyards. The average finca or holding was only about six to eight hectares (fifteen to twenty acres) here for the big ones had been divided up amongst the workers who then all shared their earnings. They cultivated their vineyards and then sent the grapes to giant bodegas where they were pressed and the liquid placed in great wooden casks to ferment. Fermentation takes twenty days, and then the wine is kept in the wooden casks until mature.

The idea of grapes and wine did not tempt me for the

going was hard and I found tea much more refreshing. On and on I went, up and down great rolling hills for another 220 kilometres to the next town which was Londres, Argentina. The Conquistador Juan Perez had named his new city Londres in honour of the marriage between Philip of Aragon and Mary Tudor of England which had happened just four years before he founded it in 1558.

I had two introductions to people in Londres, one to a journalist on the top Argentinian newspaper, *La Prensa*, and one to his brother, a man of business, who turned out to be the living image of the actor Raymond Huntley. They both showered food and presents upon me and through them I met a local Englishman, Arthur Bauer, who was married to an Argentinian. Bauer's father had been the master and owner of an American windjammer and he had been born on board in 1884 in Danish territorial waters. He was certainly the most vigorous and benign eighty-nine year old I had ever met. A brilliant photographer, he had a charming house in the plaza littered with weird and wonderful cameras of bygone years. Arthur Bauer had led life to the hilt. As a young man he had studied at Heidelberg and then in 1907 he had gone to Spitzbergen just to see what it was like when coaling was just beginning there. On returning to England he had brought some rare books at an auction for a song and sold them for 8,000 pounds; on the proceeds he had journeyed up the Congo and down the Zambezi. An eight-month trip during which time he had employed forty negroes whom he had paid a shilling a day; good money for them in 1908. He had gone down with black water fever at Mozambique and had been amazed to survive, for the mortality was ninety-nine per cent. He'd survived to join the Royal Flying Corps in the Kaiser's War and when that was over he'd made money out of diamonds in Johannesburg. Finally he had come to Brazil to die of dysentery. Forbidden to smoke or drink, he had soon been smoking cigars and downing three bottles of whiskey *per diem.*

We talked far into the night and he told me many things which on my honour I cannot relate. His adventures leave those of Richard Hannay and Sandy Clanroyden cold.

Next day, 7th August, I was given the singular honour of raising or is it hoisting the Argentine flag in front of the schoolchildren and teachers. This was a truly gracious gesture of true democracy. Although invited I declined as I felt it was not for me, a foreigner, to be so presumptuous. Arthur took a picture of me surrounded by children and later I signed by name in the distinguished visitors' book called the 'Libro de Oro', first started by Sir Michael Hadow, British Ambassador in Buenos Aires, on his visit to Londres in 1970. I hope to meet Arthur Bauer and his wife again one day; incredible people.

Leaving Londres I strolled along, averaging over forty miles per day. All the way from Londres to Santa Maria I had not been charged a dime for anything, the country and town alike were kindness itself. A smile is the universal language – *just smile.* People often came up to me horrified to learn that I camped out all alone in my little tent. Honestly I had never felt fear but as Arthur Bauer wisely said, a little pepper is worth carrying all the same.

No news came from the outside world except that Picasso and Noël Coward were dead. As I walked on from Santa Maria, I wondered what else had happened. Nearing Cafayate I entered a wine-growing region with excellent vineyards all round which looked as though they had been cultivated for centuries. I later learned that all the wine was *torrentes* which means that the grape came from Spain over a hundred and fifty years ago: it is a sweet white wine with a vintage life of about seven years. They produce so much of it that they export massive quantities to Brazil and the States. During the last thirty years they've been trying out a French-based wine called Cabernet but evidently it does better near Mendoza than here. Each locality can claim – and by God, does! – to have the best wine and considers that their particular one is the most 'individual'. This hypothesis did not appear logical to me but doubtless does to everyone else. . . .

There is an old Cafayate saying: 'He who drinks wine loses sadness'. Rubbish! I drank it and felt infinitely sad. Cafayate is also noted for its cottage industry of homespun, waistlength ponchos. Whilst wandering round the town looking at these multi-coloured ponchos, I ran into a charming Englishman, Tony Frith, who worked in Salta for the F.A.O. branch of the U.N. He had been in forestry for a lifetime, serving in all those strange hot tropical and equatorial forest lands of Africa and Central America. We dined together and over the delicious Cafayate wine I felt motivated to walk for two days and two nights to his house at Salta over one hundred and eight kilometres further north. Accordingly I sallied forth into the brilliant moonlight. Although I lost all sadness under its glowing influence my initial euphoria waned as the moon waxed. After only four hours I camped at 'doom watch' in the canyon of Quebrada de los Conchas for a brief three hours' dog sleep – then continued until eleven thirty a.m. next day – Ascension Day and a public holiday – when Tony overtook me on his way back to Salta. He brought manna and precious fluid in the form of sandwiches, biscuits, mandarins and coffee. Afterwards I passed a lazy day encamped in magnificent scenery beside the higher reaches of a muddy stream.

Next day I continued on my way through the Quebrada canyon, a labyrinth of sandstone cliffs and peaks of curious contour, fantastic form, fashioned by nature in the shape of churches and pyramids, which was very eerie by moonlight, like being on a lunar lanscape, alone, without a pick-up module.

All that day I walked along a serpentine 'dirt' road

which was hell on the feet. That evening I reached a little pueblo called Talapampa where I put up at the hosteria in order to meet people, gather information and have a square meal. Here I met Senor and Senora Walter Klinke who were on a bus excursion from Buenos Aires. I found them chairs for the place was crowded out with other predatory skirmishing excursionists pouring Pepsi-Cola or 7 Up down their frothing throats. I apologised to the Klinkes for my unshaven state, but Klinke said I was not to worry as he was *the* representative of Gillette in all Argentine; anyone less like that heavily handsome blue-jowled Victorian figure one sees on the packet could hardly be imagined. Klinke looked like a kindly bespectacled, well-shaven ferret, not a porcupine bristle to be seen, with a neat little Charlie Chaplin 'Great Dictator' moustachio.

The Klinkes were a delightful couple, insisting on paying for my dozen cups of tea. A little later a large lady with wobbly bosoms and bottoms bursting for freedom and almost achieving it, as they nuzzled up and spilt over beside me, asked how I crossed the twenty mile Magellan Straits. I replied, 'By vintage landing craft in this incarnation, but doubtless I shall do better in the next – if I live that long!' She retorted that some special shoes, unknown to Our Lord, had been invented for crossing large stretches of water. 'Made in the Argentine?' I asked tongue in cheek. 'But of course, who else could!' she replied missing the irony and catching the point which appealed to her rabid xenophobia.

The following day I passed through a small village near which there is apparently a large estancia bought, after the war, by the late Alfred Krupp; now run by his sister. Far-flung rumour has it that Bormann is pigging it there in some discomfort. I couldn't be bothered to investigate.

By the time I hit Salta my feet were in poor shape, cut, calloused and deeply blistered. Tony's wife, Myra, in whose house I lodged, had been a nurse, specialising in 'skins' (no, NOT a taxidermist) and metaphorically, virtually literally, flung me into a bath as soon as I hobbled across the threshold, filling it with all manner of detergents, deterrents and deodorants. I have an allergy about baths; I think they are bad for the pores, or something equally erroneous. It was therefore my first since Tierra del Fuego, I don't mind admitting. Anyhow, the net result of my second bath after eight months in the Americas was that my feet became even more painful, veritably crucifying. Still it was extremely kind of them and showed great courage.

The City of Salta dates back four centuries; it was colonised from the north by the licenciate Hernando de Lerma, governor and captain of the province; he founded the city of Lerma in the valley of Salta 'In the name of the Most Holy Trinity and of the Glorious Virgin and of the Apostle Saint James, the light and glory of the Spanish Empire, and in the name of His Majesty, King Felipe II'. Over the years the city became known as Salta, which means 'to leap', because in Spanish Colonial times it was a staging post for caravans bearing gold and silver from Peru to the Atlantic. The province of Salta is synonymous with high Andean plateaux, tropical forests, temperate valleys, abysses and rivers. I was astonished by the landscape, traditions, legends and mineral resources but bald and boring though statistics are, the scale of everything in Argentina is really vast. The province of Salta forms a great horseshoe encompassing about 155,400 square kilometres (60,000 square miles) which is an area as big as Belgium, Denmark, Holland and Switzerland all rolled up into one. Moreover the position of this one province is most strategically situated as it is not only on the borders of Chile, Bolivia and Paraguay but it also touches no less than six other Argentine provinces.

Folklore is deeply implanted in the hearts of the inhabitants. Man and his land are part and parcel. He *is* the land. The Saltaneans have deep-rooted pride in their valley and are very proud of their Indian heritage. Then there is the Gaucho tradition. Up to only four years ago businessmen over the age of fifty, the élite power structure of the town, went around dressed in Gaucho garb; which is *not* just a uniform for showmanship; for the Gaucho has a code of Honour and a Culture.

The Gaucho is described by one writer as 'possessing the personal bravery of the Calchaqui, the generosity, the arrogance and the detachment of his Spanish ancestors who began the reconquest of Spain in the mountains of Asturias; he is also noble, hospitable, a horseman dauntless and romantic'.

Gauchos have always been out in all weathers, deeply suntanned they like solitude and the loneliness of the wide open spaces, and above all freedom. They served with conspicuous gallantry as irregular troops in the fight for Argentine freedom under the legendary General Martin Miguel de Güemes – the Gaucho General – and with him defeated the Spaniards, who were infiltrating from the north. The Spaniards were well mounted – but the Saltanean Gauchos had sturdy little Criollo horses that could thrive on nothing. The Spaniards were first bottled up in the mountains near Salta, and then allowed through the pass and beaten up piecemeal by Güemes and his gauchos. This event is venerated annually; Güemes' death being marked by bonfires placed at the foot of his monument in the city of Salta.

The climate around these parts is extraordinary for in the north there is a freak subtropical region where temperatures go up to 50°C (122°F) which enables sugar cane and tobacco to be grown, whereas near the Andes the mercury needle plummets to –5°C (22°F). Between these extremes the province enjoys a dry healthy climate. I walked through it at what is probably the best time of year; although the mid-day hours were definitely hot, I always met a tempering freshet or breeze to cool the brow, if not to lighten the load on my back.

Along the road there were innumerable little shrines dedicated to a woman called Difunta Correa; whether these are consecrated or not I don't know. The story, as told me by the rector of the Catholic University, a trenchant American Jesuit, was that the woman died en route between Santiago, Chile and Mendoza, Argentina. The dead mother was nursed by her baby until found by a traveller. Like St. Christopher she became the patron of travellers, especially to long distance lorry drivers who light candles and put flowers at the foot of the shrines: I have also seen spare parts and tyres of vehicles at their foot. Sometimes I found a cross which marked the spot where someone had been killed. But since Mendoza I hardly saw a dead dog which gladdened my soft heart.

After Salta, San Salvador de Jujuy and then a final 300 kilometre gallop for the Bolivian frontier. I was meticulously careful to make sure that I always left a city from exactly the same spot as I came into it. If I stayed several days in a city, I took a bus or was driven round in a car by friends, but I was always, always honest about walking through it from end to end. I usually walked into a city and made straight for the British consulate and carried on again from there. I never cheated over this.

To date I had covered nearly five thousand three hundred kilometres. Multiplying by five and dividing by eight to get the mileage makes it over three thousand three hundred and twelve miles. Every centimetre from that little church at Ushuaia in Tierra del Fuego has been traversed faithfully on foot. Certainly the Argentine seemed a long country and it took seven months to traverse it alone, but I grew fond of the people and amused by their intense pride.

Every time one met an Argentinian, in my experience that is, he asked: 'Do you like Argentine?' Next he enquired where I came from and where I was going. Before I could answer he usually launched into an enthusiastic tirade on the grand scale of everything around. I was told that near where I was staying was the biggest industrial firm in the world for producing sugar cane. This firm was also the first to produce paper and alcohol of all kinds from the waste by-products.

Well, Argentina seems to have the biggest and the best of everything. Take a few examples: the biggest shearing shed in the world; the biggest vineyard in the world; the biggest industrial firm in the world; the best beaches (Manley and Bondi included); the largest remains of the oldest animal the Rincosaurio – by comparison with which the poor old Brontisaurus is a mere chicken. They are indeed a very fortunate nation. . . .

I was often questioned about the Islas Malvinas-Falklands – but always in a jocular vein! But once I encountered a very formidable, very militant middle-aged lady who informed me *categorically* that the thorny and hoary old question of the Falkland Islands was directly analogous to the equally thorny, hoary old question of Gibraltar.

'Gibraltar belongs to Spain,' she announced unequivocally.

'No, it does not.' I retorted hotly. 'We, the British, seized it and intend to hold on to it. Besides the Apes would go into a decline under Spanish Dominion.'

'But the Islas Malvinas are Argentinian,' she droned on. 'We, Argentinians, supply the Islanders with everything.'

I concluded the conversation by pouring oil on 'troubled waters' telling her, very gently, 'I am sure the Falkland Islanders are *very, very* grateful. . . .'

I knew nothing of the dispute – I longed to be informed – so I could not state an impartial opinion. But I do know that every time I looked at the map of Argentina, their territorial waters appeared to be creeping, little by little, way out into the South Atlantic, which appeared, to me, rather acquisitive. Indeed, only the other day the whole government flew to Argentine Antarctica which I learned at school to call Graham Land, to read some manifesto or proclamation – re-affirming their territorial rights.

The Argentinians are very conscious of outward appearances, and seem to me to be unhealthily conscious of money: whenever I bring out my wallet in a store all eyes scan and impale it with rapacious radar eyes.

Further, why is it that so many Argentinians' like Chileans' teeth are bad? When not bad they look like elongated and uneven piano keys; many people possess only one or two molars. Possibly it's something to do with the water; possibly it's the lack of dentists, who are probably expensive, and vast distances apart. Certainly it must have something to do with heredity.

However, enough carping. Instead, I wish to point out that the first time I was congratulated on my walk was in Jujuy.

When I arrived in Jujuy, well after consular hours, I took a chance and rang the Bolivian Consul's private address. Immediately she came, together with her engineer husband and escorted me to her consular office. Here she not only congratulated me but also gave me a ninety-day visa, whilst her husband worked out by slide rule the distance from the frontier to La Paz. Afterwards they took me on a tour of Jujuy which touched me deeply. I wondered however why Mrs. Consul kept making the sign of the cross at very frequent intervals. Was it her husband's driving? Fear of the dangers of Jujuy or was she perhaps invoking the help of the Almighty for my safe passage through the highways and byways of Bolvia? Whatever the reason she was immensely helpful.

From San Salvador de Jujuy, clutching my cherished Bolivian visa, I trekked 300 kilometres north in six and a half days, which means that I was managing to average hard on forty-five kilometres a day or over twenty-nine miles a day. For four of these days I was travelling at heights of between ten and twelve thousand feet with a forty-five pound pack on my back. Weathered by the ultra violet rays, I was now as black as night, and except for my scanty fairish hair, I could have been taken for an Indio.

All the way I was walking along a road which runs parallel to the Buenos Aires-La Paz railway line so I imagined. It was the least arduous route that could be managed in these mountainous parts. All the time I was steadily mounting towards the high Andean plateau or *altiplano* which continues from here far into Bolivia. On Wednesday 29th August I crossed the Tropic of Capricorn so knew that at eleven thirty a.m. that day exactly, I was at 23½° south of the Equator. The country round about was high, totally isolated and curiously bleak. The drivers of the few cars and lorries that passed greeted me with huge smiles and the roadmen shouted their good wishes at me from the cabins of their heavy machinery. Such gratifying epithets as *amigo, paysano* (fellow countryman), *campanero* (one of us) would come roaring out from some giant bulldozer; little Indian schoolchildren in their white dentists' coats yelled from their classrooms '*Aqui es el Muchillero*', or here comes the rucksack man. Bush telegraphy is a wonderful thing but it can also be dangerous, especially for a foreigner, unarmed and alone, whom all think must also be rich and an innocent abroad. I hoped the pepper would be useful in a tight corner.

After a forty-five-kilometre walk I arrived at about four thirty p.m. at a pueblo called Abra Pampa which was celebrating its own ninetieth birthday with a tremendous fiesta. This had already been going for eight days and I had had the luck to arrive on the last and grandest day of all, the real finale.

No sooner had I dumped my rucksack than I was whisked to the 'football' ground where an interesting sport was taking place. Gauchos and their horses in full dashing regalia were endeavouring to throw a stick in a lance-like thrust through a metal ring, not much bigger than a big wedding ring, at full gallop. Light was failing fast, but it really was a grand spectacle. Six or seven horsemen would charge all trying at once, hell for leather, to plunge their wooden stakes through the elusive ring that hung on an improvised rope, supported by two diametrically opposite telegraph poles. There was a large very colourful crowd of bystanders. It was all rather like the movies. If only I'd had some colour film: nevertheless I did my level best and stationed myself on one knee directly in the path of The Charge. I was a little frightened because I did *not* know how horses and riders would react; for instance, would they run me down in their enthusiasm? They all tried but I never budged, the horses looked to my safety.

However, I stationed myself some three yards from the rope and ring – alone. A sharp shout rang out and on they came at full gallop churning up the dust. All of them made for the ring, but some were faster than others. I stood my ground and hoped for the best, and that the film would come out.

I reached the frontier post between Argentina and Bolivia feeling slightly tired but in great spirits: my first real objective achieved: a total distance, by my route, of close on five thousand six hundred kilometres. The last few miles were incredibly painful on the feet and to date seemed the worst day of my entire journey. Was it the effect of the height? But I had come through, which is all that matters.

Now for Bolivia.

Rio Abuná
Rio Ortón
Rio Madre de Dios
Rio Beni
0
100
Miles
Rio Guaporé
PERU
Rio Mamoré
L Titicaca
BOLIVIA
Illimani Peak
COPACABANA
CORD REAL
LA PAZ
PORT GUAQUI
TIAHUANACO
Rio Grande
Rio Desaguadero
COCHABAMBA
CORD OCCIDENTAL
ORURO
L Poopo
CHALLAPATA
POTOSI
VITICHI
COTAGAITA
R Picomayo
TUPIZA
VILLAZON
LA QUIACA
CHILE
PARAGUAY
ARGENTINA

CHAPTER FIVE

BOLIVIA

In the end I stayed at the border town of La Quiaca which is still one kilometre on the Argentinian side of the actual frontier. Here I endeavoured to get maps of Bolivia from the Bolivian Consul which seemed a sensible thing to do, but he had none, which was just as well.

I bought a kilo of long thick nails in lieu of tent pegs which I thought ought to serve just as well and I also bought two rolls of Ferrania film, a wild extravagance. I tried to get a lens hood filter but failed. I had my right ankle bandaged at a chemist. It was rather embarrassing, removing filthy, stinking stockings in public but I could not explain what I wanted in Spanish. I also bought toothache tablets. After siesta I crossed the frontier to Villazón without a passport. A very courteous Bolivian policeman called Rodolpho Vera, escorted me around the town, where I bought a couple of irrelevant maps of Bolivia to show interest, and a very cheap and very small watch plus a magnifying glass to see it with. Rodolpho Vera actually strapped it on for me. Clearly he wanted to keep in with me, at the same time asking the woman behind-the-counter if it was Czech made. Obviously he believed himself to be no fool. He was. He also asked if I was armed, adding he was constantly in touch with Scotland Yard; he looked at me sharply but got no change.

I was heavily stoned by a phalanx of a couple of hundred bowler-hatted Quechuan ladies, but luckily not very accurately. They were registering annoyance at being photographed on the frontier bridge which spans a slow-flowing, smelly and dirty stream. I was to find this resistance very prevalent among the Quechuan and Aymara women. If they didn't resort to chucking actual boulders, they would turn their heads away or sink them into their ponchos. This time, however, I continued to shoot, until a demented Vera rushed up and said it was against the law. So after taking a snap of Vera and Liberator Simon Bolivar's bust, which I felt I ought, I retraced my steps to La Quiaca.

Later in the evening, after dark, I crossed the frontier again (without passport) to soak up a little atmosphere, but got picked up by Vera who, ostensibly, was on his way to see a sexy gun-toting Racquel Welch at the Ciné. The people of Villazón are very much poorer, even the dogs are very much poorer, much more ill-kempt and scruffy, poor dears, than their counterparts across the bridge, but better mannered, I'm glad to report.

I left very early on the 4th September and got angry with the Argentinian Emigracion Dept. because they said I had overstayed my ninety days' tourist allowance. But, I pointed out, I had been given an extra nine days in Bariloche. The Bolivian Emigracion Officer was late on parade, so I did not wait for him and went and dumped my rucksack at the Pan Americano Hotel, costing the equivalent of ten pence all found, then returned to the frontier as leisurely as possible to find the Emigracion hopping mad. However, the Bolivian Aduana were most friendly and helpful; they did not even cast a radar eye over my *muchillo* – despite my insisting it was crammed with bombs. In fact, the entire Bolivian Aduana were very interested in my walk to La Paz, they seemed to understand its 'motive' much more readily than the Argentinians. They carefully totted up distances to La Paz which all varied considerably; very friendly.

Around four thirty p.m. I strolled down towards the frontier bridge to photograph the colourful scene around me, and found my friend Rodolpho Vera furtively reloading his Smith and Wesson; he looked rather hot and bothered. I asked him if he had had any luck. Obviously he had not for he shot me a savage look. The Colonel of the frontier police gave me a letter of recommendation to the Teniente of Police in Tupiza.

Next morning I was away at seven a.m., sun rising behind hills, big black dog shitting on railway track – no one else was making motion. A signpost to Tupiza said ninety-two kilometres; an easy two-day march. The countryside is high, flat plained pampa with the mountain Cordillera far to the right. There was a certain amount of traffic early on, and I passed through two control points within ten kilometres of each other, neither of which asked for my credentials. They appeared more intent on searching baggage for contraband, especially keen on peering into those clumsy sacks on top of buses.

For about twenty kilometres I crossed a high flat desolate plateau, on either side low scrub bush was widely dispersed in sandy soil. After some twenty kilometres I reached a crossroads, no signpost but I hoped for the best, and turned left for Tupiza. Near the crossroads was a lonely cemetery where a great number of people seemed to have been buried, which was strange because there were only a couple of mud and straw houses at the crossroads. Could it be the result of accidents? No. I dropped in at one of those mud and straw dwellings, thatched with bamboo and tied together with goatskin and twine. A middle-aged lady in a brown bowler, lots of skirts and a no-nonsense air sold me a couple of cups of strong black coffee and took a couple of jolly snaps while I drank; but, like all Quechuan and Aymara women categorically refused to be photographed herself.

However, every itinerant one passed on the road nearly always greeted one with a warm smile and always said '*Buenas Dias*' or *Buenas Tardes, Caballero.*'

Continuing, I arrived at a little village where there was a military fort, reminiscent of P. C. Wren's *Beau Geste*, and a charming Major – with a wonky mouth as if he had just eaten his teeth. He asked if I was armed? Was I not afraid? Did I have a lot of medicines? He invited me to stay overnight for safety, but I said I must proceed.

Further on under an incredibly blue sky I was given a welcome cup of tea in a civilised house by a civilised very middle-aged lady. By the time I arose to leave she ardently pressed ten Pesos Bolivianos into my paw and told me to get a good square meal. Just the sort of thing my dear old Nanny would have said.

By now I was getting very tired, the dirt road, uneven, circuitous and steep made every step an act of will. I finally staggered on legs of rubber the final few kilometres into a *pueblito* where there was a customs control post. I showed my passport; no difficulties. 'What was in my *muchillo?* 'Bombs.' No difficulty. I pitched my tent near the Aduana office, in a sloping corral that had very recently been used as a public convenience. Some local schoolchildren dressed in little white dentists' coats helped erect my tent with brio. Later I was invited to dinner but pleaded fatigue. Night comes down at about six thirty p.m. so I soon settled myself into my sleeping bag, the children then proceeded to throw stones with some effect on to the tent. Enraged I emerged from the tent with my torch, flashing it for culprits, but all had disappeared into the night, or so I thought until my climbing breeches fell to my knees, a spectacle which raised a laugh in the darkness.

I was away at six thirty a.m. without coffee or any warming beverage. Fast downhill walking virtually all the way to Tupiza. A bloody hot day. I eventually arrived at five p.m. exhausted.

A young Indian boy passed me on his bicycle and said, *'Que Sacrifico. Que Sacrifico! Senor!'* I asked for the cleanest and newest 'hotel'; called Hotel Mitru it certainly was the newest – it was still being built. Showers of dust fell on one's head in a slapstick sort of way as one entered the front door. After dumping my rucksack I had tea and then took my note of introduction to the Teniente José Padilla at the Comisaris de Transito. Young and courteous, he gave me another note to the Comisaris de Transito at Cotagaita, some eighty kilometres north. Later, after dark, I was picked up in a street leading off from the Plaza by a couple of plain-clothes detectives (Mr. Brawns and Mr. Brains I christened them). 'Show me your warrant,' I demanded curtly. They did, and I was conducted like a recalcitrant steer to the office of the sinister sounding 'Direccion de Investigacion Criminal' colloquially known as 'El Dic'. Here I had to produce my passport for the third time that day and then was escorted back to my hotel where all my effects were frisked for drugs and arms. I had plenty of drugs, prescribed by my doctor, but not the ones they were looking for; nevertheless they took away a couple of specimens of Valium and Lentizol. They appeared satisfied, I was not . . . I was bloody angry as they threw all the contents of my rucksack across the room and did not have the elementary courtesy to pick them up.

Another detective stood outside my bedroom door for an hour or so, smoking cigarette after cigarette like fireflies in the night, until he got bored and took himself off, with a couple of genteel farwell coughs, presumably telling me I was harmless. God knows what he had thought I was going to do! A bad night's sleep – dripping tap and a fetid bathroom did not help.

Tupiza is a great mining centre soon to celebrate its four hundredth anniversary; this will no doubt mean a mighty fiesta, for it is a rich area with antimony, zinc, copper, lead, bismuth, I believe, wolfram, all in the surrounding neighbourhood. Although located at an altitude of over two thousand seven hundred metres (9,000 feet), it still manages to nestle in a valley encompassed by vertiginous, jagged, red, yellow and violet sandstone hills; and it basks in a climate of eternal spring.

I met two young Mormon Evangelists – both amiable, and not too earnest. From them I learnt that the surname Snow is quite common round that Mormon stronghold,

Salt Lake City. Indeed, there was apparently a fairly recent prophet called Lorenzo Snow.

Almost ten thousand Bolivians here became Mormons in seven years; one of the young men I was talking to, called Douglas, was only twenty-two and had converted twelve families in fifteen months. Mormon young men undertake a two year missionary tour; they then go back to their careers, in Douglas's case Electronics. Before becoming a Mormon, he had been a confirmed atheist and drug addict. Douglas told me that Ché Guevara was killed in his sleep at Valle Grande by an American Green Beret; the local Alcade cut off his head and his body was dragged around the streets and buried in an unknown grave. I place no credence on this claim. I think he was shot by a Bolivian soldier. I asked Douglas if he had read Burton's book on the Mormons. He thought I meant Richard Burton. I did.

Immediately – but immediately – I fetched up in Cotagaita, fifty kilometres north of Tupiza, the acolytes of the Jefe de Transito swooped down on me, like predatory vultures, and demanded documents in a rather drunken fashion. I produced the note, the *laisser passé* from Senor Teniente José Padilla to the Teniente Jefe de Transito here, at Cotagaita. It was all the minions needed; they did not ask for my passport and one of them gave me a note to a relation of his in the next village – Tumusla. The Jefe de Transito was 'indisposed'; in fact, he was endeavouring to recover from one helluva hangover, poor man. Scarcely coherent, he shook my hand and asked what I wanted, then slumped back on his bed again without troubling for a reply. I liked him. It was not surprising he felt as he did because apparently every house here fabricates Singani de Higo which is Bolivian whiskey. I've never seen so many large packets of Alka Seltzer for sale. I stayed at the only little pension; I was the only occupant, except for a detective who was a charming man, gently polite but thorough. He had come expressly from Potosi to look me over. He particularly admired my Italian boots. Such good leather, he said, all the time feeling for drugs, diamonds or God knows what.

Next day I passed through three *pueblitos* – for the most part the inhabitants spoke only Quechua. These little hamlets nearly always have a *tienda* or shop where one can purchase soda, which comes in large bottles and is a non-alcoholic gaseous fruit drink with many flavours, and round loaves of bread, often very hard.

Halfway along the road I got picked up by yet another detective; he pretended to be visiting relations in another *pueblo* but I was not convinced. He was quite pleasant however and accompanied me all the way to Tumusla – with a sack over his back like Dick Whittington. He told me that the first clarion call of independence in all Latin America came from a place called Chuquisaca in May 1809. Freedom at last arrived with General Sucre's defeat of the Spanish in Peru on August 6th 1825 which was followed by the famous Battle of Ayacucho on December 9th assuring independence for Peru.

Spanish Resistance continued until Sucre's victory at the Battle of Tumusla, now a small, rather triste, passé village in which I lodged. Bolivia has had a rather raw deal, she lost large areas to the three contiguous countries. She may still sport ten stars on her coins but now she has only nine provinces for she lost the tenth to Chile in 1884 together with her only port. Antofagasta, rich nitrate fields and copper mines. Already without access to the sea, at the turn of the century, she lost more land, rich in rubber, to Brazil, and after a war with Paraguay in 1932, Bolivia lost nearly one hundred thousand square miles of the Gran Chaco. Nevertheless she is still a large country – about the size of France and Spain, or Spain and Spain put together but with a population of only about five million, seventy per cent of which are either Quechua, Ayamara or Guarani Indian, twenty-five per cent Mestizo (half and half) and five per cent European.

From Tumusla I walked over barren shale rocky granite mountains, where only the thorn bush and the cactus thrive; the only animals being red and grey fox and small rabbits. There were many different types of cacti everywhere, some of which I knew produced edible fruit called tuna but I did not sample any. Over this rugged stretch I became extremely aware and alert to the 'speaking silence', rather eerie for the lone traveller, loaded with a vast amount of dollars.

At Vitichi I had an introduction to the local Mayor but instead stayed with a very kindly Canadian Evangelist and her Bolivian husband.

I lodged at their house for a couple of nights and was told about a local Jesuit priest who once stole an Indian woman and went to live in a cave to the west of Vitichi. He was called Martinez and his descendants founded the town, so now there are a great many families called Martinez in the vicinity, just as there are still many Fletcher Christians on the Pitcairn Islands who are descended from those Bounty mutineers.

A number of years ago evidenly, not far from this place, a man, a foreigner, was killed because the Indians thought he had a syringe that took the fat out of a person. I decided I had better beware.

Then I was told all about patron saints for animals. If an animal gets lost, a mass is said and a candle is lit to that particular animal's patron saint. The patron saint for donkeys is St. Peter, for cows and oxen it is St. Luke, dogs St. Roque, cats the Virgin Mary and for sheep and goats it is St. John. On their special saints' days, dogs and cats are decorated with coloured ribbons round their necks. The village's own patron saint was St. James, represented in the town on horseback in a most heroic attitude. I forgot to ask if the same saint looked after horses and cars but was told that if someone buys a truck, the priest baptises it and gives it a name, it is tied up with ribbons and covered with confetti. They also told me that in La Paz one of the more unusual ceremonies is the Rooster Mass or Misa de Gallo; this is a special midnight Mass at Christmas time when the country people from far and near drive their sheep and llamas to the famous old church of San Francisco. The fiesta then continues for eight days, turning finally into an alcoholic nightmare, for the Indians dance all night and drink *chicha,* brewed from maize. First the Indians are said to enter the parrot stage of drunkenness when they are just very talkative, then they pass on to the monkey stage when they leap about like monkeys, finally they reach the pig stage when they roll grunting into the gutter.

To this benign Canadian the high rate of infant mortality among the Indians was most depressing. She felt that was the result of low nutrition and lack of sanitation. Nappies were made out of a piece of old sweater or old trouser leg and were only washed perhaps once a week. When the child was bigger, it was provided with a dirty shirt and no pants because it would wet pants. It was not unusual to see a child suckling from its mother until it was two years old or more. Lacking proper nourishment, weak and underfed, the children were slow to learn to walk.

Two days later I reached Potosi, the halfway mark between the frontier and La Paz. Potosi is probably, almost certainly, the highest town of its size anywhere in the world for it lies at just under four thousand two hundred and eighty metres (14,000 feet). Over it towers Cerro Rico which contained the largest silver deposits in the world. The old Indian workings were discovered by the Spaniards in 1545 and by about 1600 Potosi had become the biggest and richest city in the Americas with a population of over a hundred and fifty thousand: its name echoed throughout the world, becoming like Croesus, synonymous with riches. Potosi was made an Imperial City by Charles V of Spain and a mint was constructed there to coin the silver. 'It's a Potosi' is still an expression used in Spain for anything phenomenally rich. Indeed its fame girt the world even as far as China.

Potosi, like Manaus on the Amazon at rubber boom time, inevitably became a city of culture and vice. However, by 1800 the wealth of Cerro Rico began to decline as lodes came near exhaustion, and just as Malayan rubber undermined Manaus, so the silver finds of Mexico and Peru led to the collapse of Potosi's importance. I did not find it an attractive town, its streets were narrow and smelly; Indian women wore tall black hats here rather like those of Guy Fawkes. With an American girl, I visited the famous mint at the Casa de la Moneda which was built in 1572 and rebuilt a couple of centuries later, when they turned it into a fort and prison combined; now it's also a museum. It's rather an awe inspiring place and I felt definitely uneasy as we were herded around. My thoughts turned to all the forced labour of both men and animals that had made this place what it was. We were proudly shown the huge wooden machine that made the silver coins from the sweat of human and animal labour; the sand so clean and unsullied now beneath where the toilers did their daily treadmill. I rushed Karen, the American girl, around for the atmosphere, emanating from so much sacrifice of blood, tears, toil and sweat alarmed me. I was pleased to get into pure cold sunlit mountain air again and pulled Karen along to have an ice-cream.

Karen and her friend Mat then nobly offered to transport some of the heavier bits and pieces of my rucksack direct to the British Embassy in La Paz in their Volkswagen. I had been carrying far, far too much, loaded like a poor beast of burden and they relieved me of my spare pair of boots, and my briefcase. So after leaving Potosi, I went well. My pack lightened, I felt like a horse without a rider.

At a small town called Challapata the famous *altiplano* really begins, a hard, harsh land; a dreary windswept wilderness, a monotonous high solitude caged between the two cordilleras, the Cordillera Occidental and the Cordillera Real. A dusty windswept plateau where the air is crystal clear, the infra-red rays very penetrating and the vault of sky a fantastic firmament of blue that I have seen nowhere else in the world, a sort of a basin like a lunar landscape. It is approximately five hundred miles wide. It is heavily populated not only with people but with flocks of llamas, alpacas, guanacos and vicunas. The latter is almost extinct, even though it is 'protected' by law for its fur is the most valuable of all the llamoids. I saw lots and lots of llamas and alpacas, tended mostly by Indian women, spinning wool, in bowler hats and innumerable skirts; sometimes the herdsmen were little boys, sometimes, but rarely, lone black dogs. Both the llama and the alpaca are tame and domesticated: they will let you photograph them close up as they regard you with a haughty supercilious air as if you were a bad smell. The guanaco and little vicuna are wild. The llama, especially when stretching its neck to eat the coarse, sharp, *'ichu'* grass looks like a small camel without humps. Its eyes are large and bright and masterful rather like a dowager's with a lorgnette at her daughter's coming out dance. It walks in a rather prissy kind of way, like a pansy in the Kings Road but is capable of leaping up and down hill like a chamois. Not a friendly creature for it is inclined to spit through its hair lip and split nose. The llama is employed as a pack animal but can carry only about a seventy-five-pound load and has, like some mules, strict Trade Union hours of travel, but it can carry water like a camel, once tanked up. The alpaca is wool-bearing and virtually indistinguishable from the llama.

At Challapata I climbed a big tree in the main plaza in order to take pictures of a fiesta where the Huayno dance was being performed by Indians in from the surrounding country to the music of a brass band and a big trombone. The Huayno dance, which I first saw near the Amazon in 1951, is frenetic with eyeryone following their own particular rhythmical, or non rhythmical, steps and movements.

Also at Challapata I misguidedly got myself in trouble with the army. In the sacred cause of photography I endeavoured to form up a troop of soldiers in the position of a firing squad, firing at me, while I took the photograph. The soldiers entered into the spirit of the thing with gusto but suddenly their lieutenant came down the street . . . I walked off but was soon arrested by two soldiers with rifles and brought before the lieutenant like a naughty boy, which I was. The lieutenant, a young kindly man, asked me a few questions, but I refused to answer until the two soldiers with rifles at the ready left the room. However, all ended on a happy note and we shook hands. As I went out, the platoon of soldiers, who when I went in were lined up with their field grey backs towards me, the prisoner, turned, faced and gave broad grins which I reciprocated by giving a *Sieg Heil* salute. I was not re-arrested and was told not to be funny. I laughed.

I dined with the Alcade and the headmaster of the school who stamped my passport needlessly and waxed very nationalistic about Bolivian beer. Certainly it was very good, rather like German beer. It was the only occasion, unlike my time in the Argentine, when I ever heard a Bolivian become nationalistic about anything.

I had a gang of local boys erect my tent in the centre of the town but the place was so noisy I moved it to the periphery. Next day, I walked on under a very hot sun which was a little unpleasant as I had lost my nautical German U-boat commander-type forage cap so my bald head was exposed to the infra-red rays which burnt into my skull as if I had a magnifying glass held over my pate. Also I had woken up that morning to find my right eye completely closed, suppurating and highly inflamed. I had tried to find a doctor to no avail, so went to the dentist instead who prescribed some special ointment that the local chemist did not stock.

The following day I encountered the tail end of Lake Poopo. It is a big lake covering over seven thousand seven hundred and seventy square kilometres (3,000 square miles); it is deep too, nearly three hundred and twenty-eight metres (1,000 feet); an amazing vast expanse of water to find at over three thousand six hundred metres (12,000 feet), but it's not nearly as large as Lake Titicaca from which it gets much of its water. At the nearby village of Poopo I was told to report to Interpol in La Paz; I did not know Interpol lived in La Paz. I think that they imagine that I am a paid up member of S.M.E.R.S.H., for why else should a dotty unarmed Englishman loaded up like a burro, traverse their state in Italian boots?

Skirting Lake Poopo, I reached Oruro, a biggish little railway centre which seemed full of smelting works for silver and tin. I stayed there a day in order to have something done about my eye. I found an oculist at long last who told me that I had cut my eye rather badly just under the pupil. Probably a stone thrown up by a passing vehicle was responsible.

Only 229 kilometres from Oruro to La Paz. The road was asphalted and I made good time. Buses and lorries on their daily runs got to know me in the four days it took me, and they always waved or tooted a friendly greeting to the mad dog of an Englishman. I have never gone so well in my life, averaging over forty kilometres a day for four days at a height between three thousand and fifty and three thousand six hundred and fifty metres (10,000 and 12,000 feet). But soon after arrival I had a relapse, finding I could hardly stagger upstairs at the pension. At first I feared that it was the start of a dreaded bout of altitude sickness which I had had before on previous visits to Peru but I think the main trouble was my rucksack which was too heavy in proportion to my own weight. I had lost three stone and it was heavier than a soldier's pack. At only nine stone, it was too much.

La Paz is rather a shock to come across suddenly, virtually without warning. Situated in a sheltered canyon which forms a Cyclopean natural amphitheatre around it, it is a city of roller coaster streets, overlooked but not dominated by Illimani and other lesser peaks. Surprisingly, although La Paz is the actual or *de facto* capital of Bolivia, Sucre is the legal one.

At the same pension I met Bill Smeaton-Russell and his wife Eve who were making a documentary film of *Tschiffley's Ride.*

In April 1925 Swiss-born Aime Tschiffley set off from near Buenos Aires with Mancha and Gato, two Argentine Criollo horses. Almost three years and ten and a half thousand miles later they arrived in Washington DC. In fact when they did so there was an amusing incident. Tschiffley and the horses were due to appear at Capitol Hill at a certain time, but he got lost. So he tied the horses to a lamp post and went into a café to telephone for directions. On emerging he was confronted by a large, red-faced Irish cop who snarled, 'What the hell d'you think this is, bud, the Wild West or sumpin?'

Now, nearly fifty years later, Lieder Films Ltd. of London were attempting to recreate the epic ride in a six part television series. Bill Smeaton-Russell had already won several documentary film awards, including an Oscar. His wife Eve, who hailed from Inverness, had spent two years working her way round the world in 1960. The other two human members of the film unit were Norman Noy of Derby, ex-racing driver and oil company executive who was to double for Tschiffley, and Alec Campbell, a fifth generation Argentine Scot. Until eighteen months ago he was a pupil at St. George's School in Buenos Aires. Of the equine stars, Mancha Mark II, a sweet mare, had somehow managed to get herself pregnant, which proved, in time, a lot of fun for the unit. Gato Mark II was a gelding, so Macha's condition was not his fault.

The two horses looked very much like the originals but were much younger; Mancha II being six and Gato II eleven. The first Mancha and Gato were both sixteen when they started. They lived to be forty years old and are now embalmed in the Transport Museum outside Buenos Aires.

The whole story was well-known to me for I had myself once thought of repeating Tschiffley's classic ride, but my knowledge of horseflesh was limited which complicated matters. I had in fact started out from near Buenos Aires on horseback with a gaucho companion but it had not been a success so I had sold off the horses and decided to travel alone on foot instead over the same route. In those days I had not been as fit and plodding along the Argentinian pampas in temperatures of over 32°C (90°F) had burnt out my enthusiasm for the whole enterprise, so I had retired. However this brief episode in my life gave me an added interest in the Smeatons' efforts. They too had run into trouble.

The superb Argentine obstructionist bureaucracy held up the filming for some months. The Argentine Embassy in London assured Smeaton-Russell that there would be no difficulty in buying a suitable truck in Argentina, which could be exported. In Buenos Aires it was discovered that while this was true for private cars, there was a ban on the export of commercial vehicles. So, Norman had to be sent back to Britain to buy and ship out a suitable vehicle. Similarly, the Argentine Embassy supplied really beautiful-looking importation documents, which had to be paid for, for the film equipment. In Buenos Aires the customs laughed gaily at these, tore them up and the equipment went into bond. Six weeks and a bank guarantee for the full value later, the equipment was released.

Kodak Argentina assured both Lieder Films and Kodak London that they could supply the necessary colour film stock, but, again, in Buenos Aires, it was found that a quota had been enforced and the government department responsible was adamant that it could not allow the film stock necessary for the series to be imported. The stock had to come from London by air and then there were the usual weeks of negotiation to get it through the customs.

Apart from the truck, which had stalls for the horses,

the unit also had a jeep; but Bill Smeaton-Russell thought that he would probably need yet another vehicle just for the paperwork. Already, the horses alone had files over a foot high.

The Smeaton-Russells, who had been there over five weeks plungd in bureaucratic troubles, had been told that Klaus Barbi, who in his Gestapo time was known as Altmann, was in La Paz. Altmann was Gestapo chief of Lyons and was said to go around the streets there with two tough German bodyguards, all armed. It was said that if he was harmed, Jews here would have suffered.

Incidently, my teeth had been giving me pain; they had been giving me pain as long as I can remember, but as soon as I make up my mind to go to a dentist the pain stops. However, a girl in La Paz gave me the antidote, brandy down the earhole. She also told me that apparently in the Crillon Hotel, La Paz, article fourteen of the Bolivian law is written upon the wall and it states that single gentlemen cannot entertain ladies in their rooms without a chaperon. Some American had written 'Why?' Another American had written 'because of the altitude, it is no good' . . .

I finally left La Paz after a nine day stay on 9th October 1973. I was, up to the very last moment, in two minds which way to go to Lake Titicaca: there are, thank God, only two routes, one via the world-renowned ruins of Tiahuanaco and the small port of Guaqui situated on the southernmost shore of the lake and one by Copacabana. Titicaca is the highest navigable, heavy emphasis on 'navigable', body of fresh water in the world: 'fresh water' is also open to question as some ninety-five per cent of the water flowing out of the lake, into the River Desaguadero and so into Lake Poopo, is lost by evaporation.

The route to Lake Titicaca by Copacabana (the place which gave its name to the famous beach at Rio) enables one to visit Desaguadero, which I'm told is an interesting place, a small red-roofed town with a singular church harbouring the magic miracle making Dark or Black Virgin of the Lake, alias the Virgin of Candelaria, which to me smacked of idolatry or paganism, but it is hard to refuse a Virgin, even if she is black as pitch, let alone a nun. Hundreds of pilgrims come out from La Paz every year to pay their respects. In addition, there are the allegedly picturesque Straits of Tiquina from where they say one can descry the entire backdrop of the snow-clad Cordillera Real – with at least four peaks over six thousand one hundred metres (20,000 feet). If I had not been on foot I would have opted for *this* route into Peru . . . but as the Straits of Tiquina are over a kilometre wide, and the lake probably bloody cold, I decided to go by way of Tiahuanaco. I can scarcely swim however buoyed up, let alone with a full pack, cannot *yet* walk upon the water and have not yet got around to buying some of those very special footwear which that nationalistic Argentinian lady with the bosoms and bottoms had recommended for the Straits of Magellan. No doubt the Straits of Tiquina would be child's play, but I was not risking it and anyway it was cheating if there was another route round, which there was.

I was escorted out of La Paz by Bill and Eve Smeaton-Russell and Alec Campbell. Bill had kindly offloaded my old diaries, old maps, old brochures and other useless bumph that was no longer current. He also very sportingly undertook to smuggle 500 dollars' worth of Peruvian local currency which I had exchanged at a very favourable thirty per cent gain above the official rate at Peruvian banks. Under current Peruvian law, one is only allowed to take 1,000 soles into the country (about ten pounds) – *which is ridiculous*. At first I thought I would secrete the 500 dollars' worth of soles somewhere about my person, but as I am a 'walky', 'The Rucksack Man', I stand out like a sore thumb and am clearly up to No Good. In a word, I would almost certainly be searched painstakingly. Bill on the other hand had many hideaways in his big van transporting Macha and Gato, and was going to leave my bounty at the Embassy in Lima. I also bought a couple of alpaca sweaters with the loot, which would be four times the price in the United Kingdom.

As I trudged along the *altiplano*, I realised that I must be walking the ancient Inca road that linked Cuzco, their capital, with the outlying empire and which the Spanish had also made use of for transporting silver between Potosi and Lima. Every now and then there were small villages, founded as resting places for the mule trains no doubt. I stopped at one to shelter from the cheerless wind; as I ate my round hard bun and drank my strong black coffee (decreasing the efficiency of the nervous system according to the tenets of Mormonism), I felt decidedly breathless. I reflected that if Argentina has the biggest and the best of everything Bolivia assuredly possesses the highest: the highest ski slope in the world (rather dangerous due to crevasses), the highest eighteen hole golf course, the highest tennis court, the highest ping-pong table – special high altitude balls are provided . . . for all activities . . . you need them, I can tell you.

During the next three hours practically the entire Bolivian Army passed in a pall of dust; at least twenty – thinly plated – armoured cars, dangling long wireless aerials; they looked like Saracens, but probably were not. Anyhow, they cloaked me in dust and I cursed in vain; but vociferously. Then I reflected perhaps they were moving up to have a jolly little frontier skirmish with Peru or at least a punitive raid. I hurried on hoping to be an 'eye-witness'.

I arrived at the village of Tambillo at siesta time; no one about except a few poor scruffy dogs and a shop cum drinking den that sold no tea, at least not in Spanish. I pitched tent on the northern side of the *pueblo* and started to read Herman Wouk's *Winds of War* (over eight hundred pages) and *The Prince of Seduction*, simultaneously purchased in the only book-shop in La Paz that sells a modicum of heinously expensive English language paperbacks; practically all are American publications, many of the pornographic type that would make Lord Longford wilt. The only exception was a lone British thriller by Miss Elizabeth Lemarchand; a charming middle-aged spinster from Topsham in Devon whom I had in fact once met drinking tea at the country house of a friend.

Around four-thirty p.m. my tent and I came under bombardment, fairly heavy, but ill-directed. This time I got very angry. I grabbed the nearest little bastard and took him by the shirt collar to find his headmaster. He appeared to have four headmasters, each of whom I informed in my execrable Spanish, eeked out by mime, that I would thrash them if the gutter behaviour of their pupils did not cease, *at once, pronto*. By God it did. I was amazed.

I passed a very good night, the best for many a moon, sleeping the watch round, from dusk until dawn. Ironically I felt very, very lethargic on waking and very, very apathetic packing up and pushing off – but a vibrant bright sun soon shucked off the malaise. Almost immediately I had to climb the one and only hillock between La Paz and Guaqui. Fairly short and fairly steep I passed two pathetic looking very old Aymaras gazing sadly, steadfastly at a little cross . . . Their son? A daily pilgrimage, perhaps? I was touched and doffed my hat. At the unadorned top of the serpentine Tambillo 'pass' there is a large shrine, not created in good taste, the back wall is blue tiled, like a public convenience. I do not want to appear irreverent, but that's how it looked. From the top of the pass I stood, panting and breathless, marvelling at the entire unfurling central chain of the Cordillera Real looming up in the morning light. Illampu on the far left, Huayna Potosi pyramid-like flanked by 'outriders' more or less in the centre; the hefty triple-peaked hulk of Illimani – custodian of the roller-coaster busy-bee honeycombed life of La Paz – nestling unobserved in its huge canyon. Unlike Ruth Draper's garden, proverbially never in bloom at the right time on visiting day, this stunning panorama before my very eyes was at its best.

Reluctantly quitting my perch on the pass I glissaded down ski-like the other side of the hillock until I happened upon a very large group of Aymaras selling all kinds of country fare under little white awnings. It was market-day held every Thursday. I bought a couple of cups of coffee and had myself photographed drinking it. I then followed the narrow gauge railway track for about ten kilometres to Tiahuanaco – the South American Mecca of archaeologists. En route I 'cut camp' (as the phrase goes) and un-hobbled a poor old donkey, having hellish difficulty, painfully limping around, searching for the very scanty fodder. I was chased by a brown-bowlered lady aged about eighty who shouted imprecations and chucked stones, that fell short. I laughed, while the dear old donkey bolted with the belligerent old lady in hot pursuit. Poor dear. I was sorry for them both.

Tiahuanaco is, I suppose, meant to strike the tourist all of a heap, as my old Nanny was wont to say: but ruins to me are just any other ruins, anywhere. They leave me apathetic and cold. I just don't register their importance, significance, symbolism or what have you; it makes no impression. Tourists rave at their wonders, but as far as I'm concerned they might be talking to themselves.

After lunch at a rather seedy little pension I hobbled, for I had a game right ankle, through the narrow cobbled down-trodden smelly *adobe* street to the ruins – *in the cause of Duty*. Bloody Hell. Almost immediately I got picked up by a gold-toothed peak-capped pimp who tried to sell some filthy old bones for an exorbitant price: '*Autentico*', he kept re-iterating. *Balls*. However, he came in handy when I asked him to take a photograph of me at the 'Gateway of the Sun'. The pimp operated my 'Olympus' with dexterity and panache, tut-

tutted and asked why I did not possess a couple of Nikons and a Leica for good measure. I gave him a peso for his pains, he looked at it three or four times, before anguished credulity crept over his vulpine features; clearly Americans were more his meat. I got myself photographed in various other places to provide circumstantial evidence that I had indeed been there, philistine that I am. Nevertheless, I did get interested in one monolith – an inscrutable old gent with a flat nose that bore more than a passing resemblance to pictures I have seen of those on Easter Island in Thor Heyerdahl's book *Aku Aku*. In fact, I believe it as the Bennett Monolith (named after the man who excavated it) in Museo Tiahuanaco in La Paz that gave the Viking his initial inspiration, that there was a link up between the peoples of Peru and Polynesia; a plausible theory as testified by the Kon-Tiki expedition, but I prefer the hypothesis of mass migration from Mongolia across the ice bridge that once spanned the thirty odd mile Bering Straits, followed by a gradual infiltration through the Americas. Tiahuanaco is nothing like as impressive or dramatic as the remains of the Aztec, Inca or Mayan cultures; but its appeal lies in its mystery.

Dr. Arthur Posnansky, now deceased, first awakened the world in general and Bolivia in particular to Tiahuanaco's rich cultural past and archaeological *bric à brac*. Carbon dating artifacts found from the Tiahuanaco civilisation have been jig-sawed into roughly – very roughly, one suspects – five 'epochs', stretching between the First Epoch from 1200 B.C. to 360 B.C. and the Fifth Epoch from 724 A.D. to 1200 A.D.

In 1940 Dr. Posnansky built a hotel near the railway station which was later turned into a museum. I tried to get in but the wicker-gated main entrance was bolted and wired up. In theory it is open to the public but in practice no one can get in because there have been so many robberies. It wore a passé air. There is little left of Tiahuanaco; at its zenith it is alleged to have contained nearly one hundred and fifty thousand inhabitants in a tiny space of about six hundred acres which is incredible, if true. Assuredly the most densely populated area the world has ever known. *Certainly* it is the most ancient culture in the Americas; it has no apparent antecedents, and what is more extraordinary, the civilisation 'vanished' as it began – without real trace.

The remaining wall, pillars and monoliths have been restored and restored; vandals have taken a heavy toll. Materialistic iconoclasts have employed much of its masonry for 'bedding' on the La Paz to Guaqui railway, while other archaeologically priceless bits and pieces have gone into neighbouring farmsteads. Luckily some of the very best artifacts have been wisely taken into the custody of the Tiahuanaco Museum in La Paz.

Still the tourists come in their hordes like on-coming savages. I photographed taxis and buses in line hard by the Gateway of the Sun, while child-vendors, appearing from nowhere, like Tiahuanaco itself, tried in vain to sell me genuine rubbish, long tapering polychrome pottery vases, unexciting ornamentally, but, I suppose, useful for long thin flowers of the delicate sort or for some intoxicant. In addition other infants begged me to buy long copper spoons of no very intricate or artistic design; a diminutive but disproportionately heavy figure of an old man in copper; an entirely naked hunch-back with his penis thrust out at half mast. However, the old gent was so bent, as if he had retreated to his mother's womb, that I am inclined to think he (or his facsimile) were buried in that sort of defecating position, probably in a shroud, as people were interred in Britain centuries ago. I was asked twenty dollars for his purchase.

Back at the seedy pension a young school teacher or professor as he called himself rather grandly, very courteously offered me his garret to sleep in. At least it was a roof over my head. No bed, but I was very comfortable in my blue Swiss sleeping bag placd on top of my tent. The young 'professor' did not possess a bed either just a sheepskin and a few blankets. He was on the tiles most of the night, finally shuddering in on his knees at doom watch, like some shagged-out Cinderella. In the next room (very thinly partitioned) a young couple played an ancient gramophone, no doubt with that charming little short-haired terrier cocking his ear into the trumpet, with an ancient needle, an ancient record . . . guess what? 'Red Sails in the Sunset'. I had not heard it since my childhood. I think they played it, over and over again, for my benefit; also for their own to tone down their love-making, which at twelve thousand feet sounded like one long *cri de coeur* or an old Puffing Billy, expiring for lack or water.

Next day I moved off early after strong black coffee and the usual hard round loaf of bread to the Bolivian port of Guaqui, some twenty kilometres distant on the southernmost shore of Lake Titicaca. A gentle stroll under a very bright sun with a little cumulus fluffing the really extraordinary blue vault of sky; the dirt road, flat and as red as the clay of my native Devonshire.

Guaqui (pronounced Guakey – like Crackey) must be one of the highest ports in the world, hard on three thousand six hundred and fifty metres (12,000 feet). It is not a very lovely spot, not an idyllic place for retirement: in fact it is probably the filthiest, dirtiest, smelliest dump I have ever had the misfortune to hit upon. The port area is one shit-laden dung heap exhaling under the torrid mid-day sun like a pissoir.

Still I can't complain because I had a rather interesting time.

On arrival I was drawn, not of my volition, into conversation by a very kind, very charming, very thorough detective. He didn't actually *say* he was one, they don't you know, but I could by now smell them a mile off, in more senses than one. As a child I had always been fascinated by the story of two British-made boats – the B/M (Buque Motor) *Yapura* and the B/M *Yavari* – that were transported piece by piece on the backs of mules from

Africa to Puno, the principal Peruvian port on the world's highest inland sea, Titicaca, half of which is in Bolivia and half in Peru. This was in 1861, nearly fifty years before that redoubtable American engineer Henry Meiggs constructed his high-altitude, push and pull, pinion railroads.

The B/M *Yapura* and B/M *Yavari* are not, alas, still on active service; they have been honourably discharged and superseded by the *Coya* (350 tons) named after a group of Indians in northern Argentina and brought up from Mollendo to Puno in 1905. The *Coya* still plies between Puno and Guaqui, although they say the lavatories are not *so* workable as they used to be; and the S.S. *Inca* (680 tons) in 1929, the T.S.S. *Ollanta* in 1936 and very recently the *Manco Capac* in 1971 . . . all sailing under the Peruvian flag.

As it happened both the S.S. *Inca* and the T.S.S. *Ollanta* were in port, drawn up to the mole bow to stern.

I hurried my corpulent detective to the quay at a smart hand gallop. On arrival the Bolivian naval policeman told me I could not enter the port area without my passport and then only for five minutes. I endeavoured to cajole him by saying Bolivian sea power is known throughout the world as second to none. Guaqui is their only port since they lost Antofagasta so it seemed a plausible enough statement here. No use, the policeman turned a blind eye and I hectored my shadow back to the pension where I was staying; fished my passport out from my anorak pocket where it was protected with layers of waterproof sheeting which took at least five minutes to undo and returned to the sentry box. The naval policeman in his white American-styled helmet didn't even bother to ask for it this time, let alone peruse it.

I had a field day amongst the dock installations photographing everything I could. Grabbing my shadow by his flabby paw I pulled him aboard the S.S. *Inca*, while the captain was not looking, and had him take a photograph of me pointing at a plaque, amidships – which read 'Earles Shipbuilding and Engineering Co. Ltd. S.S. INCA, No. 489, HULL'. We did the same on the T.S.S. *Ollanta*.

Then I spotted a very small, very ancient crane swinging very large crates ashore for S.S. *Inca*. I noted that the crane was also made in Britain, or rather Yorkshire, for the legend read, big and bold, 'THOMAS SMITH & SONS (RODLEY) RODLEY NR: LEEDS'. Thrusting my Olympus into the hands of my *alter ego* I told him to take a picture of a crate precariously dallying over my head at zero feet. He said it was dangerous, as did the naval policeman. 'Balls,' said I. 'Can't you see that crane is British made?' my innate xenophobia reaching new heights. The sleuth pleaded with me, but I was adamant; the naval policeman registered belligerence but I got the pictures taken, thanked the sleuth and the policeman for their co-operation then tapped the latter on top of his tin helmet as much as to say, 'That didn't hurt, did it?' He laughed with mule-like teeth; as he did so I took the golden opportunity of taking a photo of the entire Bolivian Navy – three small patrol launches. I saw three matelots, too.

By this time my shadow looked rather hot and bothered and suggested we visit a church. . . .

Next day, it rained without stop, that kind of all-penetrating cloudburst that no waterproof can resist. The clouds were dark, low and lowering; pregnant with more to come. I stayed in my pension, saw no more of my shadow, ate heartily and wrote my obituary in two lines which reminded me of the time when, not having an overdraft, I had had a pair of shoes made at Lobbs and they had measured and indented my feet around a musty yellow obituary column page of *The Times*.

The next day was dull and overcast but the rain had ceased so I walked the final twenty kilometres to the Bolivian-Peruvian border.

The land around Lake Titicaca is very fertile – and the Aymara Indians make the most of every nook and cranny. They are prosperous small-holders, agriculture is good because there is a sufficiency of rain for crops of wheat, barley, potatoes and quinoa, while the big variation in annual water-level of the lake, together with its more or less constant temperature of around 51°F, in turn make for a moderating influence on the littoral, and extremes are avoided. The Indian *adobe*-aluminium roofed shanties between Guaqui and the frontier were all situated well away from the lake, at the base of and up the hillsides which I presumed was to avoid inundation.

The Aymaras are a fine people, kind, jovial and bold; they look you straight in the eye in a man-to-man kind of way. Passing them on the road driving sheep, hogs, llamas and donkeys before them they never fail to greet one with a courteous *'Buenas Dias'* or *'Buenas Tardes'*. To this greeting they can add *Caballero, Maestro, Hermano* or *Jefe,* whichever they think appropriate. The women are rather more timid, sometimes rushing past one at a full gallop as if expecting rape. Some of them are not deliberately unattractive but their bowlers do nothing to enhance their petticoat appeal. They go to church in bowlers and remove them like a man on entry; whether or not they take them off when they go to bed I know not, they are probably born with them on their heads.

Aymara school children are full of high spirits, bumptiously calling out *Gringo! Gringo!* as one passes them, often chucking a sod of earth or a boulder at one's retreating figure manifesting their *joie de vivre*. Unlike their counterparts in Argentina and Bolivia they do not wear little white dentists' coats – but grey trousers and grey sweaters, rather like prep school boys at home, with shirts hanging out. The Aymaras are stubborn fighters too; they were the last tribe to be conquered by the Spanish, putting up a very stiff resistance, until the end of the sixteenth century.

I finally arrived at the Bolivian-Peruvian frontier at

noon at a place called Desaguadero after a river of that name which flows very slowly, hundreds of miles south into Lake Poopo, Titicaca's largest and only significant outlet. The Bolivian border control post was un-manned so I strolled across the bridge that spans the river to the Peruvian border control post – where a couple of young policemen were sunning themselves and reading the Sunday papers. They took not the slighest notice of me until I told them the Bolivian border post was un-manned, therefore I could not get the mandatory exit stamp on my passport. Returning to the Bolivian side I asked some locals the whereabouts of the official for on the door of the Control Post was inscribed *'Ministerio de Migracion Horario de Atencion* [Hours of Attention] *Mananas 9 a.m. a 13 p.m. Tardes 15 p.m. a 19 p.m.'* Where was the man? Reports were conflicting: one person said, lackadaisically, that it was Sunday, another said a woman was keeping him; another said he was playing football miles away, pointing towards La Paz; another said he was dead. This last piece of news maddened me for I envisaged weeks of delay before he was replaced.

I sent three small boys in search of him: after about one and a half hours he turned up, excusing himself by saying, very, very piously, that he had been attending *Missa* (Mass). He then stamped my passport with the utmost expedition, wished me a happy journey and went off to lunch, and, no doubt, a well-earned siesta.

I crossed into Peru.

COLOMBIA
ECUADOR
Rio Putumayo
Rio Napo
Amazon
Rio Yavari
Rio Marañon
Rio Ucayali
LOJA
SULLAN
PIURA
BRAZIL
TRUJILLO
CHIMBOTE
PERU
CHANCAY
MATUCANA
LIMA
HUANCAYO
MACHU PICCHU
OLLANTATAMBO
LIMATAMBO
ANTA
ANDAHUAYLAS
CUZCO
URCOS
SICUANI
LA RAYA
AYAVIRI
JULIACA
PUNO
L. Titicaca
AREQUIPA
DESAGUADERO
GUAQUI
PACIFIC OCEAN
0
100
200
Miles

CHAPTER SIX

PERU: MACHU PICCHU

As the Peruvian Consulate in La Paz would not furnish me with a tourist card because I was entering Peru in an unconventional manner, I had taken the precaution of providing myself with letters of credence from both Peruvian and British Embassies in La Paz. On foot like a mendicant monk, instead of by car in the accepted way or by plane, rocket, ship or zeppelin, my position was somewhat similar to Bengt Daniellson's who had been the only Swede amongst the five Norwegians on the Kon-Tiki expedition. On being asked how he entered Peru, he replied simply, 'I came in by canoe and am departing by raft.'

The letters of credence struck just the right improbable Latin histrionic note: they winged me through no less than ten control points between the frontier and Puno, a distance of 150 kilometres, on a magic carpet of bonhomie. Only at the frontier at the filthy village of Desaguadero, which smelt like one big latrine that had never been emptied since it was first used, was my passport required.

I could in fact have easily smuggled in my illicit 500 dollars' worth of Peruvian soles I bought in La Paz; for I entered Peru without the least trouble, without any awkward questions being asked. Was this perhaps because it was Sunday, the day of *manana* of *siempre manana*.

At a large village over forty kilometres from the frontier the police, Guardia Civil as they are called, instead of demanding documents entreated me to spend the night at their *puesto,* which I did.

'Don't you want my passport?' I asked.

'No, only your money,' they replied briskly.

But this did not stop a diligent young policeman on a bicycle asking very courteously if he could possibly accompany me. Was he hoping for promotion or did he want to see if I really could walk? I think he left me, convinced of the latter, for by the time he took his departure he had fallen in the ditch twice and was sweating freely.

Some days I felt like a poor old blinkered 'Shire' horse who has not long to go before he makes his last journey to the knackers' yard. Neither looking to the left nor right, I just clippety-clopped along into the limbo of never-endingness, harnessed both physically and mentally to a burden, that at times was scarcely supportable. Indeed, by some transcendental process I seemed to take on the characteristics of a Shire, my head lowered, resolute, I just plonked one foot in front of t'other; mentally munching nothingness, until the long day was at an end and I was freed from the metaphorical treadmill; repeating to myself, as the road stretched into boundless infinity, over and over again, 'We shall arrive, when we shall arrive'; for some reason I always used a plural, possibly I was alluding to my rucksack and I, in lieu of company. However, this kind of equine philosophy did not prevent me shaking my fist, with impetuous ferocity, in impotent and open defiance of vehicles which drove straight at me, just for the hell of it, often literally brushing the sleeve of my anorak, covering me in a thick pall of dust like a shroud, that choked me and rendered me temporarily sightless. This sort of bovine behaviour caused such insufferable pain, to someone like me who wears contact lenses, that alas, only too frequently, I swerved drunkenly off the dirt road into the ditch, temporarily absolutely blind, unconscious of my surroundings, reeling and blubbing with agony as little microscopic stones foregathered inside the lenses like micro-dots; a savage hate stole over me, ironically making me the more determined to never say die.

Why in the devil wear contact lenses? Why indeed? But vanity is strong in man and is capable of taking the worst of beatings, again and again, and in my humble experience is rarely vanquished. *Amour propre* just will not let one take things lying down, and so one goes on.

Fortunately, purely physical suffering is soon forgotten, but at the same time is swiftly recalled, often with additional poignancy, paradoxically strengthening one to fight another day. This provided a continuous self re-generating motivating force that became a habit, the *spirito animo* that throve on adversity; the more the better, perhaps.

It constantly amazed me why I had *not* been shot, or at least robbed, because my Argentinian body belt, bulging with literally hundreds and ofttimes thousands, of dollars, cheques and 'greenbacks' was only too obvious. I resembled a pregnant elephant to the sharp-eyed and most South Americans are incredibly sharp-eyed where money is concerned. Moreover, lots of people knew that *'El loco Inglés'* is a minor gold mine. Was all the world that honest? Still there was plenty of time yet, especially in Colombia, I undertood. Let's live in hope.

Continuing my way round Lake Titicaca still, I came to Puno, the capital of a Peruvian department situated on the north-west shore of the lake, at over twelve thousand feet. Here I was almost certainly the only tourist who did *not* visit the one and only tourist attraction, the locally famous Uru Indians who live on floating islands on Lake Titicaca fishing for salmon and eating the totora plant. They are apparently completely self-sufficient and rarely, if ever, set foot on *terra firma*. Small boats took indefatigable blue-haired rimless spectacled ladies ('Daughters of the Revolution' to a man) and earnest puposeful Germans for the three-hour round trip. The Urus were, by now, highly tourist-conscious of their value and asked for money before they would let themselves be photographed making their papyrus balsa rafts. I did not venture forth for two reasons: – *First,*

I had *no* intention of voyaging across river or lake unless I *absolutely* had to as I did over the Straits of Magellan. *Second,* I have a 'die-hard' aversion to tourist hordes, corralled like sheep, ruthlessly exploited by pimps who have about as much mercy as Attila the Hun. Instead, I wandered around the bazaar, streets of wooden stalls, sheltered by awnings like the Kon-Tiki sail-head; trying to get myself memorably photographed with a pretty bowler-hatted dame. I didn't have much success because they are all *so* coy and so shy. Incidentally the stink in bazaars is indescribably horrific, sewage is emptied in the streets which have no outlet for drainage; and the Indians never take their myriad skirts off from one year to another, or so I am told. The slops are trampled into the beaten earth streets.

Leaving Lake Titicaca I slogged forty kilometres of asphalt roading, almost dead straight all the way, in *perfect* walking weather, under a beneficent sun to Juliaca, where one can buy the best and cheapest alpaca goods in all the world. I met a young Englishman here, called Tony, who was purchasing ten thousand pounds' worth of alpaca multi-coloured caps with ear flaps, gloves, ponchos of all hues like Joseph's coat, and superb thick sweaters. A sweater bought here costs approximately two pounds, as opposed to four pounds in Lima – Heaven knows what it would fetch in Europe.

My new found Englishman turned out to live in Catalonia and was not a business man but a theatrical producer and director of plays in mime, who was buying the alpaca wool for a friend in London. Whilst photographing me with the local sorcerer or witch-doctor surrounded by a massive pot-pourri of herbal remedies and spells, undoubtedly spurious, he told me that both the Aymara and Quechuan Indians spin the wool directly from the alpaca's back; then send it to Lima or Argentina to be dyed. They then knit it up into the chosen garments, be it caps, gloves, ponchos or sweaters, wash it, then leave it to dry in the sun and afterwards stretch it into shape, turn it inside out and sell it for an average price of about four dollars direct from their alfresco stalls in the Plaza de Armas, Juliaca. Here much haggling takes place; the Indians are clever, sure-fire mathematicians, but they did not outsmart Tony, who was not a theatre director for nothing and generally beat them down by saying things like, 'Darling, you *know* that's an outrageous price'. The Indian bowler-hatted ladies keep their small change in their wide cleavages, between their ample delta-like ding-dong breasts one of which always seems to be gelt. It is an amusing sight watching them rootle around searching for their money at the same time endeavouring, without avail, to keep their knock-kneed bosoms in position, occasionally, in a fit of irritation, together with their long plaits, they seemingly throw them over their shoulders in a brisk businesslike manner, giving their neighbours a nasty black eye en route.

Tony also informed me that until recently the Quechuas would drive their llama trains over the mountains to trade their wares of salt and other foodstuffs. Owing to the long duration of these treks they found themselves sexually deprived, but soon resolved this little problem (which we all have to face *de temps en temps,* but most of us can walk off) by employing the female llama whose sexual organ is very similar to that of a human being. However, this pernicious piece of buggery has now ceased, I'm glad to report, although it seems rather hard luck on the protagonists in that inclement climate where there is not much else to do. Just as well perhaps for the llama is a highly syphilitic beast, much more than Columbus and his merry men who barely touched the sub-continent. Now the government in their infinite indulgence have been kind enough to pass a law disallowing llama caravans to travel without women, who take on the role of chaperons, duennas and quick 'dip' mistresses, which I suppose is better than catching a dose. These Indian ladies waste nothing of the alpaca. They weave their voluminous skirts and clothes from his wool, use his dried dung for fuel and finally eat him when he gets too senile and is unable to shit. Unlike some people I know, they really do make ends meet.

The same day, I scooped up Duffy of San Francisco from a bench in the main square where he was sitting disconsolate and destitute. It seemed that it was impossible to change a traveller's cheque in Juliaca. Duffy had a train ticket to Cuzco but no place to go for the night, so I found him a bed in one of the state tourist hotels, and over dinner, helped on by a delicious cocktail of white of egg, gin and sugar, known as a Pisco Sour, he opted to walk with me to Cuzco.

I got up in the middle of the night at five a.m. sharp and had some communal coffee with some communal Germans on a package tour, ably marshalled by their group Führer.

Duffy almost immediately had trouble carrying his hold-all, he tried every position but the right one and found it impossible long before we had even left the smelly suburbs. I endeavoured to balance the recalcitrant hold-all on top of my own rucksack but it was reluctant to stay put. Finally it broke the straps of my rucksack which annoyed me. We could do nothing but make an ignominious, humiliating volte-face to the hotel for repairs which wasted an entire day.

That evening we witnessed an ancient dance in the main square called Sardanas. It originated from Rome, some two thousand years ago; but the accompanying instruments originated from Catalonia. A fine spectacle, superbly executed.

At last Duffy and I started our march again; I chivalrously carried most of Duffy's belongings because he had sustained a bad car accident earlier in the year, leaving him with an injured back and traumatic shock, as he had gone through the windscreen and back again. After a scant twenty kilometres poor Duffy bleated that he hadn't walked so far since he was a boy scout. Fortunately we soon found a co-operative *finca* where we passed the night; me in the comfort of my tent; Duffy in his sleeping bag *in the open,* brave man. There was a heavy hoar frost during the night and Duffy looked like a frozen mummy in the morning.

We plodded on to a dirty filth-ridden village, noted for its pottery, where we slept on the floor of a seedy pension that advertised beds, but didn't have any. Around midnight we witnessed some strange and frightening Indian ritual involving a llama's foetus, or somebody's foetus, that left us sleepless.

On again another twenty kilometres north. Duffy's back was playing up so he took a lift into the town while I walked every bloody step; dotty purist that I am.

I met Duffy in the main square; he looked very wan and very ill. I suggested he hitched a ride on a truck Cuzco-bound and get to Lima as soon as possible for an X-ray. However, he gallantly said he would see how he felt next morning. Next morning he felt worse for in addition to his back he thought he was suffering from hallucinations. Poor Duffy. He was an interesting guy, a writer, very well read. For about two hours I carried all his baggage in addition to my own until he said he must give up before he became seriously ill without the right medical care to hand. Carrying eighty pounds at over twelve thousand feet for two hours was certainly no tea-party.

Duffy had come to South America in order to find out more about the Villas Boas brothers and their great humanitarian task of helping to protect the Indians of the Brazilian hinterland from exploitation. He had also come hoping to be able to interview the Nobel Laureate Pablo Neruda, but the latter had died just before Duffy got there. In addition he wanted to find out for himself what was really happening inside Chile after the fall of President Allende. He found an eerie calm, like the lull before the storm, a weird tacit premeditated silence. At the innumerable checkpoints the military had looked at his passport, seen he was a writer and raised their eyebrows, as much as to say 'you are not a writer, you are the spider', as Malcolm Lowry put it in *Under the Volcano.* A writer to the new military rulers of Chile is tantamount to being a Communist for they had apparently desecrated Neruda's house, pee-ed on his books and opened his furniture with bayonets. Incidentally Duffy told me that Communist Neruda had said that the Chilean bourgeoisie were the enemies of poetry. Referring to the view from his house, he is alleged to have said, 'Civilisations come and go – but my ocean remains the same'; a banal remark even I could have coined.

The day before I managed to perform a ritual double-barrelled pee on a watershed divide over four thousand three hundred metres (14,000 feet) up. The water from this black peat bog, where sheep were grazing disinterestedly, flows half into the Pacific and half towards the Atlantic.

Some seven or eight kilometres further down the road, in the direction of Cuzco, I happened on a High Altitude Alpaca Research Station tucked away in a beautiful lush green valley with high hills on either hand. It is the only high altitude alpaca research station in Peru and is directed by thirty-two year old Doctor Sumar, a charming man who gave me the run of the place.

The Station is partly supported by San Marcos University in Lima and partly by the Ministry of Agriculture. It has 11,000 hectares (about 30,000 acres) of high pasture on which graze 7,000 alpacas, twenty llamas and 125 vicunas plus ordinary domestic animals. Alpaca husbandry is economically a very important activity in Peru together with other South American countries along the Andean Chain. Peru possesses approximately three million, two hundred thousand alpacas – mostly raised at over twelve thousand feet. They produce valuable fibres and nutritious meat. The fibre has a price about three of four times higher than the wool of sheep and is even exported to Britain. I learnt that there are two kinds of alpaca: Suri characterised by long straight hair and Huacaya which has shorter curly hair. The colour of the hair of both varies from white to black and all combinations in between these two – but white has the most commercial value.

The alpaca's sex life is interesting; both males and females come to the age of puberty at about twelve months, but the age of breeding is postponed two years in females, three years in males. (The apotheosis of good breeding.) The alpacas show a tendency to seasonal breeding; however, when the males are separated from the females they are sexually active all the year round. Females are continuously on heat; ovulation is induced by copulation. Sterile copulation is not followed by pseudo-pregnancy. Females return to being on heat within eighteen days after sterile copulation. Multiple births have never been reported.

The gestation period is about three hundred and forty-two days: a long almost elephantine wait. There is, alas, a high incidence of embryonic mortality – within the first thirty days of gestation. Artificial insemination can be, and is, performed in the alpaca; 'spunk' is collected by electro-ejaculation, as in Shepherds Market after a drunken evening, I'm reliably informed by hearsay of course.

The alpaca management practices currently used are similar to those in sheep farming. Sheep, incidentally, do not do so well at altitude as they do at sea-level. Alpacas are kept in herds, usually classified, which I saw done with a blue dye, according to the colour of hair, the type, whether Suri or Huacaya, sex and age. The usual breeding season is from January to March during the rainy months; there is nothing else to do, I suppose; therefore the young are born when there is a good food supply. They are dependent entirely on the local coarse natural grass and are never specially fed.

I witnessed alpacas being sheared which was a helluva of a hullabaloo; watching gave me a ghastly headache.

This is done every year and on average about four pounds of fibre is obtained per animal. An adult alpaca weighs approximately one hundred and sixty-three pounds and is the very devil to hold down while being shaved.

'*Crosses*' of the wool-bearing alpaca and cargo-carrying (thirty pounds only – strict Trade Union rule) llama are called 'Huarizo'; and the alpaca with the vicuna are called 'Paco-Vicuna'.

I must admit I was most interested in the beautiful, wild, untameable vicuna which I had never before seen. Nowadays, alas, there are very few vicunas left, their numbers are variously estimated at between ten and fifteen thousand. Virtually on the verge of extinction they are only just maintaining their own by the constant care and vigilance of conservationists. In 1966 an especial National Vicuna Reserve was established called Pampa Galeras; a 15,000 acre farm where approximately six thousand five hundred vicunas find peaceful sanctuary in ideal conditions and surroundings, at an altitude of over twelve thousand feet, protected by armed wardens. There is also another farm, Cala Cala – a private one – near Juliaca which cares for a further 1,300 of this rare species.

Originally, before the Spanish Conquest, there were over a million vicunas free, roaming at will, protected by the Incas, who were also conservationists and very good ones too. But the brutal Conquistadores with the sword in one hand, and Bible in the other plus fear of the Inquisition at their backs, slaughtered them in thousands; their metaphorical golden fleeces fetching a very high price.

Not until 1825 did the Liberator Simon Bolivar declare vicuna-killing illegal – but in practice the law could not be enforced; the killing continued, unabated, down the centuries.

The vicunas here have to be fenced in. I found them very timid, very difficult to stalk and photograph without a telescopic lens. They are constantly on the alert and the siren never seems to sound the 'All Clear'; their large lustrous dark eyes are distant and wary, yet their gaze is compassionate, gentle and tender. Their ears are tuned-in to every alien sound on whatever frequency. Their necks are long, graceful and statuesque, taut as a bow string. They rely on speed for escape; are perhaps at full stretch fleeter than a hartebeeste; can climb as nimbly as a chamois and resemble, at a distance, something between a baby giraffe and an antelope. Their natural foes are the fox, dog, puma and man. At bay they will attack the fox, dog and puma but avaricious man, their deadliest enemy, never. Thus their extreme vulnerability.

The vicuna lives a patriarchal family life. The male quite rightly controls every activity with a firm hand, like a Victorian father. For instance the male chooses the best living, feeding, sleeping and watering places available. He pegs out, figuratively, his domain according to the size of his seraglio. He wields the sword of Damocles freely and can expel a young male or female from the clan without compunction. The young male will probably form his own clan; the young female join another. Vice-versa, if a resident female tries to leave the harem, it is the omnipotent male who either compels her to stay or lets her go. The vicunas are creatures of fixed habits; for example they always sleep on top of hills and feed in the valleys below until a late hour and then return to the tops again.

I was surprised to be told here that the whole camel genus evolved on the grasslands of North America, millions of years ago, then migrated across the Asian and Mongolian Steppes and so across the Bering Straits, which in those days formed a 'land' bridge. I always thought it was the other way round.

Dr. Julio Sumar, head of this High Altitude Research Station, coughs exactly like an alpaca. My grandfather's Keeper called Damon looked exactly like a pheasant. I can only conclude from the above that one comes to take on the habits of one's nearest and dearest.

When Dr. Julio Sumar told me that the source of the longest tributary of the Amazon, the Ucuyali, Urubamba, Vilcanota river was within easy striking distance from the farm I jumped out of my skin with excitement for I had visited the other source of the Amazon, the Maranón over twenty years ago. He most kindly seconded a ghillie called Domingo, who was equipped with a pair of binoculars, to help me. A most excellent man, very sound on the hill.

Off we went. Some four hundred metres from the dirt road and one and a half kilometres below the divide at La Raya where I had just pee-ed, there was a lake called Gomer Cocha, which in Quechua means green lake, but as I am slightly colour blind I could not tell whether it was emerald green or Irish. It's not really a lake, but a large pond about two hundred metres long by one hundred and seventy-five metres wide although it is notoriously difficult to opine distances over water; this lake was shaped like the orifice of an ear and was encircled on three sides by a natural auditorium or amphitheatre of closely cropped paramo grass. It looked dirty and shallow, which it was; but it harboured trout weighing between eight and fourteen pounds plus a couple of ducks. Having found an outlet, a scarcely perceptible flowing rill, I leapt across it to demonstrate its insignificance and fell in.

Domingo and I circumnavigated the lake in the approved exploratory manner, falling into a bog and getting stuck as we did so. Here, in this lake, the source of the longest affluent of the Amazon begins: it is not the main source as it does not supply the most water. The water which fills the lake comes in its turn from higher up, from a glacier called Chimboya which is at approximately seventeen thousand feet.

Domingo and I scrambled up over scree and shale until we reached the snowline and the insignificant but dangerous glacier. Between the glacier and the lake far below there was no ostensible connection; we scanned and scurried in all directions looking for one. However, we both heard the strangely eerie wheezy gurgles of subterranean streams insinuating, passaging and pursuing their timeless courses beneath our feet like a lava flow. I was convinced that the Chimboya glacier was the birthplace of the Amazon's longest tributary; unless Dr. Sumar has got his facts wrong; but I am by no means convinced it is the actual or true source of that mighty river. The determining of a source depends not only on what criteria one applies, but many other concomitant hydrological factors of which the layman is ignorant and only the qualified hydrologist can venture an opinion. I have now visited both the main rival candidate aspirants with claims to be the real Amazon source: the source of the Maranón where over twenty years ago I spent nine weeks at more than fifteen thousand feet, and now the source of the Vilcanota/Urubamba/Ucuyali.

Personally, and I repeat personally, I have no hesitation in saying (not being bigoted or a hydrologist or both) that the Maranón is the 'true' source. It is much shorter, *but* has infinitely more volume of water; the locale is far grander and more impressive, hemmed in as it is by the high mountains of the Cordillera Huayhuash (pronounced Why Wash). In a word it looks the part with its adjoining and attendant cirque of lakes. I may be partial, but the cap fits or at least it did when I was there.

After leaving the High Altitude Alpaca Research Station I marched on down the road to the small town of Sicuani – an agricultural centre, where Indian ladies sold beautifully woven rugs dirt cheap. But I was only conscious of the wind and dust (a sharp reminder of my Patagonian days) which whirlpooled around the streets, like blinding spindrift.

The sacred river of the Incas, the Vilcanota, breathes life and vitality into its valley. I saw large herds of contentedly grazing cattle together with equally contented flocks of sheep and goats tended either by spinning women or knee-high little girls and boys and sometimes just by a dog; while the men-folk ploughed the fields and scattered either by hand or with oxen.

The faces of the Indians seem to undergo a kind of sea-change; instead of the dour, lack-lustre triste looks one encountered on the other side of the La Raya divide. I met happy beaming faces, laughing eyes, flashing teeth, bounce and joie-de-vivre. On every hand I was greeted with genuine warmth, *'Buenas Dias Cabellero, Jefe, Maestro'* – and even papa by young comely girls together with an incredibly aged Indian gent supporting himself on a Harry Lauder 'Keep Right On To The End Of The Road' knobbly cudgel. Cohorts of children chanted 'Gringo! Gringo! Gringo!' in strident altissimo in rather a monotonous manner, exhibiting petulance if one absentmindedly forgot to acknowledge. The word 'Gringo' is not meant to be derisive, it is simply applied to anybody of the Caucasian race but phonetically, according to intonation, it sounded as if one was being mocked, which one probably was. I must admit I got very bored, and often alas very off-hand, with every Tom, Dick and Harry asking, 'Where have you come from?' 'Where are you going?' – so I adopted the effective expedient of replying: 'From *la luna* (The Moon) to *la luna – hasta la vista'*. This means 'Ta-Ta for now' in jargon and on occasion 'fuck-off', I am sorry to say. It had a mesmeric effect and after all as far as the Indians were concerned it was practically true.

All Saints Day turned out to be a good excuse for a great many Indians to get very drunk and very pathetic. I happened to be passing through a small village around eleven o'clock in the morning on All Saints Day and a very intoxicated Indian gentleman took exception to me in a mildly belligerent manner. His face blazed with aggression, I stood my ground and he stood his until he fell flat on his face, poor devil. I was never molested or interfered with although my fists were often balled in my pockets, ready for the slighest real provocation.

I covered over sixty-five kilometres that day, hell-bent for Cuzco, shaking hands with innumerable Indians, very amiable but very tipsy, en route. That night I slept at the police post at Urcos. The day following I reached the former Imperial City, a tired but happy man.

I found Cuzco (140,000 inhabitants) choc a bloc with German and Japanese tourists, on package tours, taking over entire hotels, en masse. I met one Englishman. Impossible to squeeze into a pension hotel, I only got into one fortuitously, solely because the manager had seen me marching down the road towards Cuzco in a brisk military manner, fly buttons undone, shirt tail billowing like a sail. He told me he admired my 'goose step' – the bastard.

The day after I arrived there was, to put it mildly, a meeting in the main square. Throngs of people poured into the centre from all quarters of the compass to demonstrate their approval for the government's agrarian reform programme. Column upon column of Quechuan Indians wearing their home-spun work-a-day clothes marched in good-natured, orderly groups bearing banners *'VIVA LA REVOLUCCION'*! With the exception of one rogue banner that bore not only *'VIVA LA REVOLUCCION'* but also support for the down-trodden brethren in Chile. This caused a dealy hush. The Minister of Agriculture, inevitably a general, fixed the crowd with a glassy eye and gripped the rostrum as if driving on a serpentine mountain road that was a real white knuckler. Plenty of trigger-toting troops and colt-carrying cops in evidence plus squad cars and the occasional ambulance but there was no trouble, no signs of a struggle; except for a little girl of seven or eight locked in a caged Black Maria looking very pleased she had been arrested. We winked at each other and I wrenched the door open and let her out: we bolted and I took her home.

Cuzco nestling snugly in its valley is situated topographically not too unlike La Paz except the latter's valley is infinitely deeper. A very ancient city, probably, if not certainly, the oldest in the Americas, it has been inhabited for well over a thousand years. It is a typical Spanish Colonial city built up on Inca foundations. From the hills above one decries a mass of gabled red-tiled roofs plus a clutch of Colonial churches that blend very well with the terra-cotta of the surrounding countryside.

The name Cuzco means 'heart' or 'navel'. I met Aunt Emma, sixty, and attractive Anna, twenty-nine, in the centre, which in Inca times was the heart of the universe, on their way to a Yoga convention at Sao Paulo. I quickly persuaded them to walk with me to the old Inca fortress of Sucsahuaman and later to Machu Picchu.

Aunt Emma was a great trouper in the very best Australian tradition. She did not speak a word of Spanish and had no intention of doing so. She was the sort of person who, 400 years ago, would have envinced a profound contempt for Spaniards and scurvy and undoubtedly still does. She closely resembled one of Sir John Peel's original Peelers.

Game for anything, she and the very attractive Anna accepted my invitation to march to Machu Picchu with alacrity and some excitement. But first we trekked up to Sucsahuaman, about a mile and a half up and above the city which took us about a similar length of time to achieve.

Aunt Emma became very red in the face, which I thought might well harbinger a heart attack, but was more likely the effects of the post-prandial potent pisco-sours which Aunt Emma had never imbibed before, and which, like vodka, is inclined to hit hard on emerging into the cool mountains after propping up the bar. Anna went well; she knew the ropes.

The world-famous fortress guarding Cuzco is a really formidable, massive pile of vast cyclopean granite boulders constructed in three parallel zig-zag shaped bastions.

No one seems to know the date of its construction – but it is said to have taken 200,000 men fifty years to build. I can well believe it.

Next day, Monday, 5th November, we set out on our pilgrimage to the Mecca of South America – Machu Picchu via Anta, Urubamba and Ollantaytambo.

The first day to Anta (twenty-four kilometres) was very hot and muggy and Aunt Emma's feet played up so she and Anna got a ride with a truck-load of Indians about halfway.

The second day we had a march of some fifty kilometres to the village of Urubamba situated in the ever-deepening canyon. After about twelve kilometres Aunt Emma's feet again gave her pain so she and Anna once again hitched a lorry down to the *pueblo* while I trudged on, alone.

On arrival, I was greeted enthusiastically by Anna who dashed out to meet me, as if I had risen from the dead, and escorted me to Aunt Emma firmly ensconced, arms akimbo, kindly eyes a-twinkle, behind a bottle of near empty, pink champagne which I quickly finished off and ordered another. Aunt Emma was prone to premonitions; for instance she knew I would arrive when I did.

Later, while I was writing up my diary a middle-aged American surgeon introduced himself and asked in a very earnest and serious voice if it was safe for him and his wife to walk the streets of Urubamba village. Deep in my work I replied in an off-hand manner, 'Well, a few people were butchered yesterday in a particularly nasty way but you might get away with it. Let me know if you get strung up to a lamp post, I'll come and cut you down.'

After dinner Aunt Emma retired to bed; afterwards Anna and I sat on the banks of the Urubamba and looked at the river. Next day we rested and watered Aunt Emma while Anna spent hours patching my poor old ventile anorak, marvellous girl.

The following day we marched on down the Urubamba valley in the direction of Ollantaytambo some nineteen kilometres distant where there are some Inca ruins. After a few kilometres Aunt Emma slumped down beside a stream, muttering something about the sound of running water always making her want to squat. She did. But, indomitable as ever, Aunt Emma completed the leg to Ollantaytambo. I relieved her of her rucksack which I carried in front of me, like a kangaroo, feeling ludicrously pregnant.

At Ollantaytambo there was no room at the inn, so we camped in an idyllic glade of lush verdure beside a torrential little tributary of the Urubamba, cocooned by tall eucalyptus trees gently, almost caressingly, unfurling their top-most leafage to the will of the wind. Anna, although far from well, insisted on helping me erect the tent, while dear Aunt Emma propped up a tree, absolutely spent, poor dear, by the day's exertions.

It then began to rain hard. Anna and I thrust Aunt Emma into the tent head first; on reaching the lower end she found she could not turn round, the dimensions being rather restricted. Anna dived in after her and somehow tugged Aunt Emma back into position; it was as if the *Q.E.2.* had gone prow first into the wrong dock. They thrashed around like rhinos in a most indecorous manner until I feared for the future of my one-man tent. I slept out in my Swiss sleeping bag comfortably sheltered from the rain by Duffy's waterproof plastic yellow poncho. I was soon saturated. Anna, although ill with a stomach upset, repeatedly emerged from the tent to cover me up, undeterred by heavy rain, thunder and lightning flashes which crashed through the valley like a bombardment.

On one of these missions of mercy Anna told me she did not know what had come over Aunt Emma all of a sudden. Apparently she had been fiddling all over the place with Anna's shapely curves, forgetting on which side she was lying, mistaking Anna for the tent. At least Anna hoped so.

None of us slept and next day Aunt Emma and Anna entrained totally washed out for Machu Picchu, fifty kilometres distant, while I slogged along the tracks. Even today, despite the tourists, the approach to Machu Picchu is highly spectacular. I descended the picturesque, incredibly awesome Urubamba canyon amok with sub-tropical vegetation, bath-clothed by snow-capped mountains ever narrowing, ever tightening its clammy claustrophobic clasp upon the intruder, painfully shuffling along the railway line in my worn-out boots and Charlie Chaplin breeches like some down-at-heel mandarin; slowed by sleepers placed too near together for comfort and beset by sharp fist-sized pieces of granite that further retarded progress. I did not descry the ruins, literally to the very last moment, to the very last bend, to the very last turn, until I emerged from the very last tunnel into the sinking sunlight and found myself blinking, incredulously almost opposite the little white utilitarian station that lies like an incongruous eyesore amongst the jungle green amassed at the foot of the man-mountain that is Machu Picchu.

Considering the terrain, the rough hewn ghetto-like tunnels are masterpieces of engineering prowess. Within their maw water drips in a seemingly calculated and sinister manner, which I am sure would filter through the brain like a Chinese torture if one tarried.

There is, it is claimed, an old Inca trail leading to the ruins, but I saw no sign of it so had no option but to trek along the tracks, punctuated by sporadic sad little crosses, some very up to date, marking the spot where some poor railway ganger had met his Waterloo; either swaying into the train or swaying out into the Urubamba: between rail and river there is, far too often, only a three or four foot margin of error. To maintain a nicety of balance was not always easy, especially on the curves of which there were many. Here the prehensile Moby

Dick like tail of the penultimate carriage automatically swings outwards, like a backlash, necessitating the rare walker to retain a steady eye and steadier nerve to avoid premature demise. At times the roar of the river was indistinguishable from the roar of the oncoming train which led to a long sequence of frightening moments. The horrendous white waters of the Urubamba thrashed about like a school of killer whales directly below.

Fortunately, the tunnels were never more than one hundred yards long and were often much less. Notwithstanding I shuffled through them at a hand gallop, if a Chinaman can shuffle at a hand gallop. I noticed, in the semi-darkness, little niches, grottos and crypts where *in extremis* I could take cover from the oncoming juggernaut of blindly disposed peregrinating pilgrims but they were not deep enough to encourage one to linger with my highly pregnant rucksack. Probably the best thing to do would have been to lie supine on the track in an emergency.

From Machu Picchu station, little grey microbuses meet the trains and transport the tourist pell mell up the Hiram Bingham Highway, and eight-kilometre serpentine white knuckler, to the state tourist hotel squatting demurely at the top of the eighth wonder of the world. From an eerie above, the road looks like a protracted series of concertinaed serpents whose tails practically overlap at the bends, doubling back on themselves.

I finally weighed in at Machu Picchu station around four forty-five p.m. – daylight was teetering on the abyss of night. With no time at all in hand I grabbed the driver of the nearest microbus, told him to transport my knapsack up to the hotel while I stormed up the hill diretissima which was like escalading a medieval castle. This was presumably what Senator Hiram Bingham and the Yale Commission who originally found it had done. Finally I popped out of the undergrowth, like a wandering rabbit out of his hole, into the muted light of the

1 The author with his basic equipment which made up into a thirty-three pound load

2 Coming off the ferry at Punta Arenas

3 Fiesta time in Northern Argentina

4 Looking towards Bolivia

5 Mancha and Gato Mark II in La Paz

6 Travelling headgear – an Aymara Indian hat

7 Bolivian Sunday

8 One of the headwaters of the Amazon

9 New Year in Lima

10 A desert road on the coast of Peru

11 A llama on the *altiplano*

12 Boys in Puno

13 Chris Bonington on the third day out in Ecuador

14 The road through Colombia

15 With Don Leo and his mule train

hotel's terrazza, as Anna said, 'appearing from nowhere'. I was back in civilisation.

How ironic to hit upon a hotel with running hot and cold housemaids, figuratively speaking, out of every tap, at the summit of the most famous lost city in the world. Anna doctored my hands, bathed my feet and cut my toenails. I took a shower and for once had no regrets, except contrition.

Why had Machu Picchu been built? Was it the sun worshipper's equivalent of St. Peter's or the Mecca of Mohammed? Or had it been a seasonal retreat of the Inca dynasty, like the Pope's summer residence of Castel Gandolfo? Was it a fortress, and if so what was it defending? Was it beset by punitive incursions of newly conquered peoples to the north and east of the vast Empire? I spent two days at Machu Picchu wandering round the ruins puzzling them out.

I would have dearly liked to have been of Hiram Bingham's company when he discovered Machu Picchu in 1911. One can only speculate what it must have been like then, before the semi-tropical jungle was cut back and the buildings cleaned up. The initial impact of discovery on that winter day of July 24th 1911, of a lost Inca stronghold, religious centre, self-sufficient city in the clouds, must have made the explorers' minds boggle with the enormity of their find. Or did the very magnitude of it only register by degrees?

The skeletons dug up on the site, interred in caves or under large rocks, represented in numbers, ten women to one man, so some historians think that the virgins of the Sun God escaped from the capital at Cuzco and took refuge here, but this theory is only a piece of the mysterious mosaic of the unfinshed jigsaw puzzle that is Machu Picchu.

The site has myriads of buildings which archaeologists guess must have been temples, houses and palaces. Not only were there quarters for women, but also for soldiers, industrialists, intellectuals and learned men. The latter were well-versed in their knowledge of astronomy and astrology. They possessed a lunar calendar of twelve months and could calculate the equinoxes and solstices but their methods of mathematical calculation are unknown.

Like Rome, Machu Picchu was not built in a day. The man, or men, who (metaphorically) first staked it out must have been endowed with an unerring eye for country plus a sound bump for locality. He or they could not have chosen better – both stragetically *and* tactically.

Well nigh inaccessible from all quarters of the compass – a handful of resolute men could have held a whole army at bay until the end of time; furthermore the approaches form perfect positions for endless ambuscades. Situated astride a saddle-like ridge, over a thousand feet directly above the boisterous, horrific, roaring white waters of the tempestuous Urubamba, which describes a 'U' or giant hairpin around it, it is virtually impregnable. I have seen and been on a powerful deal of rough water in my life, but have never seen, or been on, anything approaching the volume and velocity of the Urubamba at Machu Picchu.

Surrounded by perpendicular scrub-covered peaks of white granite, it is dominated by the almost hypnotically omnipresent Huayna Picchu, standing sentinel on the periphery of the Amazon jungle and the most eastern chain of the Andes.

In addition to being either a military base or a sun worshippers' religious retreat, it is assuredly a winter's Shangri-La; still paradoxically a Lost City, but a paradise nearly lost by the mounting tide of tourism, that laps over it in ever bigger waves every day that passes.

Only a mere seventy miles north-north-east of Cuzco the Conquistadores never found it, thank God, and therefore it was never wantonly desecrated, looted, pillaged or sacked by an avaricious Pizarro as was the unhappy fate of the Sun City, Pachacamac, on the Peruvian coast near Lima, that fell to the predatory Gonzalo, half-brother of the Conqueror, Francisco. Gonzalo, like his brothers, lived by the sword and died by it.

After a day spent among the ruins, wondering about those who had once lived here, Aunt Emma and Anna departed for Brazil. Before she left, Anna wrote up her diary which she showed me. I think her description of me conveys a spontaneous graphic word picture from an unsullied eye and an unsullied mind so I am including it:

> We were sitting in the Plaza in Cuzco watching the people come in from leagues around. Indians were pouring down the path towards me, four abreast On and on they flowed seemingly never ending until the place was crammed.
>
> Suddenly amongst this mass of heaving Indian humanity there bobbed up an incredible figure. Heavy scuffed walking boots, long blue stockings tied below the knee with bright red plastic garters to a pair of breeches which may once have fitted him when he was three stone heavier. The alpaca pullover was rubbed blue on the back and under the arms; obviously a rucksack man. His good-looking suntanned face with sky blue eyes was crowned with a yellow and brown tea-cosy with pompom. His rather unlikely activity was furious snapping of the crowd, into which he disappeared.
>
> More Indians flowed by, and sometime later the figure re-appeared, introduced himself as Sebastian Snow, made a couple of unprintable remarks about 'smell' and 'sanitation', suggested a drink at the Cuzco Hotel. With rather a stunned 'Yes' from Aunt Emma and me, our adventure began . . .

I stayed on one more day after Aunt Emma and Anna had gone. I left my second pair of boots at Machu Picchu, not out of symbolism, but because they were worn out. I then walked back the way I had come along the tracks.

On the way back, at Ollantaytambo, I entered the little restaurant where Aunt Emma, Anna and I had dined. The proprietor asked what had become of my two Senoras with touching courtesy.

'Oh, I ate them.'

'Both?'

'Both,' I replied, reverently.

Clearly he was a man with a sense of the absurd and took this banter in his stride for he brought countless cups of extra tea, presumably to help wash my two dear Senoras down that 'little red lane' as my Nanny used to call it, when she doled out the tablespoon of linctus, or syrup of figs. After which he said I was a bigamist.

'No, I'm not – I'm a cannibal.'

I stayed at the really enchanting little township of Urubamba situated in a beautiful fertile valley with its narrow, cobbled streets and glaring whitewashed houses encompassed with gum trees. Nevertheless I felt lonely, out of sorts, I missed my dear friends and good companions.

The only other English-speaking person I met during my sojourn was a vivacious young and dusky Brazilian girl who came, of her own free will, and sat beside me in the little garden. She told me she had been 'finished' at the Monkey Club, so had my sister – small world – fairly animate, she had that undeniable simian look, she also had an invisible young husband lurking somewhere in the foliage chatting up a tree.

Oh, yes! I also met a bearded young American, yoked to a vast brass cross that reached from his neck to his navel. He said he was a Child of God and that his name was Abraham: 'Call me Abe.' Feeling in a sacrificial mood I replied, 'I'm Isaac.'

'Farewell, Brother,' he said as he passed on – fly zip of his blue jeans at half-mast.

From Urubamba I cut across old Inca trails towards the formidable gorge of the Apurimac River which was once crossed by the greatest bridge ever engineered by the Incas which also inspired Thornton Wilder's famous novel entitled *The Bridge of San Luis Rey.*

The Incas were amazing bridge builders: suspension, pontoon, cantilever and permanent stone types were all known to them. But the one over the Apurimac was their finest achievement and was known to them as the sacred bridge of Huaca Chaca. It was made by plaiting together fibres from the maguey plant; these were then twisted into giant ropes which formed the suspension cables. Llamas with or without loads could get across but the Spaniards' mules and horses found it terrifying, as did the Spaniards themselves. Historians seem to think that the first bridge was probably constructed about 1350 A.D., it was then kept in working order for over five hundred years.

Every village in the Inca Empire had to pay a service tax called mita which could be paid in transport or military equipment or by service as litter bearers. For the village of Curahuasi, however, it was the upkeep and maintenance of the great sacred suspension bridge (Huaca Chaca): namely the restringing of cables which took place every two years. Because it was the village nearest the bridge, the villagers of Curahuasi performed that task right through the Inca period, the Spanish occupation, Peruvian Independence and well into the Republican regime. They strung the suspension ropes for the last time in 1879.

Knowing all this I was most disappointed when I finally reached the site, for the waters of the Apurimac, which means 'great speaker', seemed to me to be *notably* muted at the point which the famous bridge once spanned. The gorge seemed comparatively low and open here although further downstream the canyon did narrow and tighten. The Apurimac at this sacred spot is more or less on the same latitude as the Urubamba at Machu Picchu and compared with its terrible and turbulent twin is a veritable millpond.

In fact, I crossed at the modern bridge of Cunyac

scarcely realising I was crossing the formidable Apurimac River. The modern Cunyac bridge was probably built when the road was constructed in 1932 and is not unlike the George Washington Bridge in New York on a diminutive scale. I don't know how many bridges have spanned this gorge but the one celebrated by Thornton Wilder was a Spanish Colonial structure linking the main arterial highway between Lima and Cuzco. 'On Friday noon, July the twentieth, 1714, the finest bridge in all Peru broke and precipitated five travellers into the gulf below,' begins one of the alltime greatest classics.

The old etchings and engravings I have seen of the Apurimac gorge at this historic point of fact and fiction show it to be an extraordinarily awesome, extraordinarily narrow canyon. But in reality this is just not so. The remains of the romantic bridge are still there – showing pillars or abutments deeply embedded into either side of the gorge. From a couple of photographs which I took I estimated the distance from bank to bank just below a tame watershoot to be seventy-five to one hundred yards. I felt let down.

I continued my way by old Inca trails, off the beaten track to the village of Limatambo which lies in a deep, narrow, rather muggy valley under the shadow of the sublime Mount Salcantay, which according to the locals few people have ever climbed and even fewer returned from. The village was formerly a *tambo* or rest house in Incan times on the great Imperial turnpike stretching between Cuzco and Quito in Ecuador, a distance of 2,000 kilometres (1,250 miles).

I was sitting in the one and only roadside transport café nobly writing up my diary. I had just penned the facetious entry, 'Met no one I knew' when a Volkswagen drew up decanting a young Swiss couple. Taking a long look at me they exclaimed sotto voce, 'Isn't your name Sebastian Snow? Didn't you meet an American schoolmaster and his wife near Lake Argentino in Patagonia? We met them and they talked a lot about you.'

I replied, 'I had indeed' – the schoolmaster had taken a whole roll of films of me. Small world – getting smaller every day.

The next day (18th November) proved to be one of the very hardest of my entire trip; not because of the terrain or of any untoward incident but because of the listless condition in which I appeared to have sunk. My legs felt flimsy and rubbery and my rucksack seemed to weigh a ton; clearly I had been over-doing things of late. In fact, it was the very first time I had *not* met my immediate nocturnal objective, the cable-stringing village of Curahuasi, situated high above the Apurimac defile. I camped approximately three kilometres short, utterly spent, scarcely able to erect the tent, even in slow motion, replay of a replay of a replay.

I finally made Curahuasi the next day and tottered miserably into this sad passé place. In pre-Inca times this was the central point for the Quechua tribe who were large and dominant when the Incas were still struggling down in the Cuzco valley. The Quechuas were first brought low by the powerful Chancas and then conquered and absorbed by the increasingly expanding Incas. Nobody knows what language the Incas originally spoke but after overthrowing the Quechuas they took over their language and used it ever after. The name Curahuasi turned out to have nothing to do with their bridge-mending activities but to mean 'house of gold' for the winds are so strong in the afternoons hereabouts that the Incas found them excellent for fanning fires to smelt gold, employing the winds like punkahs.

I now began to cross directly over the mountains by muddy horse trails (the rains had now begun in earnest), marching as the condor flies, instead of making endless serpentine turns which overlapped and ran parallel to each other. For the highway snakes over the hills in a long limitless series of low gradients for the convenience of unacclimatised vehicular traffic of which there was a marked paucity. Crossing by trail in a more or less straight line, often arduous and exhausting, halved the distance although seeming to treble it at the time. I never consulted a compass or anything brazenly avant garde like that, although I had one with me, one of Anna's many magnificent gifts. Most of her other presents were underclothes, of which she had few to spare!

After a hardish, rough and tumble journey of ten and a half hours from my last stop, I arrived in Huancarama and the very first person I met in this otherwise entirely Indian village was a young jovial Irish priest, Father Desmond, who at once invited me to stay with him and Father Raymond for as long as I liked. These two missionaries belonged to the Missionary Society of St. James the Apostle based on Boston and founded by Cardinal Cushing in 1958. The Society had seventy priests spread over Ecuador, Peru and Bolivia. Together with one large parish that included seventeen churches and twenty villages.

Huancarama means in the Quechua tongue 'the man who sings' but was colloquially known amongst the Irish brethren as 'little London' because of the pea-souper that so often shrouded it in a mantle of dense November fog. The locals called it cover pot, a significant appellation that underlined its notorious lack of hospitality; however from my point of view this was more than compensated for by the bounteous generosity, goodwill and joie-de-vivre of the charming Irishmen.

During my stay I learnt many things: that the illiteracy rate in the Department of Apurimac was nearly eighty per cent; that professors often lived a long way from their schools and took days commuting to and fro (they probably only actually taught about three days a week); that children naturally did not turn up at harvest time and that many had to journey a long way from their homes in the outlying fastnesses of the Sierra without, of course, the benefit of any school bus.

I asked Father Desmond to explain to me why the Indians had stuck very ornate and garish crosses up on the roofs of their dwellings. Evidently it signified that one, two or three godfathers, according to the number of crosses, had helped build and finance the house. A large black cross on the door meant that the family was in mourning for a dead one, inside.

At Corpus Christi, he told me, there was a procession of all the thirteen districts of Cuzco; each district brought the statue of their patron saint into the great cathedral and afterwards all processed around the main square; vying with one another to see who had the best decorated 'float'. At Pentecost a statue of the infant Christ was taken to the summit of the huge 6,100 metre (20,000 foot) mountain Ausengate – some climb!

I enquired about local agriculture and was informed that the Indians cultivated many varieties of potatoes, corn, maize and a cereal they called quinoa. Their diet was potatoes and corn plus the occasional guinea-pig, once a month as a special treat.

I stayed a couple of days with the hospitable Fathers. When I left Father Raymond gave me a note to their American confrères in the small town of Andahuaylas which read as follows: —

> The undersigned deputy acting ambassador of Her Majesty's Royal Government at the Court of St. James in Huancarama does hereby ask and require that all persons of good will – if such there be in that Godforsaken town of Andahuaylas – afford the bearer of this note all the hospitality he deserves as a loyal subject of the Crown. Up the I.R.A.

Very Irish.

Through the good offices of the Governor, and through no fault of his own, a guide was dredged up from skid row to conduct me across the circuitous route to Andahuaylas. This was Don Arturo, aged fifty-two, the very antithesis of what an upstanding Quechuan male is supposed to be. Instead of being sturdy and thick set with a large well-developed chest for breathing at high altitudes and good strong legs, he was a jobless, incredibly ragged little wizened scarecrow, with a decidedly venal visage, who could have found employment anytime by simply standing motionless among the sweet-peas in anyone's kitchen garden.

During our brief thirteen and a half hour Sunday stroll over the hills and far away Don Arturo tentatively put forward a number of wanton excuses for not journeying further.

First it was aguadiente, the local firewater, fabricated from fermented sugar cane; highly potent. 'Would I like . . . ?' Then it was cerveza, the Cuzco made beer. 'Would I like . . . ?' Then it was chicha, fermented maize/corn, tasting rather like bad cider. 'Would I like . . . ?' Then it was coca. 'Would I like . . . ?' Finally I was offered the services of a young, comely Indian girl, her dog and her shaggy llamas, grazing peacefully on the *puna* – fortunately they all bolted as if the furies were at their heels at the sight of Don Arturo (or was it of me?). He offered them as a sort of package deal – a kind of convenience meal. This last made me howl with laughter, as I recalled the well-known rhyme, so heinously applicable at the time:

There was a young man called Arturo
Who said about shacking I do know
A woman is fine
A boy divine
But a llama is numero uno.

I allowed Don Arturo none of these delights except coca which I thought would put a tiger in his tank and speed him up. It did.

Don Arturo, like about five million other Indians, was an addict. He stuffed a quid of wad of coca leaves into the side of his mouth adding a pinch of lime. This combined with his own saliva to give the desired effect. His lips turned green, his cheeks bulged and his eyes glittered in a remote, unearthly kind of way. He looked grotesque.

Author Harold Osborne, says the Quechua has 'A high degree of physical insensibility which is now artificially enhanced by masticating the natural anaesthetic coca, rendering him impervious to the effects of hunger, cold, exhaustion and pain to an extent which perhaps is unequalled in any other race'. Hence no doubt the comment, 'If coca did not exist, neither would Peru' which was made by the Spanish chronicler Pedro de Cieza de Leon.

As far as I could gather coca-chewing over a protracted period did lead to addiction and to a general physical collapse. The most immediately obvious effect could be seen in the eyes and it was clearly a strong anaesthetic; eventually the Indian's whole manner would become apathetic and benumbed until he could no longer lead a positive way of life. Once completely addicted, deterioration was only a matter of time.

Poor Don Arturo looked as if he was born an addict; indeed, he looked as if he had been inducted into coca-chewing in embryo when he was little more than a foetus.

Nevertheless, the Incas called coca 'the divine Plant'.

Eventually I did make Andahuaylas. Don Arturo told me its name meant 'balmy land of copper' but that the locals had long ago nicknamed it 'lazy town'. Here I was given a magnificent welcome by Father Bill and Father Vic, both of whom said 'You can stay as long as you like', even though I had turned up out of the inky night, djinn-like, soaked to the skin, and had shaken myself like a wet dog all over their sitting room floor.

'I guess you could use a shower,' said Father Bill.

'I guess I could,' I replied hesitatingly – and I really did . . . have a shower.

One rainy evening while sitting around chewing the

cud, listening to Handel's *Messiah* with Father Bill and Father Vic, the latter had this interesting anecdote to add to my collection.

'Sebastian, what do you think of this one? On returning to Andahuaylas from vacation in Bolivia last year, I learned that one of our town beggers, a charming alcoholic, by the name of Santos, had disappeared during my absence. Santos used to sleep in a lean-to in our churchyard and came around daily for his ration of food. On checking at the local police station, I was told by the Captain, "Ah, yes – Santos. He went off to Lima to work."

' "Officer," I replied, "you and I both know that Cantos was physically and psychologically incapable of working. Do you know what everyone in the town is saying? That he's been used as the *pagapa* in the new bridge that was just built on the Abancay road."

'At which the Captain burst into peals of laughter. *Pagapa* is a Quechua word that refers to the custom the Incas had of burying a person alive in a bridge or arch under construction, so that his spirit would support the structure forever.

'The day that Santos had disappeared, 17th August (a night or so before the concrete was poured in the bridge) a shopkeeper claimed to have seen him, stone-drunk, forced on to the back of an engineer's pick-up.

'Whether or not Santos was used as a *pagapa*, Sebastian, I don't know. But I do know that the year before, I saw with my own eyes a complete human skeleton in the substructure of the colonial arch in our church, while we were re-inforcing it. However, I keep telling myself, "But that was the seventeenth century!" '

Surely the very acme of pathos.

I was glad of my few days' rest with the priests for I was becoming increasingly aware that Peru is twice the size of France. It took me six days to climb out of Andahuaylas which is situated at approximately eight thousand feet. I climbed to over fifteen thousand feet, then abruptly descended to a mere three thousand, then up again to over twelve thousand, then down to seven thousand three hundred feet.

My immediate and longstanding lodestar was Lima but I still had over five hundred and fifty kilometres to cover and only nineteen days to Christmas to cover it in over rugged country. I might just sneak down someone's chimney on time but it would be a close run thing.

The trouble was the difficulty of the terrain, the rain and the weight of my pack, plus the rapid change in temperature that involuntarily slows progress and saps energy. I seemed to creep along the Inca trails toiling every kilometre. I did in fact achieve more than eighty kilometres in fifteen hours' very hard pounding and the previous night I was still walking in my sleep but at least I was pointed in the right direction and in good spirits.

I might have had to spend Christmas on the road but hoped not. All the towns around were making their preparations for celebrating the twelve days of Christmas. Originally this was, I think, a Greek custom and the twelve days began on Christmas Day and ended at Epiphany but here each town chose a day. For instance the three small contiguous towns of Talavera, Andahuaylas and San Jeronimo had each chosen 25th December, 1st January and 6th January so that the fiesta time would continue with great gusto for the whole period. The Spanish missionaries encouraged these fiesta periods for they felt that they enabled them to care for the religious, spiritual and temporal needs of the people without too much travelling. All the Quechuas came down from the mountains in droves on these occasions: to confession, to communion, to get their children baptised in great numbers and to get married, also in great numbers, and the priests were waiting. It saved them wandering the sierras in search of their flocks; it was a great social event, with much dancing, until they dropped; much drinking, until they dropped; but above all much goodwill was manifested. The very spirit of Christmas.

Lima
Peru
28th December 1974

Dear J,

I am absolutely head over heels with delight that Christian is flying out to meet and walk with me on 21st February. Tell him to meet me at the Banco de Londres y Montreal in Guayaquil on the 21st. It is through the Ecuadorian Andes towards Quito.

Kindest regards,
Sebastian

P.S. Do tell Chris that I could not possibly walk him off his legs . . . in Tierra del Fuego a ninety-two year old poodle (ninety-two in doggy years) walked me off my feet.

P.P.S. I am woefully short of reading matter, any paperbacks by Mark Twain would be a God-send.

Ancon
Peru

3rd January 1974

Dear J.,

Today lost *vital* contact lens. Would you please be very, very kind and telephone my optician in Exeter (Prescott, 14 City Arcade) and ask him to make ONE LEFT EYE contact lens as soon as possible. Send it out with Christian when he meets me on the road between Loja and Cuenca, Ecuador on 22nd February.

Otherwise all going very, very well.

Kindest regards and best wishes,

Sebastian

CHAPTER SEVEN

PERU: DESERT

I had not envisaged Cuzco to Lima as being such a hard slog. It had not looked so rough from the map. One moment I was crossing a col at 15,000 feet in a snowstorm and the next I was down to 3,000 feet sweating with energy-sapping humidity.

I made Lima at long last on 23rd December. Well over half of a continent covered in ten and a half months. Lima turned out to be incredibly expensive and I decided to quit as soon as possible as I had no intention of becoming sybaritic at this price. My small English-run pension cost approximately three pounds sterling a day, all found. It was on the sea and so healthier and less polluted than central Lima which is a huge metropolis of 3,000,000 souls.

In Lima I had a letter from my father who, although virtually blind and practically unable to write, said among other wonderful things, 'I pray for you every day and have fanciful ideas of angels flying over you to protect you.' He is eighty-three and the kindest of men.

I picked my way out of Lima with unaccustomed facility as far as the airport. A brand new airport said to be more splendid than Orly. I dropped in for a cup of coffee at the snack bar and then had to scramble to the lavatory helter-skelter where I was caught with my trousers down, with a virulent attack of squitters and no bumph – just like Orly.

From the airport onwards I marched through sandhills on either flank; hard going, very hot and very humid, probably about 32°C (90°F). I was carting nearly sixty pounds of rucksack and wearing a double ventile jacket simply because it was too big to pack and too awkward and heavy to carry so the net result was a daily nine hour long sauna bath which I presumed was destined to last for the next thousand kilometres or so.

The sidewalk adjacent to the good, well-cambered asphalt road was sandy and sometimes soft, even inviting in patches, but much more frequently riddled with a plethora of small loose sharp stones that contrived and succeeded in making life one long bloody *bastinado* as if one was literally walking on hot coals or across an active lava flow à la Sangay.

I tried to accept this kind of *auto-da-fé* (Dr. Scholl would have had apoplexy) for I knew it to be my lot for the next month or so: I even endeavoured to enjoy it in a masochistic sort of way. My legs stood up fairly well: thank God they did for I would not have known how to do without them.

There was much traffic, all going full bat, causing one to be constantly vigilant. I found it best, on the whole, to face the oncoming vehicles like oncoming savages. Close calls, however, were part and parcel of life – or death; as inevitable as the rising or the setting of the sun.

At one point I did not know where in the hell I was except that I was in one of the very few and far between wayside restaurants which was run by a very middle-aged buxom Dutch woman closely resembling Queen Juliana; maybe she was Queen Juliana for all I knew but where was that bicycle and that man perennially wearing dark glasses? Maybe every very middle-aged buxom Dutch woman resembles Queen Juliana? In the midst of this coastal desert was Ancon 'THE' beach and summer resort for well-to-do and famous Peruvians. As Copacabana is to the Brazilians; as Punta del Este is to the Argentinians and Vina del Mar is to the Chileans so Ancon is to the Peruvians. The Bolivians have not got a beach resort only because they have got no beach.

Do hope my letter and cables get to England as I urgently need that contact lens and am very much looking forward to seeing Christian. It's so difficult explaining the topographical location of the United Kingdom.

The postmistress produced a battered old school atlas, rifled through its yellowed pages, found what she wanted and then pointed a stumpy finger to the United States.

'No, no,' I yelled, impatiently . . . that's the Colonies.'

'Same thing,' she yawned – she was really with it.

'No, it is *not* – we lost them in 1776.'

'Que lastima (what a pity), she replied.

'Yes,' I lamented, *'Que lastima* – always, always progress – but one must move with the U.S.A.'

'Sir, Senor, but I have no stamps for the United Kingdom.'

On Saturday, 5th January 1974, while lodging in a very passé hotel in a place called Chancay, I was rudely awakened at three-forty a.m. by an earthquake; fortunately it only proved to be a severe tremor. Nevertheless, everything shook, as if hell was a poppin', bed, wardrobe, walls, ceiling vibrated in unison. I fully and fatalistically accepted that the entire tenth-rate hotel would collapse on top of me like a pack of cards. Curiously I did not register fear – *at first;* I just felt horribly sick without being able to vomit satisfactorily as I always do on the calmest of millponds, be they the Serpentine or the Dead Sea.

Then, and only then, the proverbial penny dropped with a vengeance. I groped for my Argentine torch which is an old friend; I always kept it handy in one of my boots. I then thrust myself into my khaki shirt, grabbed pictures of my family, held in a plastic container, and rushed for the door. Mere details such as trousers, pants, passport and money appeared superfluous. I charged along the narrow passage to the administrator's office cum bedroom. He was fast asleep. I awoke him saying there was an earthquake or something rather nasty going on and asked rather plaintively if he thought there would be another. He shook his head and went back to sleep. Peruvians are seemingly hardened to seismic disturbances, especially after the 1970 holocaust when over fifty thousand people were killed in the Cordillera Blanca region.

Feeling rather foolish, I returned to my bed on the spurious assumption that lightning never strikes twice in the same place; at least that's what I was led to believe in the nursery. I pulled the bedclothes over my head and pretended to be an ostrich – some ostrich, some neck. However, I could not help hearing the pandemonium going on in the main square below; people leaping into cars and zooming off in all four directions of the compass, and all points in between; gears crashing, tyres screaming, children crying, dogs barking, as if the furies were in hot pursuit. They probably were.

The tremor, I learnt later over the radio, was *felt* in Lima, all the way up the coastal littoral and in many districts in the Sierra. The epicentre, according to one report, was in a small town some fifty miles east of Lima in the mountains called Matacuana where I had stayed a couple of nights before reaching Lima. This was my very first experience of a severe tremor. Although it only lasted approximately forty seconds the feeling of *utter* and *complete* helplessness was omnipresent; some uncanny agency enacting its strange drama, beyond the realm of orthodox metaphysics. I think fear of the unknown, with no weapons to combat it, is the worst kind of fear.

Once before, many years ago, I had been involved in a very minor tremor in Quito, Ecuador, where I was with a friend. It had occurred in the middle of the night and my friend's first reaction had been to yell, 'For God's sake, Sebastian, get the bloody car out,' instead of 'For God's sake, Sebastian, get the wife and kids out!' Of course he had had his priorities right, none of that bloody avant-garde stuff of women and children first as the ship went down.

Chancay was a small fishing port of some ten thousand inhabitants situated in a fan-like fluvial oasis irrigated by a small river of the same name where sugar cane, cotton and vegetables were grown. Once out of the oasis, and this applied to all of them, I got the feel of the desert heat, a punkah wallah was obligatory, a parasol mandatory, a mandarin's fan optional.

On the day following the tremor, I was breakfasting at a wayside restaurant when a bearded gent asked very politely if he could sit at my table although all the other tables were unoccupied. After discussing the incipient earthquake he asked me what I was doing. I replied that I was walking to Panama. Unlike other Peruvians he digested this piece of information with complete equanimity as if it were a run-of-the-mill little toddle. I was even slightly piqued. He never told me his name, but I put him down either as a gentleman of the press or a detective when he insisted on paying for my huge breakfast.

Later the same day a young and very animated Peruvian girl throttled down and pulled up her car near me in the desert. She sauntered over to me wiggling a very engaging bottom, presumably wishing to take a closer look at this unusual sight.

'Desert driving is very monotonous,' she announced without preamble.

'Desert marching is no sinecure,' I replied. Her English was colloquial and flawless except for a faint Spanish accent which she would never lose, even if she had lost everything else, which by the look of her she had already done without dissent.

'Where did you learn your English?' I asked.

'At Ascot.'

'I was at school near Ascot,' I said.

'How near?' she asked.

'Near enough, Slough Grammar.'

'What on earth is an old Etonian doing here in our desert?'

'Making his bed.'

'What for?'

'To lie on it – what else; would you like a quick peep inside my tent, it's a very special tent?'

'How many people can you squeeze into it?'

'One and a half – at a pinch.'

'Well, it would be a welcome change from etchings: I've always wanted to meet the Sheik of Araby,' she joked. 'Where have you come from?'

'Down the road.'

'Where are you going to?'

'Up the road,' I replied.

'Do you belong to an organisation like S.M.E.R.S.H. or anything like that?'

'Naturally.'

'Have you a Bentley and a Beretta?'

'Both – but not with me.'

'You interest me. What's your name?'

'A four letter word. Guess.'

'Bond.'

'No – Snow.'

People in general are friendly and vivacious on the coast; the very antithesis of those of the Sierra. For instance children do not shout 'Gringo, Gringo, Gringo' every other minute becoming cross when they get no reply. Nor do grown-ups perennially ask where one has come from and where one is going. In a word they are not curious, this is partly due to climatic conditions, partly to race and partly to the practical attitude they have developed towards the exigencies of the Pan-American Highway with its constant current of traffic, day and night.

The day before I crossed a large fifty mile slice of pure unsullied desert and I had a further fifty miles in front of me: a barren, sterile terrain of large sandhills and sand-dunes that sometimes encroached and dipped down on to the turnpike in drifts.

I still marched by the watch, which I found a morale booster, stopping for five minutes every hour. Temporarily I took the weight off my feet and shoulders, lay on my rucksack surrounded on all sides by seemingly limitless desert and drank three or four mouthfuls of water from a bottle labelled GIN which was practically at boiling point by mid-day.

While on these arduous desert marches where heat benumbed thought, I frequently simulated the matador against the unending bulls that entered my arena, namely, the terrifying traffic. These irresponsible actions I found salutary to my state of mind: shock tactics.

Often I walked head-on into the line of the oncoming juggernauts blindly disposed to speed for speed's sake. Whenever I considered a car or a long distance lorry driving too dangerously or too fast I would will myself to head straight for them. Ninety-five per cent scrupulously avoided me, but there was the odd five per cent who were not to be moved from their chosen course. At such times, and they were often, I knew real naked terror as I leapt towards the verge at the last moment.

My real reason for this masochistic behaviour was somehow to break down the awesome accidie and ennui that pervaded my mind during these monotonous marches. These risks were coldly and calculatedly taken, for each evening when I went to bed I steeled myself to meet them on the morrow. This was a very personal antidote against despair, of throwing in the sponge. There were innumerable crosses beside the road where fatal accidents had taken place, sometimes twenty or thirty in a single spot, to alleviate my jaded spirits. I did *not* want to become one more victim.

When I took a rest, vehicles of all kinds hurtled by. I steadfastly gazed at a sand-dune, in a vacant kind of way, thus making it clear to motorists I did not want a lift. A rather anti-social attitude, but too many drivers were too kind in the desert for obvious reasons. I probably looked rather ludicrous dressed in the heavy double ventile jacket, sweater, shirt and vest in addition to climbing breeches while everyone else was sweating freely in lightweight shirts and lightweight trousers. I wore those clothes because they were to hand. The desert was not very breezy, the only breeze I encountered was from the slipstream of passing transports.

In the midst of this seemingly endless monotonous desert strip, halfway between Lima and the frontier, I came across a great river valley oasis. The area was first irrigated by a network of channels way back in the obscure fourth century. These early people built the great adobe city of Chan Chan which once allegedly contained a population of 40,000. Adobe is a very friable substance – making its preservation over the years all the more remarkable. Inevitably, it has suffered at the hands of avaricious souvenir-hunting tourists, and from contiguous hacienda owners and householders who can put the adobe to good use, in addition to Nature itself who unleashed the great floods of 1925. As an intact adobe city Chan Chan has no peer, neither in the middle-east nor far-flung Tartary.

Chan Chan and its kingdom were over-run by the Incas in about 1460 when the latter were nearing the plenitude of their power; before they themselves were conquered by the Spanish in the mid-sixteenth century.

The Spanish needed somewhere to halt in this desolate spot, so they built the city of Trujillo in the well-irrigated valley and I found the place full of early colonial houses with grilled gratings and projecting wooden balconies.

I decided to rest here for a couple of days over my birthday in order to celebrate being forty-five in a garden-like ambience before hitting the desert again. For desert marching was hell. The sun made my feet swell. At the end of each day's march I spent at least a couple of hours simply rubbing out the pain, almost delectable in its intensity. The humidity sapped my energy; all day long my body was bathed in sauna-like sweat; rivulets poured down face and neck emanating bead-like from my eyebrows and sweat burned the corners of my eyes. My dry lips were stuck together, trapped by a filthy combination of adhesive glutinous saliva, salt and sweat which congealed and was the very devil to get off.

As I marched along the periphery of the tarmac or, of necessity, on the tarmac itself, I hardly had time to look to my left or right for I was blinkered, constantly having to keep a very sharp look-out to watch what was ahead; listening to what was behind. A moment's aberration could be my last – and very nearly had been many times. All my senses were keyed up through the heat and burden of the day. Indeed, I had reached a point where I could almost smell danger.

The Pan/American highway was alive with traffic of all sorts and sizes. It was not a very wide arterial strip but quite sufficient for two large trucks to pass each other in safety.

However, often deep sand encroached upon it, forming herring-bone like dunes fashioned and furrowed by the cool nocturnal breezes. At these places there was absolutely no latitude for error. One mistake – either a trip caused by the turning of a tired ankle, or a slip in a moment of absentmindedness could be – so easily – my last.

I had already decided that it was on the whole best to walk like a good Highway Code pedestrian, facing the oncoming traffic, of which there was a great deal; although it was the vehicles that stealthily and noiselessly crept up behind me to overtake that were the most alarming. The right sleeve of my voluminous double ventile jacket was, literally, brushed on three separate occasions – by two cars and a lorry – travelling at high speeds. My automatic reflex action was to rub my sleeve petulantly.

The only alternative to this risky business was literally to wade through the desert, more than ankle deep in hot, soft sand and totally exhausting; progress would have been impossibly snail-like dressed, as I was, like a pregnant polar bear on safari.

Crosses in the sand were sobering and too frequent for my liking. Some were stark and sombre, others ornate, even festive. Every single one that I passed without exception made me involuntarily make the sign of the cross in homage to the dead and hope for the living, for there but for the grace of God went I. In addition to the crosses I came across many little shrines situated at significant and specific topographical points.

Oddly enough the whole way up from Lima, I had seen the remains of only two dogs both of which were barely discernible as they had become part of the tarmacadam as if a steamroller had been at work.

I have invariably found lorry drivers considerate, courteous and kind. They were constantly trying to give me lifts; I had the greatest difficulty making them *understand* I wanted to walk. This was made all the more difficult to explain becauses of the limitless expanses of desert. For instance when I said *'à pied por favor . . . muchissimo gracias'*, they more often than not switched off their engines and stared at me fixedly in total disbelief, as if I had come from some other planet. This action had its comic side too, because on occasion, vehicle after vehicle pulled up, one behind the other – until a long queue was rapidly formed, all gazing with overt incredulity at this curious 'Gringo' dressed as if he were in Siberia. Some drivers actually pleaded with me to take a ride saying they were lonely, that the way ahead is long, dreary and waterless. They spoke the truth. At other times, my Spanish completely exhausted, I simply pointed to my feet when they invited me to jump in or jump up according to the conveyance; hoping this little mime would have the effect desired. Often it did not for they switched off their ignition leaving the vehicle in the road causing a blockage, got out, crossed over and asked what was wrong with my feet!

Slowly as I walked north the countryside changed from desert to no desert, little water but sparse vegetation, then scrubby trees and bushes on hard beaten earth appeared, goats and donkeys abounded. The climate became steadily hotter and more humid as I approached Piura, the very first township to be founded in 1532 by Francisco Pizarro, who called it more formally, San Miguel de Piura. He stopped here before marching on to capture and hold the great Inca Atahualpa to ransom. Pizarro garrotted Atahualpa at the last minute instead of burning him at the stake, even though he had turned Christian and paid the required ransom in gold. Piura is well inland – a large oasis, entirely dependent, until fairly recently, on the very temperamental Piura River which runs through the town. Colloquially it is known as the mad river for it swiftly changes mood: at one moment it's a raging torrent sweeping everything before it, next it's a mere trickle, causing a widespread drought in an otherwise verdant fluvial valley. It never reaches the sea but ends up in a large depression in the midst of the Sechura Desert, *tierra despoblado,* where no one lives, except for a few fishermen on the coast, so that it has remained in the main quite undisturbed since pre-Inca times.

When I crossed the Piura River it was very low, in fact it is very low and dry most of the year. So now it is to be linked to the nearby Chira River by a fifty-four kilometre canal and the Chira River itself is to have a huge eleven kilometre dam built across it which will make a vast reservoir. The water so obtained will be used to irrigate long-abandoned cultivated land where the best-quality cotton in the world used to be grown. Lately the land had become saline, however, owing to lack of water but soon all will be changed. Yugoslav engineers were constructing the dam but the whole project was being designed and supervised by the British.

Quite fortuitously I met an old friend, Hew Fanshawe, whose father, a Major-General, had once taught me to keep broiler chickens. Hew turned out to be engaged on the design side of the £60,000,000 dam project.

I stayed with Hew and his wife Colina, enjoying great hospitality. Among other peculiarities regarding Piura, they told me that vehicles have the right of way over pedestrians when the road is parallel to the river; this must be very confusing to the tourist who has never been to Piura before and does not know which way the river turns or where it is. Also vehicles can only be driven five days a week for some reason.

One of Hew Fanshawe's acquaintances, on being told I had come from Tierra del Fuego averaging overall twenty-five kilometres per day including multifarious 'stop-overs', asked what sort of car I had driven? The Fanshawes were not as surprised by this comment as I was for when Colina had bought a donkey for her small son Rupert, she had been asked, quite seriously, why she wanted a donkey when she had a car.

Not far away was Cabo Blanco where Ernest Hemingway's little masterpiece *The Old Man And The Sea* had been filmed – once it had been one of the very best angling centres in the world for marlin and tuna but now the 'big ones' had left the area, either because of the vagaries of the current, or more probably as a result of over fishing.

From Piura to the town of Sullana was thirty-eight kilometres of pure unadulterated desert, barren and sterile, except for two bordellos, or happy houses as they were colloquially referred to by the English-speaking community. One brothel was situated exactly five kilometres north of Piura and the other exactly five kilometres south of Sullana; they looked like Saharan Beau Geste forts. Apparently they were much frequented by Yugoslav construction engineers whose wives could not or had not joined them yet. I had occasion to stop at the bordello south of Sullana for I was very thirsty – *SHORT OF WATER* – and had some difficulty disengaging myself from the blandishments of the occupants. Fear of the consequences strengthens the will. A girl showed me a necklace of imitation pearls a French gentleman had given her – thus displaying her price and availability. I fled.

Whilst in Piura I had tried to find someone who would change my superfluous Peruvian currency into Ecuadorian sucres for officially I was only allowed to take the equivalent of about ten pounds sterling out of Peru and I could not afford to jettison the rest. I was most impressed with myself when I not only found someone who would change my money for me, but also someone who would then take it into Ecuador. I carefully wrote down his address, name and passport number on the fly-leaf of a quasi-pornographic paperback which I specially purchased for this reason. I then made my go-between, or smuggler, make a note in his own handwriting of the amount in the same paperback. He wrote, 'Lolita pay bearer 14,800 sucres (37,000 soles)'. I was pleasantly surprised that my accomplice in crime had written it the right way round.

The novel was called *The Golden Girls;* on the front cover were three naked blondes titillating, on the back cover the legend read, 'Seven marriages and a string of millionaire lovers gave them a taste for luxury that could only be gratified by the subtle exploitation of their nubile bodies . . . and the hungry men who craved them.' Stupidly I thought that this innocent bed-time story would be the very last thing the frontier police would bother about when they should have been scrupulously searching for arms, drugs or forged passports. *The Golden Girls* was, of course, the very first thing that held and riveted their attention. Thumbing through the name, address, passport number and details of the amount of money of my accomplice were quickly perceived . . . without the least interest.

One of the guards said, 'You want good woman?'

'No thank you, not today.'

'I find good woman . . . you get "it" good.'

'That's the trouble,' I replied, for I had visions of trekking south, back down the desert to Lima, in scorching search of an 'understanding' physician.

Realising I must come clean, tell all, for my smuggler lived on the other side of the frontier, I innocently asked the guards if they thought my accomplice would pay up, not up-sticks and bolt, as a sensible man would do.

'No, no,' they replied in unctuous unison, as if I had mortally offended their amour propre. 'We know him *very well,* he is a *very honest man.*' This piece of unsolicited news pleased me greatly for it confirmed I was a good judge of character and knew 'a very honest man' when I saw one for once.

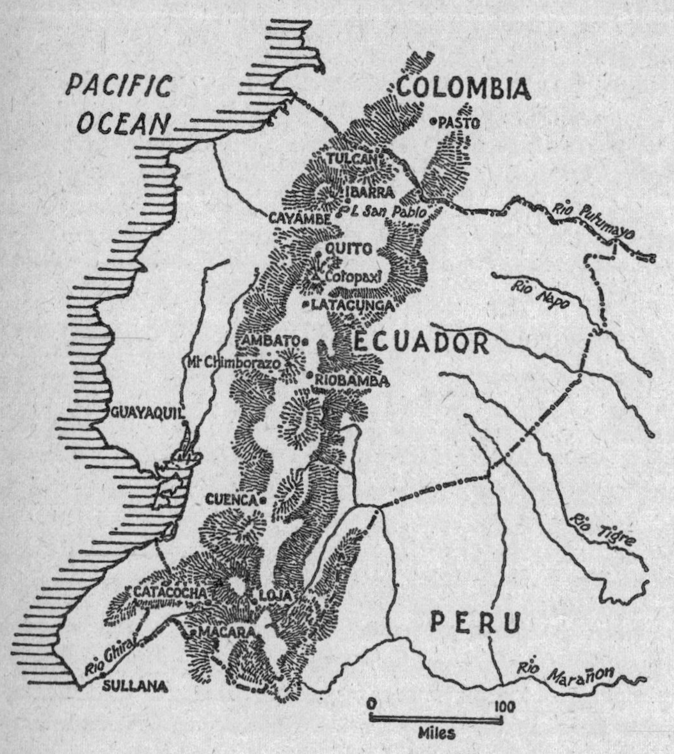
PACIFIC
OCEAN
COLOMBIA
PASTO
TULCAN
IBARRA
L San Pablo
CAYAMBE
Rio Putumayo
QUITO
Cotopaxi
Rio Napo
LATACUNGA
AMBATO
ECUADOR
Mt Chimborazo
RIOBAMBA
GUAYAQUIL
CUENCA
Rio Tigre
CATACOCHA
LOJA
PERU
MACARA
Rio Chira
SULLANA
Rio Marañon
0
100
Miles

CHAPTER EIGHT

ECUADOR

Ecuador at long last: I had been walking for over a year now. At Macara, on the Peruvian-Ecuadorian border, it was hot, about 29°C and bloody humid. But I had a very easy border crossing and the frontier police gave me permission to stay the night in their station. I slept very comfortably on a couple of rifle butts chained and locked to the bed, covered with a couple of shirts which made an exemplary pillow. I was given a solemn warning about bandits and robbers which I did my best to take to heart.

By now I can instinctively tell whether a slice of country is potentially hostile or not, whether it is subject to rustlers and thieves, by the way the local dogs behave towards me and the way they bark. Their size is also a good indication of the honesty of the place and the way they approach a man of the road.

The distance to the first town in Ecuador of any size, Loja, varied in the estimation of geographers and savants from one hundred and twenty kilometres to two hundred and eighty kilometres. No map was available in Macara, but the Ecuadorian Consul in Sullana had given me his; it was a very elegant map but unfortunately the distances from place to place were marked in such small print that I could not see them without a microscope. Finally an eagle-eyed little gamin, whom Fagin would have at once employed, read out the numbers to me while I toted them up: sum total, 210 kilometres – which made it about four days' march.

As soon as I left Macara to climb up into the wooded hills with their bushy-top trees, far apart and not very tall, I passed a number of pastoral *casas* where all the dogs, without exception, proved most courteous and friendly, as did their owners.

After about two to three hours of trekking I called in at a small wayside hacienda where I was warmly greeted like a long lost blood brother and immediately proffered delectable slices of Fuller's sponge cake and endless cups of Nescafé. I showed the owner some photographs of my father and of my son and he said, 'Very good stock, very significant'; the very same words Father Vic had uttered on seeing them in Andahuaylas, way back between Cuzco and Lima in Peru.

For the second night running I slept in a police post, but this was a rather energetic place so I did not get much sleep as the policemen always seemed to be changing watch every other minute and clomping around the wooden floors in their heavy boots and shining torches with searchlight-like beams which woke me up. Their watch replacements yelled in whispers like the chiming of the bells at Notre Dame, trumpeting into the 'deaf' ears of supine shapes and forms.

Despite such a restless night I went on to cover forty-five kilometres in a long, rather arduous eleven-hour march, finally fetching up at Catacocha just as the light was failing. This time I slept in a dormitory with two non-commissioned and ten other ranks who received and welcomed me with the greatest possible graciousness. The day following I was asked where I had lodged the previous night.

'I slept with the Army,' I replied pompously.

'What all of it?'

'Yes, all twelve of it.'

Four hard days of clambering up and down hills brought me inland up into the mountains of Loja. Here I felt the cold after so many long days spent in the desert under a pitiless sun. I had had to stop to put on my combs and winter woollies.

Propping up the reception desk at the Hotel Rio

Amazonas, talking to the young desk clerk was an American writer called Grace. 'Suddenly', as Grace put it, 'I heard the clomp, clomp of heavy boots, the front door crashed open and heavy boots fell flat at my feet. Sebastian had made his debut.' This was nothing new, being my usual form of entry into a town after a hard day. I had just covered fifty kilometres in pouring rain up and down some very steep hills. The desk clerk too seemed astonished at my mode of arrival but then I discovered he always had curiously shagged out sheep's eyes by day as he went to night school and had only opened his eyes so wide to make sure he was awake and not dreaming. He had about as many rings around his eyes as he had on his fingers and that was going some.

Soon afterwards Grace and I were drinking delicious café con leche together. She was an American author who had recently flown in from Washington in order to see the very old people who lived near Loja at a place called Vilcabamba. Out of a population of 800 a census taken in 1971 showed that nine people had lived for over a century. As in Hunza and the Soviet Caucasus where there are other long lived people, there was no apparent criteria, no yardstick for such long lives. Some people smoked, some didn't; some drank, others did not; they apparently had no fixed diet but ate just what was available, such as bananas, rice and yuca which is a potato substitute. Height above sea level did not seem to have anything to do with their extraordinary longevity either for Vilcabamba is only 4,000 feet whereas Hunza and Soviet Armenia are of course considerably higher.

Grace thought their ages might have been exaggerated by the officials in Loja in the hopes that this might encourage tourism but there was no doubt that the people were old and were remarkable. They showed no signs of senility but kept active, kept working until they died. They were, she felt, a generous, cultured people who showed no signs of superstition. The old people were of both sexes, and all had white hair. The old men had white beards which indicated strong Spanish influence. They all spoke Spanish and appeared to be Spanish for the most part, not Indian or Quechua. They were poor peasant-type people who had no doubt once been victims of the cruel hacienda system with its master-slave relationship for workers. But these people had clearly learned to cope with stress in their lives and were proof that the best anti-ageing pill is exercise: keep moving. For brains and bed, there is one rule: use it or lose it.

Grace turned out to be an altogether fascinating person who had led an adventurous life. She had worked at the White House; had taken special medicine, turned her skin black and been to live in Harlem and the Mississippi in order to find out exactly what it was like to be treated as a negro; she had also lived with the Navajos Indians; she had written a best-seller and was now doing a bit of freelance journalism.

She told me that whilst she was coloured black and working as a domestic servant in the Southern States, the master of the house had wanted to assault her because as a black she was more desirable, not in spite of, but because she was black. I found her most companionable to talk to and full of intriguing pieces of information so I suggested she walk with me for a while. She explained that she had lost her suitcase and was wearing a pair of cheap ninety cent shoes purchased locally which would be unsuitable for travelling far in. I always seem to be buying people shoes so I offered to buy her a pair.

'I have bought my own shoes since I was sixteen,' she replied. 'I have struggled to win my independence and am now making my own way round the world.' Still I felt that she was tempted to accept my offer. For, as she said, a woman enjoys having her shoes paid for by someone else.

We walked in the central square mingling with the mestizo women, balancing bundles on thir heads; with horse drawn carts; with Indians carrying bundles of alfalfa for their donkys and with students. These later explained to us that Loja had a technical institute and a university of jurisprudence: it was a town full of lawyers and dentists seemingly, for if we had understood them aright there were over two hundred lawyers and as many dentists in a town of only about fifty thousand people.

I could not linger too long in Loja despite the delightful company for I had promised Christian Bonington that I would meet him on the next stretch of road before Cuenca on the 22nd February and I was determined to keep my rendezvous. Pleasure at the thought of seeing such an old friend again quickened my spirits and I raced along at a handsome pace.

Christian found me about ninety kilometres south of Cuenca. He arrived by taxi and leapt out with a great cry of surprise. What a most warm and welcoming sight he was in his bizarre T-shirt, shorts and umbrella. How delighted I was to see a real old friend after 383 days of walking alone. There had been many kind people who had helped me on my way but talking to strangers and fellow travellers was not at all the same as gossipping with someone I knew well, someone with whom I could talk about old friends in England, times we had spent together; here indeed was a link with the past.

I felt so enormously grateful to him for bothering to come: I had so looked forward to his arrival that now he was here, I felt almost incoherent. There was so much to ask, to say, to hear about that we stopped at the first village we came to for lunch and as I'd already covered twenty kilometres that day, I felt we might as well stay there for the night too.

Christian and I had known each other for eight years and together we had climbed that most active volcano, Sangay, also in Ecuador, and had hunted together with the Eskimos on Baffin Island. He was always teasing me about my lack of practicality, my absent-mindedness and my idiosyncrasies. I could see him now eyeing my, to him, outlandish garb of anorak, heavy sweaters, tweed breeches and Afrika Korps style hat and he soon started laughing at my stories; he roared hilariously when I told him that I'd already lost two wrist watches, two cameras and pairs of contact lenses without number on this trip. It confirmed his worst suspicions of my muddled madness.

Oh! but it was good to laugh and to gossip again. We quickly slipped into our old relationship and nattered together all evening. My tent was too small for both of us which was a pity, but Christian had brought his own sleeping bag so he curled up quite happily in that.

I had explained to him that I did not drink on the march but filled myself with endless cups of sweet black coffee at first light. A few old stale rolls to munch and we were on our way. As we trekked up the road between scrub-covered hillsides in a series of S bends, Christian suggested we take a short cut by walking vertically up the hill. I knew that the moment we hit rough ground Christian would be faster than me for he is essentially a climber, a coverer of uneven broken ground, used to the rocky Himalayan approach marches with their defiles and gorges. Over the last year I had established a relentless rhythm. I preferred the road where I could keep up my steady stride, so I said that I would stick to the tarmac. Several times that day he cut across into rougher terrain, but after a while I think he came round to my point of view, if not for himself, at least he came to see that it was essential for me, after thousands of miles to keep up my unchanging rhythm. He found it monotonous, but then walking is monotonous: only by making it into a disciplined pattern could I possibly march a continent. Walk for one hour, rest for five or ten minutes, walk for another hour, rest again: on and on with the same swinging pace, for hour after hour: I could keep this up for twelve hours or more and had even done it for sixty-eight kilometres at a stretch for by now I was a superbly attuned walking machine. It was the going-on-for-everness that attracted me. Lorry drivers offering me lifts, the loneliness, the fear of being knocked on the head, none of this deterred me: I did not feel any temptation to give up, to jump into a car, walking had me in its grip. I did not keep harping on how much more there was to do but of how much I had done. It did not matter either how quickly I travelled for speed was totally irrelevant in the context of the year or more I had been walking. What difference did it make if I made the next village that morning instead of that afternoon? I would make it eventually. Short cuts of minutes, hours or days seemed pointless. If the going was good and I felt in good form, I travelled in higher gear. If it was uphill wet and windy, then my pace was inevitably slower but the stride, the rhythm and the smooth steadiness remained.

I had not really thought much about this until Christian joined me but having to explain it all to him brought home to me how important my private disciplined world had become. Christian soon got tired. He leapt from tussock to tussock up the hillsides at a tremendous pace and then stood waiting for me to catch him up by the road. After sixteen miles on the first day he was footsore, bored, weary and jaded. Moreover he was hungry and thirsty, but I carried no food or water with me. Instead, I preferred to scoop what I wanted from a ditch. Christian's horrified look and his reproachful: 'Don't you use sterilising tablets?' reminded me of England, of nannies, of all I'd left behind me – the trappings of civilisation.

We were up at about two thousand four hundred and fifty metres (8,000 feet) now and the sun beat down hard at mid-day. I had become accustomed to the great temperature variation and seldom removed any clothing however hot it got, preferring to stay as I was even if it made me sweat freely. My jerseys and anorak were as useful against the sun as against the wind and rain and my jaunty cap kept my head cool. Christian's T-shirt and shorts offered him little protection against the sun's rays however and by evening he was blistered, burnt, weary and limping, only too happy to crawl into his sleeping bag in someone's garden shed and curl up for eleven hours.

Christian's company was a joy but his restlessness was disconcerting. On the second day he succumbed to a passing car after thirty-two kilometres so I was left to plod on in my accustomed fashion. I felt no desire to cheat by hitching a lift. Walking had become my way of life: to fall for temptation now would negate all that I had accomplished. It was a great pleasure though to find him waiting for me when I arrived at the next village and to find food and accommodation all lined up. He'd chosen a splendidly cheerful place with accordion and guitar accompaniment to our meal. So delighted was I with his company that I celebrated his presence by giving them all a demonstration of the eightsome reel. It had been an easy forty-eight kilometres that day, my leg muscles were well attuned and I've always been light on my feet. Dancing is such good exercise.

I think Christian found it hard that even by his third day he had not as yet covered his taxi ride out from the airport at Cuenca. The road bored him and his feet were not yet ready for long mileage. His bizarre garb seemed unsuited to the climate and I feared that his brief shorts and his long bearded face would make the authorities take him for a hippy. Remembering some of the comments I'd received at hotels earlier on I tried to persuade him to put some long trousers on but he seemed most unwilling. It would not have mattered to me for I could easily have found shelter in some back street inn but he longed for a bath and all the comforts of a luxury hotel, cleanliness, a lavatory that worked and a good meal.

After a day's rest in Cuenca we both kept on in our curious tortoise and hare fashion. Christian always plunging off the road on to railway tracks, rough paths and open country, myself plodding along the tarmac oblivious of the noise and the passing cars. Yet although he always arrived first, he seemed so much more exhausted. This did not surprise me, for I knew that walking along railway sleepers with their uneven spacing makes for a broken stride which is a greater strain on leg muscles. Pushing through mud, stumbling over rocks, struggling over scrub, wending your way round bushes requires constant weight shifting so that muscles are always tensing and straining, tightening and taking weight. Your mind has to be on the job in hand the entire time and your eyes ever watchful for jagged stones or sudden ruts. It's an easy way to sprain an ankle or pull a muscle. My humbler, drearier, dogged slog covers the ground more slowly but is less of a strain on the body and the mind. The eye and the brain are completely relaxed and at rest, the legs take over like automatons.

Despite our disagreements over speed, it had been so wonderful to have Christian with me, I only wished he would stay a little longer. The ten days I spent walking with him had been such a joy for me. What a wonderful man he is: how he can do three jobs simultaneously beggars belief but there he was writing an account of our walk together for *The Observer*, movie making, still photography taking and in addition walking with the abominable Snowman.

I was very sad when he left, it would seem lonely now for a bit until I got used to being entirely alone again. I now had to march towards Quito, Teutonic fashion, striding out.

Christian's presence had made me aware of many problems which I had not bothered myself with unduly before. Not only had he brought home to me what I was doing and the way I was doing it but he had made me think of the other risks I ran: how vulnerable I was to being robbed, how likely I was to be knocked down and killed by a passing truck and how easy it was for me to pick up some infective illness. I suspected that I was pretty tough by now and had built up considerable resistance but he'd explained to me that hepatitis and typhoid were prevalent all over South America.

With these dismal thoughts in mind, missing his company and feeling at a low ebb, I chugged along for the next three days towards Riobamba, covering between thirty-five and forty kilometres a day.

Riobamba was a considerable metropolis and here I experienced great difficulty in even getting into the seediest of hostelries; the sort of place where the owner pays one to cross his filthy threshold. The trouble was that all the better class hotels were bursting at the seams with Latin-American Womens' Basket Ball teams – strapping great ladies, at least eight feet high, with powerful muscles bursting for freedom, under their degagé tracksuits. As one knee-high Ecuadorian ventured to remark in a rather melodramatic aside, crossing his heart in deepest piety, 'I would love to be their "masseur" – until the day I die.' By the look of him it would not be long! However, the following day I managed through the connivance of an Englishman (who ought to get the V.C.) to be squeezed into a respectable hotel where these giant double-breasted Amazons bounced about like India rubber balls, in a disgustingly healthy manner, awaiting victory or elimination. One interesting little facet about Ecuadorians is that when their side is winning, be it at basket ball, soccer or any other game, they cheer like hell. When they are losing, they cheer like hell for the other side. A charming trait.

From a little eminence above my hotel I managed to glimpse Chimborazo, the monarch of the Andes at 6,272 metres (20,577 feet), but only in the early mornings, for it was totally obscured by a stratum of cloudbank that visibly and palpably crept up over its eternal snows. Chimborazo was an old friend, I had been there in 1953. Edward Whymper with his Swiss guides, the cousins Carrel, were the first to ascend it in 1880.

As late as the middle of the last century it was thought to be the highest mountain on earth. Even the great Alexander von Humboldt who scrambled part way up its slopes during his protracted tour de force in South America, thought it to be the highest peak on the globe

– until the day of his death. This of course was before the Himalayas were surveyed by Colonel Everest.

At Riobamba Mr. and Mrs. Martin Slater, both mountaineers, motored down from Quito and most hospitably invited me to stay with them at their house, romantically called La Escapada, near the village of Tumbaco some four hundred and sixty metres (1,500 feet) below Quito, the Ecuadorian capital. This was on Francisco de Orellana's route when he travelled east and which eventually led him, and about sixty other Spanish, to be the first discoverers of the mighty Amazon. They had come across the Amazon entirely fortuitously in 1541 having descended the tributaries Coca and Napo. Five years ago I also had followed Orellana's route and had travelled that way, but I had come to a watery end on a home-made raft which was smashed to matchwood a few minutes after embarkation on the torrential Coca River. I had then spent nine days on a beach not knowing whether my companion would be rescued or not.

I accepted the Slater's offer with alacrity and said that I hoped to be with them in about three days; three days of marching through an avenue of volcanoes, either active or dormant, and all old friends. But I did not get sight of any of them because of cloud. Instead I had to make do with memories and imagine them standing sentinel all around me. I skirted Chimborazo over high bleak moorland and felt dizzy in the head for the very first time on my whole trip. Even in the altiplano of Bolivia I had not felt groggy like this. I thought that maybe I was in for a bout of Soroche or mountain sickness for it is usually heralded by feelings of nausea and dizziness but as soon as I was over the col and had started the long descent into Ambato, I shucked it off.

At Ambato I stayed at a German-run joint owned by a powerful piece of German womanhood, who marshalled one and all with an all-seeing Aryan Sergeant-Major eye. Chris and I had stayed there before in 1966 when we were on our way to climb Sangay.

From Ambato I had a lazy day of forty-five kilometres' easy-going to the small, attractive townships of Latacunga where I had a shave and a wash and brush up.

Up early next morning (13th March), I set out in the direction of Quito with the avowed intention of passing the night at Machachi, a place noted for its mineral water which emanates from a spring. After bottling it is called Guitig and is circulated throughout the republic. It was not the justly famed mineral water that attracted me, but the situation of the town which afforded a comfortable spring-board for a final dive into the vale of Quito.

However as I cruised out of Latacunga, I found the periphery of the turn-pike verdant and lush and so springy under my poor old feet, I revved up from second to third, from third to top gear in a matter of seconds. My sights were set: Quito or bust, that night.

After about twenty kilometres I came to Avelina, a farm belonging to a former President Galoplaza where there were two isolated wayfarer restaurants facing each other across the artery. I hove into one of these, ordering coffee and ice-cream, and across the un-crowded room I noted two Nordic-looking priests and an Aryan lady, so I went over to their table and asked if I could join them. In the course of our conversation, one of the priests, who was English, evinced an enormous admiration for Whymper, whose name, even today, nearly a century later, is legendary in Ecuador. The priest was journeying in the opposite direction to me, towards Latacunga; in other words, south. Without more ado I asked him if he would make a telephone call for me when he reached Latacunga: could he very kindly ring up Martin Slater's firm in Quito and tell him to expect me between nine p.m. and midnight that very evening, 13th March at the Hotel Quito, opposite our British Chancellery. The good padre promised to do this. I rootled about in my pockets for a token gesture to the cloth for the cost of the call but could not find any small beer so I then charged out like the bull of Bashan coming into the arena at Pamplona: head down and hell-bent I roared north.

Clearly, I was out of my senses. Nevertheless the proverbial penny had suddenly dropped for I recalled that Martin Slater had informed me at Riobamba that Whymper and the Carrel brothers had walked from Riobamba to Quito and had covered the 201 kilometres in three days. My normally uncompetitive spirit took wings. I belted through the village of Lasso and started the long steep gradient up to the Cotopaxi Col situated at approximately three thousand three hundred and fifty-four metres (11,500 feet); where there was a North American Space and Aeronautic Station that tracked all satellites as they came overhead. I scarcely glanced at it, so intent was I on my purpose; but was told afterwards, in Quito, that the Station maintained among other apparati thirty-three llamas. Presumably in its backyard but for what purpose my *limited* imagination cannot indulge. On one occasion a mad scientist is alleged to have charged through the flock of llamas, falling flat on his face as he picked his way through yelling, 'I must catch Bessie'. I feel I must add that each satellite has a code-name – or sobriquet.

Once over the col I poured down to Machochi. Not long after quitting this long ribbon developed township, ostensibly rather down-at-heel and smelly, night began to fall. Still some thirty kilometres from goal, the elements hit me. Torrential rain, dense fog and juggernauts of traffic, often with only *one* light and that on the leg side to use a cricketing term. All this on a pitch black night without a semblance of a waxing or waning moon, or even distant glow of Chaplin's 'City Lights'. I *should* have halted, reined in and *waited* in the ditch beside the Pan-American, but my blood was up. I passed three or four drenched and pathetic looking Indians who peered at me through the all encompassing blackness with large frightened deer-like eyes as if I was some terrifying hobgoblin or at least an apparition that never before had entered their orbit. I slapped them cheerfully on the back, gave a word or two of encouragement and charged on feeling like Lord Cardigan as he led the six hundred into the Valley of Death: 'Well, here goes the last of the Snows.' On and on I went into apparent never-endingness; I was literally walking blind in both senses of the words for by now my contact lenses had peeled out of my eyes. Of course I had no torch, so could not find them in the quagmire on the periphery of the highway so marched on in my most scenic dark glasses through which I could see nothing – but vanity. I think I was fairly fortunate to stay alive for I was blinded by the lights of the oncoming traffic as it poked itself through dense fog on this torrential moonless night: it seemed to me as if one long juggernaut was set on one destination – south. At last! At last! The heart-warming glow of Quito came into view.

At last I reached the Plaza Independencia, the centre of the Colonial Quarter, but I still had a considerable trek ahead, up to the heights of the Residential Quarter, to the Hotel Quito. Passing drunks and beggars, I weaved my way through; en route pausing to ask a policeman the direction of the Hotel Quito for the capital has considerably expanded since my last visit in 1968. The policeman looked at me aghast and said, '*Lejos, Lejos.*' (Far. Far.) 'Balls,' I replied in tones that must have awoken and shaken the entire somnolent city. Having orientated myself, I took the well known Avenida 12 de Octobre (the day Columbus discovered America in 1492), which was at least three-quarters of a mile long and uphill, and proceeded at a hand gallop. I slowed to a canter past a rank of predatory taxis and strolled in through the glass doors of the Hotel Quito at one-ten a.m. on the 14th March. A trifle tired but I had made a brisk walk from Latacunga of approximately one hundred kilometres (sixty-two miles) in eighteen hours ten minutes at an average altitude of 2,600 metres (8,500 feet). Now I was thankful to have fetched up at the world's highest capital bar two, La Paz and Lhasa.

Shaking myself like a wet, but happy, retriever, among a shower of late diners, I asked for a bed as I did not wish to wake the Slaters at doom watch. There was no room at the inn. Wondering what in the hell to do, I asked rather *too* roughly if there was a message for someone called Snow. There was. 'Ring 529-990.' I did. 'Give me forty minutes,' Shirley Slater answered. I slunk downstairs to what was called the cafeteria and ordered a small bottle of beer and an ice-cream, of all things. Just as I was paying the waiter sixty-four sucres or about £1.10 at current prices, Shirley came in wearing with great panache, a Russian-like green-hooded cloak in which she looked even better than Julie Christie in *Dr. Zhivago.* This splendid mantle covered a Cromwellian tunic, trousers and top-boots, thereby manifesting a subtle reincarnation of being both a Royalist and a Roundhead simultaneously. Within seconds I was in her B.M.W. pouring through the hairpins which American gentlemen from the Deep South would describe as real white knucklers for down! down! down! we went for nearly twenty kilometres to La Escapada. We had arrived.

Here we drank dram upon dram of revitalising precious fluids through the middle watches until the first cocks crowed. On top of a foodless hard day's day that had involuntarily merged into a hard day's night I became happily paralytic and was constantly astonished to find an enormous thick tumbler of neat whisky in one hand and a glass of medicinal lemonade loaded with Vitamin C in the other, punctuated by a number of muscle relaxing capsules that I was solemnly adjured to swallow. Shirley Slater then ordered me to remove my feet, or rather my stinking, soaking, blue stockings for a thorough examination. After careful scrutiny she proclaimed them satisfactory: slightly calloused, but no fluid beneath. I was much relieved for I did not think I could afford my excellent Exeter chiropodist to be parachuted in at this stage of my long walk. Shirley Slater then proceeded to read my hand as she was an amateur palmist of some note. Grabbing my left hand, as it is the one that holds all the secrets of a mis-begotten life, in a brisk Florence Nightingale no-nonsense manner, she started searching for broken lines, for the way the lines sloped and the shape and formation in which the fingers lay in repose.

Apparently, the lines on the right hand are the inherited ones, but it is the lines on the left hand which show what one does with that inheritance. It soon became apparent that she was riveted by my left hand; the one that tells all. Repeatedly she seized it for verification, to see that she was not mistaken in any particulars. Finally she looked up at me with scarcely credible penetration, eyes wide and steady, and said quietly and sonorously: 'Your left hand is *exactly* the same as mine in every particular'. An occurrence, she went on to add, virtually unheard of. This slice of news rather alarmed me, not may I hasten to say because her hand was similar to mine, but because I have an in-built peasant fear of the supernatural. After a long, silent speaking pause I plaintively asked if I had what is known as a good life in terms of longevity and whether I would reach my destination. To both these cris-de-coeurs she replied 'yes', unequivocally. By this time dawn was wide-awake and I was nearly fast asleep. Step by step I took myself painfully to bed for by this time my muscle-power had seized up haunted by the dulcet melodies of *South Pacific* faintly to be heard somewhere in the background: 'Some Enchanted Evening', 'You Gotta Have A Dream' and finally by the voice of Kenneth McKellar giving of his best to Sir Harry Lauder's immortal 'Keep Right On To The End Of The Road'. . . .

I stayed with the incredibly hospitable and generous Slaters for six days, eating and drinking them out of house and home. They deserved an especial mention in dispatches. At the week-end Martin decided he would climb, with two others, a mountain called Illiniza South

(17,500 feet). A hard climb and by a new route but Martin was Founder President of the International Andean Mountaineers, a group which had been formed in September 1972, to promote mountain climbing among English speaking peoples in Ecuador and to help visiting climbers.

The British Ambassador and his wife, Mr. and Mrs. Mennell, very kindly invited me to stay at the Residence whilst he was away. I was simply delighted especially as the Ambassador was a cousin of mine. We could not exactly work out whether we were third or fourth cousins, but finally opted for third cousin one and a half times removed on the paternal side.

The entire Mennell family were tremendous fun and I owe them an enormous debt of gratitude, not only for their heart-warming generosity, but for the innumerable kindnesses they did to smooth my path north. Peter Mennell himself furnished me with visiting cards to all his ambassadorial friends: his defence attaché went to immense pains to obtain an introductory round robin from his counterpart at the Colombian Embassy to all authorities, police and civil, throughout the land; the Consul took me personally round to the Panamanian Chargé d'Affairs and obtained what was virtually a carte blanche or open sesame for me and all worked hard on the grapevine until they had discovered that the key information man for the Darien Gap was one El Gallo Rojo.

My main object in staying so long in Quito was to have a complete rest and overhaul which I certainly needed. But somehow, I can't think why, it didn't work out that way. I moved into the Ambassador's Residence feeling rather *de trop* with my swag upon my back and sporting my rather smart but bizarre hobo costume. I hoped that they would not notice or remark upon my lack of undergarments. But I need not have worried for their impeccable manners enabled me to forget all my problems. Instead I was made to feel very much at home and that first night Peter and I sat talking and drinking until about one a.m. when we retired. At two a.m. the Ambassador woke me in the most quiet and considerate manner as if waking a child, to say that I was wanted on the telephone, murmuring something about an accident on Illiniza South. I was in the deepest doomwatch slumber and did not at first register. My initial thoughts, if you could call them that, were like those of a person coming out of an anaesthetic. I tried to recollect where I was, in what bed, in what house, in what town, in what country and indeed what planet.

Finally I jumped out of bed stark naked and hot foot made for the telephone on the upstairs landing in the most dignified manner possible in the circumstances. Picking up the receiver, Shirley Slater's voice came over loud and clear.

'Sebastian, I am worried to death. Martin and his party have not returned from Illiniza. He was due back about seven or eight p.m. I think there has been an accident, or they are in trouble, and I am organising a rescue party. I want you to come. Please be outside the gates of the Residence at three fifteen a.m.'

'But, but,' I lamely answered. 'You know I am only a walker, surely there are better men than me around?'

However, she was both very upset and very insistent. I cradled the receiver, padded back to my room, fumbled around for my clothes which were strewn all over the place like an impossibly well-organised jig-saw puzzle; floundered about, starting by putting my climbing trousers over my head and my socks on my hands in a rather dotty way – altitude does strange things to some people; got into my 'hobo's habit'; crept downstairs, undoubtedly waking the entire household, and out into the cold – and waited upon events. I stomped up and down outside the gate for about half an hour. Every so often the Ambassador's night watchman would peek and peer anxious-like through a grilled hatch in the big wooden gates, which framed his face like a picture. Clearly he wasn't sure of me.

Finally a Land Rover appeared; I jumped into the back and we disappeared into the night. Hell bent. No one talked.

We were a mixed bag of rescuers of different nationalities. There was Hans, a German Swiss, at the wheel; Howard, a middle-aged, kindly, silent American beside him, Edward, a Belgian, opposite me in the back and Shirley, a Scot, by my side, together with a rather frightening looking and very business-like stretcher, which divided the back of the Land Rover in two halves. Shirley had telephoned around all the Quito hospitals to try and get three stretchers but had only managed to get one. Although very upset, she quickly explained to me that Martin and his two companions were making a traverse of Illiniza by a new route. I was never quite sure what my particular role was to be but felt in my old bones it might well be hazardous, especially as I had no crampons, gloves, ice-axe, or anything unessential like that. One is inclined to conjure up terrifying cliff hanging terrors at that time of night. Imagination soars.

Edward and Shirley then plunged into technical talk; what they should do with the rope and who should be on it. As there were only two seasoned climbers in the rescue party, I felt increasingly alarmed, but remained silent as the tumbril hurtled towards the figurative guillotine.

We finally fetched up at the base of Illiniza, just as dawn was breaking – and what a dawn! I have never seen the like . . . All the Ecuadorian mountains and volcanoes within the ambience of Quito loomed up in perfect, breathtaking, geometrical symmetry; combined with an embryonic sun a-stirring. The scene was one of majesty and splendour, a pageant, a photographer's dream, an extravaganza in Ektachrome, awe-inspiring to behold.

The ride up in the back of the Land Rover had been

no sinecure; Shirley, Edward and I had been bounced about like bagatelle. Fortunately, during the final stages we had had constantly to leap out and direct Hans over the rough going. Left hand down, right down and so on. At last, abandoning the Land Rover, we looked upward. The snow looked crisp, conditions seemed perfect, the mountain stood out like a huge luscious ice-cream, sharply silhouetted against a light cobalt sky. Surely no tragedy could be enacted on such superb serenity, such supreme beauty?

All eyes scanned the colossus above. Nothing moved across its vertiginous face. I suddenly felt very seriously alarmed for Martin's chances, good and steady climber that he was, and communicated my thoughts to Howard, the quiet American, who felt the same.

I cannot exactly remember what we did next; I mean what our first move was, but I do recall Shirley thrusting the stretcher in my hands. Hans and Howard remained at the base while Shirley, Edward and I started upwards. After a short time Shirley told me to cache the stretcher and continue. I did.

Feeling really alarmed now for Martin and his companions, I pushed on up by myself, not in the least knowing where I was going, but searching for tracks. After about an hour or more, I saw some tracks leading off to the left side of the mountain from a cold and uninviting bleak hut. I was completely foxed by this but fortunately Edward came up to join me and we endeavoured to puzzle things out. Together we made for the hut but found no evidence, none, except tracks going in the opposite direction, on the right side of the mountain. I asked Edward which tracks we ought to follow and he said, 'the ones to the right'. So we did.

About twenty minutes later when Edward and I were about fifteen thousand feet high, there was a shout: a shout from Martin, somewhere below us. WONDERFUL. Yes, all members of the party were safe.

'Thank Heavens,' I recall saying to myself.

Next day I received a letter from my mother saying that she had had a bet on with my father that I would climb a mountain while in Quito. Well, I did, even if not to the top. My mother is prone to premonition.

It was afterwards imputed that the rescue party was not well organised. This imputation is hardly worth refuting as it can be scotched out of hand. Shirley did all that a human being could do; her organisation at the dead of night was a lasting credit to her determination and guts. The local hospitals only allowed her, in an emergency, one stretcher; and the local Ecuadorian Mountaineering Club would not make a move before five a.m. in which time anything could have happened to Martin and his men.

Undoubtedly Quito was the turning point of my fortunes. The enormous enthusiasm engendered by everyone I met was marvellous and most stimulating to my morale. I may not have had quite the holiday I expected but it had certainly been enlivening. Martin was none the worse for his escapade and both Slaters accompanied me out of Quito as I made my way to the waist-line of the world: the equator line.

In 1736 the first group of scientists ever to set foot in South America came to Ecuador. Led by Charles de la Condamine, a savant of the Acadèmie Française, their main task was to measure an arc of the meridian at the equator; and thus solve the great mystery concerning the true, or actual, shape of the globe, namely, whether it was circular, oblong, oval or square (or anything in between). In fact, whether you could fall off it, if you did not watch your step.

The Frenchmen did a good job and staked out a line some twenty-four kilometres north of Quito. There is a monument there, now a great tourist attraction, erected to perpetuate the memory of the Mission Gentifica Franco; on which is carved o° oo′ oo″, upon which no shadow is cast at mid-day on the equinoxes, namely 21st

March and 21st September. The altitude is approximately two thousand four hundred metres (7,790 feet).

However, in 1949 a Geological Institute (I do not know where from) 'moved' the equator northwards for a distance of some fifty-one kilometres. Here it rests presumably for eternity, indicated by a 'rock' globe which the Spanish call Bola del Mundo.

In fact the new waist-line of the world passes through or across Mount Cayambe at a height of about sixteen thousand feet. This is the highest point the equatorial line reaches throughout its circuit; although its traverse through or across Mount Kenya (Kenya) must run it close.

Lake San Pablo is an unforgettable place, which reminded me of Helen MacInnes's superb novel, *The Salzburg Connection* and the sinister Austrian Lake of Finistree. But unlike the latter, there was nothing macabre attached to it, no unsolved murder, no Nazi gold beneath its waters, only twenty metres deep in the middle and five kilometres long, three kilometres wide. Surrounded by hills it was dominated by a mountain called Imbabura, snow flecked on its ultimate rocky, creviced protuberance. In fact it was a very happy lake, indeed a sixty-three year old, non-combatant, very kindly German amateur landscape painter had found his Shangri-La upon its shores. I have seen his Utopia; it is not quite ready yet, but no doubt will be, one day. When I saw it I mistook it for a public convenience, but that is in no way to its detriment. Just a question of priorities.

Carp, black bass and trout are caught in the lake by Otavalo Indians who balance themselves with almost inhuman artistry upon wafer thin half water-logged skiffs made of stooked Tortora reed, as on the larger papyrus rafts of Lake Titicaca. The Otavalos are distinguished in dress by calf-length Persil white ducks their women folk wash implacably from dawn to dusk, slapping dirty linen on peripheral lake-side rocks, like old-time fishmongers, slapping old-time kippers on their old-time slab – whack

– whack – the note tone sound is identical. Other than his ducks the Otavalo wears a very dark blue dyed poncho capped by a dark brown flat trilby with an elaborate pig-tail down his back. He is known for his industry and cleanliness and to a lesser extent, his drunkenness.

All the slopes surrounding Lake San Pablo are highly cultivated in both senses. Indeed, as one strolls its shores one never seems to escape the watching eye of the 'Indian', for they are ubiquitous, really very annoying for one who wants a bit of solitary, instead of being stared at from every nook and cranny and tripping over tethered pigs into the bargain.

Some of the Otavalos, I noted, were heavily drugged, not by the Coca leaf, but by the Datura plant that produces, ostensibly, much the same effect. The eyes are remote, 'out-of-this-world' – but, paradoxically, penetrating.

Other than constantly washing, the womenfolk are constantly begging. This, too, is very frustrating for the tourist, for if you are philanthropic enough to give a sucre to one a whole regiment emerges from nowhere at your heels, and one is cornered like a miser at bay feeling a brute. Clearly, the only possible place to seek sanctuary around Lake San Pablo is on the very top of Mount Imbabura like some kind of Abominable Snowman. But as I said previously, it is very rocky up there and a long way up besides.

Nevertheless, I shall never forget Lake San Pablo for, like a person, it has become my life. A dream that does not fade for it cannot; as it cannot awaken in an awakening valley.

From the lake I staggered only some twenty-five kilometres into Ibarra – practically on my knees feeling rather tired for once, probably as a result of my two-week rest in Quito. I can always tell when I am feeling soul-weary for my boots become bigger and bigger and bigger, until they assume giant proportions. I have never been soul weary before. I hope never to be again.

Just north of Ibarra there is an expanse of water called

the Lake of Blood for on its banks the last defenders of the old Kingdom of Quito were butchered by the Incas. Nowadays, around the lake there is an excellent ten-kilometre motor racing circuit, which is the best in Ecuador.

I perked up a bit during the next few days and made the Ecuadorian frontier town of Tulcan as if 'on the wings of a dove', marching along at a good clip through rich farming land. As soon as I had arrived I was paid a gracious courtesy visit by the Commander of the Ecuadorian troops stationed there, a charming man called Colonel Luis Tamayo who had been educated at Cambridge and was a friend of our Ambassador Peter Mennell. He thought I would live. I was beginning to look so scruffy that itinerants stopped their cars and offered me money, such a change from being constantly asked for it, so maybe the famed bandits of Colombia would leave me in peace.

CARIBBEAN SEA
BARRANQUILLA
CARTAGENA
MARACAIBO
PANAMA
MONTERIA
Rio Cauca
Rio Magdalena
VENEZUELA
PACIFIC
OCEAN
Rio Atrato
BUCARAMANGA
MEDELLIN
Rio Meta
PEREIRA
BOGOTA
BUENAVENTURA
CALI
COLOMBIA
Rio Guaviare
NEIVA
POPAYAN
PASTO
TULCAN
IBARRA
Rio Uaupés
QUITO
BRAZIL
Rio Caquetá
ECUADOR
Rio Putumayo
0
100
200
Miles

CHAPTER NINE

COLOMBIA

From the Colombian border to the town of Pasto, a distance of nearly ninety kilometres, I recall very little mainly because for most of the time my trousers were about my knees. I had somehow managed to contract a virulent attack of squitters if not incipient dysentery which was nothing new but meant that I was always being caught in the act behind a leafless or lifeless shrub which afforded little cover from buses choc a bloc with curious eyes, friendly curious eyes that twinkled with laughter as they flashed past a bare behind; courteously wishing me 'good luck'.

Pasto was quite a large town spread out in a basin beneath the volcano of La Galeras, some 4,600 metres (15,000 feet) high. The volcano appeared very easy to climb if the weather was clear but it could well be hazardous in mist or fog: wild flowers flourished all over its slopes.

The climate of Pasto was temperate, mild, although the sun was astonishingly intense especially on a bald pate due to the high altitude and the concomitant ultra-violet rays. The volcano was still sporadically active, and as it was situated only seven kilometres in a straight line from the town centre, I thought that the locals might well be nervous about possible volcanic eruptions. Instead I was told that they are scared stiff of rainbows.

I took seven days to march on to Popayan, a very attractive University city with a sunny, salubrious climate. On the way, not far north of Pasto I encountered three young Colombian men who told me that they had not a peso between them and had been walking for five days without food. I was very sympathetic, gave them sufficient money to bus to Cali and to buy food en route. I also bought them new shoes. Although I felt quixotic towards their evident plight I could not believe they had been tramping for five long days without a bite to eat. It was just not feasible, I thought, especially as all three looked in very good shape.

The youngest complained of his feet in a matter of hours of meeting him so I put him on a bus to Cali where he said he lived. A day later another started hobbling badly in spite of or despite the new shoes I had so stupidly bought him. He, too, I put on a bus for Cali. The last, Sancho Panza, however, bravely soldiered on but it was not very long before he took to taking buses and meeting me in the evenings at the places I appointed. In the end I reluctantly had to sack him for taking to the bottle in a big way; all, of course, at my expense.

I carried on, alone, much relieved. Popayan to Cali took me three days (137 kilometres). En route I encountered four North American bicyclists. The first to come into my sights was a bespectacled girl of about twenty-five years old. She pulled up and asked where I had come from and where I was going. When I replied Tierra del Fuego to the Darien Gap, her initial reaction was incredulity, her second menace. She took a strong manly hold of her white bicycle pump, which closely resembled a British policeman's baton, and manifested signs of belligerence. I asked her if she had a flat tyre – to which she answered 'No' but that her husband was 'round the bend'. I sympathised at this hapless contingency but no sooner had I done so when the husband did appear 'round the bend' where he had been for the past seventeen months. I also passed a vintage Rolls Royce, or rather it passed me. I speculated whose it was. . . .

I wish to state, from the bottom of my heart, that throughout my walk through Colombian territory, from the border on I had received the greatest possible courtesy from the Colombian police and their special branch, D.A.S. They had been really magnificent. I have not met or seen their like in any other Republic I have passed through during my trip.

I 'marched' into Medellin from a place called San Gabriel, fifty-four kilometres south in ten hours heading straight for the British Consulate where I was very warmly welcomed indeed by Miss Villa, the British Consul: an extremely benevolent, friendly and efficient Colombian lady who appeared markedly Anglophile. I arrived slightly tired after a nine day, non-stop walk/march from Cali which was 444 kilometres to the south. I must have appeared a rather grisly apparition to Miss Villa, begrimed with dust, inevitably gaunt and haggard from the privations of the road. However, Miss Villa took all this in her stride, as if such an outrageous hobgoblin appeared thus every day. She sat me on a comfortable sofa and called for tea. I had fetched up on the dot of teatime.

After a very interesting general conversation and a wash and brush up, I was very charmingly bundled into a cab which was given instructions to go to Yardley's Factory where I was told to ask for a certain Senorita Delma, who would put me in touch with Dione Gervis. However, at the Janitor's Gate, Dione appeared in the flesh with Benjamin, one of her children. We then drove to the Finca Toledo in her Jeep, a fine, high chassied, robust vehicle with a good turn of acceleration.

I was fascinated by the nomenclature of the streets, or rather street system, which was numerical. For example, streets that run from east to west are known as Calles and those from north to south are known as Carreras. The numbering of the Carreras increases from south to north and those of the Calles from east to west. A very practical system, especially if the novitiate tourist had a compass handy or in-built bump for locality. In some parts of the city the nomenclature used rather alien words such as circulars and transversals. However, some streets retained their maiden names. At each corner the visitor would find a plaque signifying the name and number of the street.

The Gervis finca was south of Medellin and to get to it we drove through a very smart area of expensive country houses all set in their own grounds. A finca is a small country house, as opposed to a large hacienda, with a small amount of land immediately around it, some food production and maybe a cow or two or a horse around. In this area of eternal spring the gardens were wreathed with flora, orchids, hibiscus, bougainvillaea, avocado trees, lilies, agapanthus, amaryllis, tulip trees and of course, the ubiquitous eucalyptus.

The joy of the finca was that peace prevailed. Far from the madding crowd comfortably seated at ease in a J.F.K. rocking chair in the cool precinct of the patio with a glass of rum and lemonade in one's hand, all was quiet. Except for the strangely cadent cacophany of cicadas and crickets, the ceaseless croakings of bull frogs and muffled and muted gurgle of the children's bath water wriggling down the drain. In addition there was almost always a plethora of very varied bird-song; such as that of blue grey tanagers, scrub tanagers and palm tanagers as well as tropical king birds, rufus tail humming birds, blue and white swallows, the black vulture, the black goldfinch and many others all of whom sought sanctuary in the garden of the Finca Toledo.

The occasional darting fire-fly and flash of lightning momentarily illuminated the serenity of the scene seconds before a distant crash of thunder. Before the brief transitional tropical twilight failed, my hostess Dione Gervis came racing through the patio, hot foot, bearing a large and heavy portfolio under her arm and a Van Gogh hat tilted at a rakish angle. Some of Dione's very remarkable and very note-worthy paintings adorned the walls. Painting is her passion. She has held three exhibitions in Medellin and on various occasions exhibited in Great Britain, exploring many media, including oils, ink and gouche drawing, monotypes and ceramics.

Her forte is almost certainly the variegated Andean landscape, the broken contours and symmetry of the surrounding mountains and hills together with the small irregular plots of land that cling tenaciously to the tops. This she has expressed in the medium of monotype.

Her ink and wash drawings suggested a more domestic and more intimate scene, the perfumed gardens and the plantations, and the prolific growth of the sub-tropical vegetation within the ambience of Medellin. In her latest exhibition she evoked the very quintessence of market scenes in Colombia, Ecuador and Peru; especially Peru where her artist's eye was captivated by the Festivals of Paucartambo and Cuzco, festivals I had, myself witnessed. I was longing to buy some of her work, but a rucksack and the Darien Gap temporarily precluded purchase.

Medellin is a very important industrial town, primarily producing textiles, in addition to plastic, aluminium objects, cosmetics, Renault cars and Jeeps.

It turned out to be a large city encompassed by highish mountains but no single one dominant unlike Quito's Pichincha. Medellin lies in a valley at only about fourteen thousand metres (4,700 feet) and as far as I could judge the climate was hotter than Quito's, giving it greater claim to the title of 'City of Eternal Spring' for it does not go through the full gamut of all four seasons in the space of twenty-four hours, instead it appeared to be more rational and nearer my idea of spring. Perhaps the pleasanter climate was achieved by the ochre coloured Medellin River which flowed fast and shallow straight through the town.

I tarried rather longer than I meant in Medellin through force of circumstances. The Gervis's were in the throes of packing up house and returning to the United Kingdom so that it was doubly good of them to put up with me for so long, and to cope with all my medical problems.

Firstly, I was bear-led to a doctor to have my feet checked and told that I had a fungus or fungoid infection and that if I did not obey his explicit orders all, but all, my toenails would fall out, or off, or both. As I have never been attached to that part of my anatomy, other than to have them cursorily cut by circular saw every five years or so, the good doctor's forebodings did not trouble me unduly. He admonished me severely for my laxity, but since a man of science had just worked out that on the basis of my taking one thousand five hundred paces per kilometre, I had taken eleven million, seven hundred and forty-five thousand paces since quitting Ushuaia in the early part of February last year, I am not surprised my toenails wish to retire.

Secondly, I bravely sustained a protracted session of virulent squitters; it was not dysentery but just as debilitating. Very embarrassing, especially when I took the charming British Consul out to lunch to a smart restaurant and spent the entire meal in the Gentleman's. She was very understanding.

Thirdly, I was dragged to the dentist because the pain-killing tablets I chucked down my throat like monkey nuts for days and nights failed utterly to fulfil their function. The dentist took one look at my teeth, back ones, thank God; and announced that at least three must come out; but eventually made it five for good measure. He said that they and my gums were very badly infected due to cumulative diet deficiency. Poor man, he had such trouble with one of my molars, yanking and pulling so hard with those terrifying pincers until the dénouement became a veritable tug-of-war with both combatants in danger of disappearing through the surgery window and making a forced landing, a hundred feet below on the heads of the passing populace, bent about their business. I have kept this tusk as a talisman. Dentists in Colombia are absolutely first class, better than any I have met elsewhere abroad. I have never met any others.

Having got medically organised, I set about preparing myself for the entirely new set of conditions of climate and terrain which I expected to meet in my foray through the Darien Gap to Panama City. I had been repeatedly told, mainly by the uninitiated, that it was impossible to walk through this area. However I was in no way deterred. I ought to have been.

I have long believed that whatever the physical hazards that loom ahead, the co-operation and the services of the right man in the right place at the right time mitigates them. In Michael Hill, a geographer and naturalist in the mould of a latter day Spruce, Bates or Wallace, I found such a man, thanks to Dione Gervis. Born in Colombia, he was a forty year old Englishman and knew the area which I had to traverse as well as anyone in the land, although to date he had not walked it. He was very keen to accompany me and helped me to get organised in multifarious different ways. He also, of course, spoke Spanish like a local, knew all the relevant top brass and how to bargain with guides.

As Medellin was the springboard from where I plunged into the Darien Gap, I had to make, perforce, a few elementary but essential preparations, to face up to the last hurdle on as equal terms as possible.

Lightness and speed were my guiding lights. Accordingly I pared down my rucksack to bare essentials for survival. The rucksack was new, a superb yellow Alpine Camp Trails Pack presented to me by a charming Texan.

My Pindisport tent and sleeping bag had come to the end of the road. They accompanied me for over 8,620 kilometres from the uttermost part of the earth and proved, over and over again, equal to the strain. With me they had marched through sunlight and storm, starlight and shadow, over mountain ranges and deserts, every climatic condition, in fact. But they were rather too heavy for me to take on any further, nor were they suited to jungle conditions.

The tent and sleeping bag had therefore been put out to grass at the Finca Toledo. They appeared quite happy and at peace in their venerable retirement; cloistered on the croquet lawn, surrounded and sequestered by a high white wall. When it rained and it quite often did, the tent assumed a somewhat beleaguered and forlorn air giving the impression that a valiant Captain Oates of Captain Scott's brave company might emerge at any moment and stagger voluntarily to meet his end in the frozen wastes of Antarctica. One day I hoped and trusted we would meet again, on another lawn in another place, perhaps my native Devonshire. They were in kind hands. In their stead I acquired, again from the Texan aforementioned, a khaki, military-looking hammock mosquito net cum light mackintosh roofing, all combined in one piece which rolled up like a sleeping bag and was no heavier called a Hamma-Carpa. I bought a maroon coloured inflatable lilo, a section of which formed a pillow which fitted snugly into the hammock. In addition I purchased three pairs of Harlem Globe Trotter boots and four pairs of woollen socks, grey and white.

Wool is a must in the jungle as opposed to nylon, orlon or any other synthetic. I already possessed one woollen object, of course, my faithful Tam o' Shanter, a generous gift from Shirley Slater, which reposed on my bald pate as long as the trip lasted. I also bought a trendy, light, sky blue denim cotton safari suit, which, although appearing frail, stood up to the rigours of Darien. Amongst other impedimenta there was an umbrella, a tip purloined from Christian Bonington when walking with me through Southern Ecuador. The brolly had long been standard practice for walk-in marches in the Himalayas and indeed Generalissimo Chiang Kai-shek, together with an Old Etonian Chinese general called Long Arm Sutton, waged war with Mao-tse-tung armed with gamps, admittedly without much success, under mortar fire.

Among other items there were a brace of all purpose machetes in colourful sheaths, a twelve bore gun and an expensive Canon Camera with all concomitants plus seventeen rolls of black and white film and more to hand. The less bulky paraphernalia included my faithful and redoubtable Pindisport double ventile anorak which appeared willing to soldier on despite being cumbersome and heavy for the vagaries of jungle travel. However this disadvantage was outweighed by its copious pocket capacity. It could also prove useful on cold tropical nights. In addition I was loaded with 'armour' in the form of documentation, photostated half a dozen times, of the highest accreditation addressed to all Colombian and Panamanian police and other secular authorities through whose hands I would be making passage.

I even had maps, all Xerox copied which the reader will readily agree is going too far: the latest available maps of Colombia and Panama, together with Major John Blashford-Snell's map of the Gap, which resembles Robert Louis Stephenson's *Treasure Island,* or perhaps something more modern stepping out of the pages of a Tolkien. Nevertheless it was of inestimable value for I had every intention of following Blashford-Snell's route along the spine of the Watershed. There was also some fishing tackle and snake bite serum, neither of which I knew what to do with.

For reading matter I had a paperback copy of Barbara Tuchman's *The Guns of August* – which I believe the late President Kennedy once presented to Mr. Macmillan.

My fourth pair of Italian Sella soft, light, leather boots had also come to the end of the road. Ominous holes had made themselves felt on sensitive soles. They were being vulcanised in Medellin but this was just a temporary measure to enable them to last until I reached the jungle and had to take to American basket-ball sneakers. From experience I had always found these latter invaluable for one can wade through river, stream and swamp with facility; and however protracted their immersion, they are completely dry within the hour when all squelching ceases. They were short. and of canvas and quite unlike the Fawcett, the knee-high heavy leather boot beloved of Conan Doyle or Rider Haggard, and were therefore vulnerable to snake, thorn and stunted stakes of sharp bamboo amongst other snags. But the Fawcett-type boot was, of course, hopeless in water.

Possibly it was significant, but I neglected a medicine chest in my list of preparations. Dione Gervis took care of this, stocking up with Entero-Vioform against dysentery, and laxatives; in fact 'stoppers' and 'starters'. Anti-malarial tablets, both as a preventative and a cure, Halazone tablets and iodine for water purification, toothache tablets, snake serum, Elastoplast bandages and Band-Aids, insect repellent, foot powder, surgical spirit and medicinal brandy – unfortunately 'Napoleon' is unavailable.

Michael Hill informed me it was the best time for an incursion into Darien – although the seasons do not change radically, as they do with the coming or going of the monsoon – in India, for instance. We shall see.

As regards my itinerary, I was assured I would encounter no insurmountable problems until I reached a small township called Barranquillta, where there is a bridge over the River Leon. From then on north there is said to be swamp for sixty kilometres or so to the *pueblito* of Puerto Libre where there are a couple of *tiendas* or shops, one of which is run by a certain Don Rodrigo, to whom I had been furnished with an introduction by Dr. Hector Anaya, Professor of Logging at the Universidad Nacional in Medellin. I had been given the name of Hector Anaya as the most knowledgeable man in Colombia by Tony Frith of F.A.O., way south in Salta, Northern Argentina and by two Swedes of the same organisation.

I visited Don Hector at the University. He received me with great courtesy. Having got wind of my project to traverse The Gap on foot, in the rainy season, he told me at once that he and his colleagues were constantly in the field in that area and so they knew for certain that such an arduous, even dangerous, undertaking was impossible. He added that my only option was to go around that vital and most fascinating part of the isthmus by water.

However, seeing, and probably sensing, that I was utterly resolved to try, Don Hector made a volte-face and called for maps over which we pored with enthusiasm and vigour. When we got down to brass tacks the situation perceptibly changed and the odds against appeared shorter and shorter until I finally gave myself a fifty per cent chance of success in this endeavour.

Blaine Purcell, the charming and kindly Texan who gave me my new rucksack, was a Medico Veterinario, working for an organisation called Oficina Internacional Regional Sanidad Agcopecuaria known in brief as O.I.R.S.A. He pointed out, on Major Blashford-Snell's map, the exact whereabout of O.I.R.S.A. establishments on the Panamanian side of the frontier and showed me which villages were used by an American construction company called Morrison and Knudsen as work camps. These places, Paya, Yaviza, El Real and finally Santa Fé might contain some of the construction company's engineers who were busy building the last part of the great Pan-American Highway Project. All these places, which did not look far apart on the maps, should have radios and these were apparently tuned in twice a day to Juan Gomez at his co-ordinating office in Panama City. Once I reached Santa Fé, I should be well over the hump of The Gap, for the worst would be behind me and at Santa Fé there was said to be four or five North American Civil Engineers with 'ham' radios and all facilities. It looked therefore as if I had a sporting chance of being passed along the grapevine by the tacit free-masonry of bush telegraphy like a hot potato. I placed great reliance on Michael Hill, for I hoped that his vast experience in the field had taught him to choose the right guides at the right time. I was convinced that if anybody could see me through this, the toughest patch, it would be Michael.

I left Medellin, walking north at the end of May alone, carrying my usual weightload. Michael was going to join me later by bus with some of the heavier equipment, after he had completed a series of lectures he was booked to give to the newly elected Liberal Party on ecology, or as he called it, the study of who eats who.

My walk to Apartado from Medellin took eight and a half days. Possibly this was rather slow going as it was only 360 kilometres but the heat and humidity had to be felt to be believed. The thermometer registered 29°C (83F°) at eight o'clock in the mornings in the shade, though admittedly there was not much shade in the early mornings.

I stumbled along wearing my new bright yellow camp trails pack, my Tam o' Shanter and my last and fifth pair of Italian boots, which had very nearly come to the end of the road. I wasn't carrying as much cash as usual, only about two hundred pounds in Colombian pesos and that was carefully hidden at the bottom of my sleeping bag, wrapped in a phosphorescent bright orange coloured waistcoat. This had been a most thoughtful present from Julian Tennant, originally meant to stop me being run over. It was a nice waistcoat but extremely hot and made me sweat freely. I had been categorically informed that if I ever wore it I would be shot but it proved its worth as a cache for my dough.

There's no doubt that I lost even more weight, where there was absolutely none to lose, but my physique did not seem in any way impaired and I was going all the time at a good steady pace. To date I had completed well over eight thousand kilometres and reached the furthest point north in Colombia, indeed in the whole sub-continent and was within spitting distance of the Caribbean Sea at the bay of Uruba. In one sense I had already walked up the entire sub-continent from one end to the other, but to me reaching the Panama Canal would make this really true. Just reaching the coast didn't quite count somehow. Contrary to people's vague general impressions, the isthmus which joins North and South

America does not lie due north of Colombia but in a westerly direction. West into the maw of the dreaded Darien Gap, and then more or less north-westerly for Panama City. I would soon be journeying off the beaten track which would be a most enjoyable change after all those thousands of miles of tarmac bashing.

I stayed in Apartado, appropriately enough, at the Hotel Darien. It was expensive at £1.50 a night, in fact, rather outrageous, I thought, but it enabled me to await Michael Hill in comfort before my next onslaught. Tarmac treading is the hardest going of all, so in many ways virgin jungle would be a salutary change and most welcome. I was incredibly well-organised for once and had even gone to far as to have a yellow fever injection. What is yellow fever?

I was so scrupulous about my preparations in Medellin, mulling over every possible contingency that might befall me that I forgot my maps, compass and machete but no doubt Michael Hill would bring them along when he showed up, along with the heavy baggage, my contact lenses, false teeth and wig, the twelve bore, camera and enough waterproof sheeting to cover an entire Army Corps in cantonment plus two pairs of bathing trunks for swamp swimming. I couldn't swim but that didn't seem to matter.

Personally I thought that the alleged hazards of Darien were over-rated. Its notoriety had been procreated by bush-telegraphy over the centuries since the time of Francis Drake. I was placing my faith in the concepts I have long held of improbable daring, likely unpredictability, speed, instant inventiveness and improvisation, allowing circumstances to look after themselves, and counting on latitude for error. The pity was, there almost certainly wouldn't be any.

Michael showed up at long last, having bussed in from Medellin in ten hours which made my walking time look a bit languid, but then perhaps I need de-carbonising or tuning up?

He instantly proved his sterling worth by fixing the electrical wind fan in our room which I'd been trying to do for two days. Now the room no longer stank of rank and fetid feet. He also most nobly made the lavatory flush for the first time since my arrival. It couldn't last.

Over breakfast next morning we discovered we didn't have a compass. Michael appeared utterly unruffled, stoutly maintaining that his natural bump for locality and Kodak-like memory would pull us through; citing the observation of certain kinds of trees that lean over according to the direction in which they receive sunlight. Also his photographic memory evidently can by association totally recall places and place-names on maps, in addition to the flora and fauna and geology of the region by association. In fact there were innumerable ways of finding a route through the green mansions of the jungle without a compass: including the prevailing winds, geological trends, mountain-range trends, river trends, the position of the sun at any given time of day; direction of cloud stratification and vegetation changes – who needs a compass?

I then told him about the work sites and the O.I.R.S.A. veterinary centres. These latter had puzzled me for I had not really understood why they were there. Michael explained to me that foot and mouth disease was prevalent in certain parts of South America and that these veterinary centres were trying to control the outbreaks in this part of the country and to stop it spreading into Central and North America. The vets, people like Blaine Purcell and the other members of the O.I.R.S.A. organisation were equipped with radios and in contact twice a day with Panama City.

Human beings can contract foot and mouth so I hoped I would not get it; it is evidently similar to something known as thrush in the United Kingdom and manifests itself by suppurating sores on the roof of the mouth and on the lips and tongue. Man gets it in a milder form than cattle and it doesn't last long, which I suppose was cheering. But it needs violet water to treat it with and I had none with me in my newly organised medicine chest.

Cattle show the same mouth symptoms as humans and their cloven hooves rot as well, therefore they cannot walk and so cannot forage and of course cannot eat because of the frightful sores in their mouths. As a result they slowly curl up and die in agony.

When the Pan-American Highway is completed it will, unintentionally, be the means of introducing foot and mouth into the Central and North American Republics, a fearsome thought that must dampen the ardour of many to continue with the mammoth project which is already well in hand. The eventual construction of the Pan-American Highway link-up will also contribute, again unintentionally, to the total annihilation of important indigenous peoples, tribes; namely the Kunas, the Chocos and the Katios who dwell quietly and peacefully in the area, quite unprepared for all the problems this monster juggernaut road will bring in its wake, blindly unaware of the march of merciless materialism. When the Pan-American is open tourists from the north are not going to spend their dollars in Panama, but scorch on and far out south to visit the wonders of Chan-Chan, Cuzco, Machu-Picchu and Tiahuanaco, only using Panama City as a stop-over and thereby greatly depleting the Panamanian government's tourist revenue.

There is already considerable illegal migration of South American people north for Panama, all anxious to get under the umbrella of the dollar zone. The Highway can only help make things much easier for them.

Then there is the ecology aspect. When the great engineering feat is put through, it will cause widespread havoc amongst one of the few remaining tracts of primary forest; having a destructive effect on one of the most unsullied parts of the globe, still, as yet, available for study by anthropologists, botanists and other specialists. It will be an ecological disaster.

Given the precedent of Latin American colonisation, I

cannot envisage any constructive pattern of settlement; and readily foresee a mad scramble to stake claims on inexpensive land, which will in all probability be consumed by the most antiquated methods of agricultural techniques, that is slash and burn. This formula, though at one point the material foundation of the Mayan Dynasty, is by today's standards both economically inefficient and ecologically destructive. For the slash and burn method is precisely what it says: it means cutting down the forest and burning the scrub. The nutrients of the fallen forest, particularly the essential nitrogens, are instantly released. The immediate result is a highly prolific yield for the first year. However the tropical rains within that same year wash away the greater proportion of these indispensable nutrients and so the field must be left fallow. After a further year most of the top soil has been washed away altogether.

Sadly there seems to be something inherent in Latin American psychology that positively demands at least a token assault to be made on the virgin forest. Is it machismo perhaps which makes them so want to conquer or rape this pristine land? In Spanish such territory is alluded to as monte, a wide ranging term, which shows the two dimensional relationship between man and nature in Latin America.

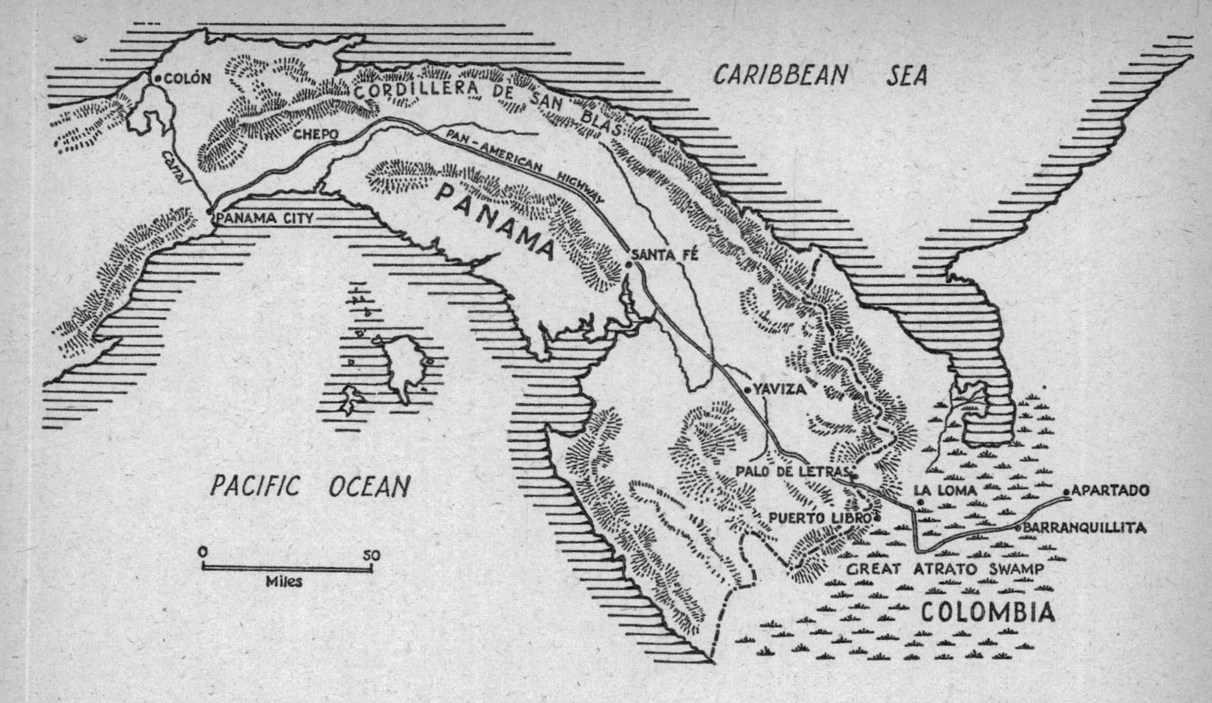
CARIBBEAN SEA
COLÓN
CORDILLERA DE SAN BLAS
CHEPO
Canal
PAN-AMERICAN HIGHWAY
PANAMA CITY
PANAMA
SANTA FÉ
YAVIZA
PALO DE LETRAS
LA LOMA
APARTADO
PUERTO LIBRO
BARRANQUILLITA
GREAT ATRATO SWAMP
COLOMBIA
PACIFIC OCEAN
0
50
Miles

CHAPTER TEN

INTO THE DARIEN GAP

Michael Hill fulfilled my expectations by introducing me to Wade Davis. Wade and I met in the cowboy film set town of Apartado full of saloons with a plethora of jeeps instead of hitched horses.

Wade, aged twenty, came from British Columbia. His father was manager of a trust company in Victoria on Vancouver Island, where Wade went to school at Brentwood College; spending his holidays logging, fighting forest fires and taking people mountain climbing. From the above activities he saved 2,000 dollars a year that went towards, but did not meet, the completion of his education at Harvard. After two and a half years at Harvard, he was awarded a scholarship for academic achievement in ethno-botany. On the strength of this he journeyed to Colombia, South America; where for the past three months he had travelled throughout that Republic, collecting different species of rare plants. For a time he lived with Aruawaka Indians in the Sierra Nevada de Santa Marta situated at the most northerly tip of Colombia. He also spent time with the Choco Indians, who live between the Atlantic and Pacific coastlines in the narrow bottleneck which runs, roughly, between the Colombian and Panamanian borders.

Wade Davis was a shrewd choice for our trip, for this young, very tough Canadian was not only conversant in Spanish, but was also a competent photographer, when his Pentax functioned properly, which it sometimes did. He could read a compass and a map and could charm the Noble Savage with his long red flute and was good at whittling things with his buck knife, some of the many vital attributes I lack, to my undying shame.

Wade was a gentle giant with very broad shoulders; a strong walker, loose limbed and long legged, with kind, blue, wide-apart eyes, capped by a rumpled mop of fair, curly hair. He had a penchant for adventure and was a very courageous person indeed.

Michael Hill, Wade Davis and I set out for Darien on 16th June; not before a Colombian English speaking friend overheard in a saloon near the small hotel where we were staying, two Colombians say to each other: 'That Englishman (me) in there must be a millionaire, . . . all Englishmen are millionaires . . .' 'Yes,' replied the other, 'I'm sure he is a millionaire, he looks like a millionaire. All the town knows he is a millionaire.' 'Let's cut him up then,' his friend answered.

'Do you think he will fight?'

'Yes . . . yes, I do . . . he looks that sort of man; all Englishmen fight, they are all that sort of men.'

'Well, that's a different matter . . . let's forget the idea.'

I howled with mirth when this slice of information was relayed, but was told it was no joke.

'Do not laugh,' said my English speaking friend.

Leaving Apartado we went south until we reached a very large rather romantic signpost on which was written in big, black, bold, block letters 'Darien'; underneath there was a large, long, black arrow pointing due west.

Off I marched in my new light blue denim trousers, Harlem Globe Trotter boots and high necked once-white sweat shirt which was already very cruddy. On my bald head rested a cheap military-looking cap – with a zip in the crown for ventilation against mosquitos and the humidity. It resembled something between an Afrika Corps and Japanese jungle forage cap. I hated it, but had to put up with it as my loving and lovable Tam o' Shanter was far too hot for those torrid regions. I kept my Tam o'Shanter like a talisman to bring me luck and by God I needed it now that the rains had started in earnest.

I had been worried about the advent of the rainy season

all the way up from Medellin. On numerous occasions I had been soaked to the skin by really torrential tempests, generally heralded by flash lightning and thunder. Nothing except perhaps heavy oil-skins can afford protection against such downpours experienced nearly every day and often three or four times a day. So far I had been fortunate with the seasons, except for the Peruvian Desert, but now I faced my Waterloo, in more senses than one.

Baranquillta was a far more salubrious place, a shanty village, whose houses had corrugated aluminium roofs and walls of the Ceiba wood plant.

Michael, Wade and I slept on the floor of the police post. During the early part of the night we were treated to a display of fearsome flash lightning followed by really terrifying thunder and buckets and buckets of heavy rain. The flash lightning came nearer and nearer, slowly but inexorably, until it was directly overhead. I blocked my ears as the subsequent thunder cracked and blasted. The scene was just like the London Blitz. I have always been frightened since a child by sudden bangs, especially at night. The cracks of the thunder sounded like a thousand stock whips cracking simultaneously on an Australian sheep station. I did not sleep at all that night, my mind pondering on the way ahead, that loomed so alarmingly before us. Crossing Darien in the dry season is no sinecure, what in the devil was it going to be like in the wet? January, February, March and April were probably the optimum months to stick our necks out, by July I thought we would certainly have them cut off. But I was utterly, totally *resolved* that whatever the season we would get through to Panama City via the Darien Gap. I had not walked all this way to be baulked *now*. Michael could not sleep either. He had a devastating attack of diarrhoea or dysentery, causing him to vomit constantly, poor man. By morning he was virtually hors-de-combat. The squitters left him apathetic, demoralised and lethargic. Only with great effort of willpower did he rise from his

Li-Lo on the floor. I saw at once he was in no condition to walk, let alone wade through swamp.

During that awful night I overheard the police inspector shout in the street, 'Do you want a bullet through the head?' to some malcontent or trouble-maker. It was that sort of place.

Once Michael had poured some hot, strong delicious Colombian coffee down his throat, he felt slightly better and said he would charter a dug-out with an outboard engine and transport all our baggage down the River Leon from Baranquillta to a spot called simply Kilometre 25 and then he would return to Medellin. Poor Michael, a brave, generous, kind man in whom I put implicit trust. The legacy of this trust was young Wade Davis. Michael could not have hit upon a better choice if he had scoured and searched the whole of Colombia. I owe Michael a very great debt, not only for conscripting Wade to my colours, but also for taking endless trouble bear-leading me around Medellin shopping and introducing me to all the relevant people.

Michael Hill made my journey a possibility; it was now up to me to make it a fact. I was determined not to fail him or anyone else.

The police inspector conscripted Don Pablo to our expedition. Looking very carefully into Don Pablo's honest, shrewd eyes, I knew for a certainty I had a very good man.

Wade Davis, Don Pablo, acting as carrier and guide, and I left the last outpost at ten minutes past seven a.m. on 17th June; while Michael chartered a boat with a pilot to meet up with us at Kilometre 25.

Once over the bridge of the River Leon we disappeared into the jungle. Don Pablo bore up manfully under the white-man's burden, which was very heavy, and directed our footfalls either through seemingly endless muddy quagmires, which in the dry season could be called tracks, or through seemingly endless wasteless lagoons, black bogs and swamps through which we waded, sometimes almost up to our necks and almost always up to our middles. Our rate of locomotion reminded me of the time I climbed Chimborazo in 1953, floundering around in deep snow up to my chest; it was like the slow-motion step of man on the moon; not because of the depth of the water, but because of the gluey adhesive mud underneath our basketball boots. Even with the help of a stout stick acting as a third leg I had found it hellishly hard going and most fatiguing.

Wade saw a chimpanzee as big as himself and then suddenly got stung very badly by seven hornets. As he dashed, yelling, past me I thought he had gone beserk, run amok or something. In actual fact, in his fearful pain, he was endeavouring to protect me. He was that sort of man. As a result of Wade's Quixotic action I was the recipient of only one hornet sting under the neck, not very painful.

At one rather difficult lagoon which we had to cross, because like the proverbial chicken we had to get to the other side, Don Pablo warned me in a rather histrionic voice, 'Many peoples drowned here.' I had not the least intention of swelling the numbers even though I can only swim a few strokes at best, being a 'non-nant' at Eton. Nevertheless I felt it incumbent upon me to do my duty and not disappoint. Luckily Wade said that he was a very strong swimmer.

I found the easiest form of locomotion was to rid myself of my light blue denims which were by now very heavy and sodden, and tie them around my neck thereby risking leeches, snakes and ticks. The other two did not follow my example. I quite appreciated their reluctance but I was fortunate and got through to Kilometre 25 without a scratch. By way of the jungle, the way we had come, it was of course nothing like that distance, that was the distance by the twisting River Leon.

Around noon we stumbled on a little isolated shack in the centre of a clearing within the all surrounding forest. A kind woman proffered large bowls of delicious lemonade to slake our unslakable thirst. It tasted like nectar: it was nectar. She categorically refused any form of payment, although obviously very, very, very, poor. We were very deeply touched by such unconditional humanity.

That night we stayed at an isolated finca at Kilometre 25 some two kilometres from the River Leon. I sent Wade and a mule to collect our heavy baggage from Michael, who had long been awaiting us. Gallant Michael went back to civilisation, he was in no condition to accompany the foray further. It was now up to Wade and me. We were very warmly greeted at the finca by a man of pure African cast of countenance and several other employees. We were waited on hand and foot as if we were on a very expensive safari in Kenya; he would not accept any money, but I pressed a few pesos into a reluctant hand. He wrung the throat of a very special chicken for us. I loathe chicken, especially as I once kept 24,000 of them, being more than content with platefuls of rice, beans and well fried eggs. He even put up my hammock and mosquito combination for me which I was too idle to do. It rained hard practically all night, a grim factor that did not enhance our chances of muddling through.

Next day after a large breakfast of strong black coffee, rice, beans and fried eggs, sunny side up we were ready; but I found my basketball boots gave me excruciating pain. Examining my feet I found the big toe nail on my left foot to be the culprit. simply because I had been too idle to cut it in recent months or years. I called for volunteers to assist me in this major operation – more difficult than it appeared – for the toe nail had become ingrown. However, after approximately half an hour and the services of all the employees of the finca, the job was done. I could walk without pain.

'Why did you not mention it yesterday?' asked Wade.

'I did not think it worthwhile,' I replied.

'Typically British,' Wade said.

We left the finca at Kilometre 25 at seven ten a.m., Don Pablo and I to walk to Kilometre 40 on the River

Leon while Wade escorted the heavy baggage around to Kilometre 40 by boat.

The going was considerably better than the previous day, the omnipresent cloying mud was not so adhesive under the feet; but the limitless lagoons we had to wade and ford through were just as deep. We got lost several times, and because of it took a very circuitous route. Lagoons and swamps stretched out in all directions. We saw a small bear high up on the tree tops and numerous monkeys, of numerous species, plus macaws, parrots, parrakeets and the beautiful toucan with its long engaging bill. Sometimes there was a patch, often nothing. Occasionally we would come across stakes which marked out the prospective route of the Pan-American road.

About one hour before reaching our immediate destination we hit upon a lonely little finca, the first habitation we had seen all day. We were proffered bonhomie and coffee. I studied the faces of the three occupants. Two of the men were young and dark skinned; the other, the owner of the small farm, was much older, older even than me, dark, dusky and swarthy.

I wanted an additional reliable man as Don Pablo had only undertaken to get us to Puerto Libre on the Rio Atrato. I liked the looks of Don Lubin as he was named. Although past middle age his body was still agile and lithe. His face radiated complete openness and honesty, coupled with an untutored intuitive intelligence. His eyes radiated kindness, his mouth small and clap-trap undoubtedly stood no nonsense.

Through Don Pablo, who had known him for years, I pressed Don Lubin into service. He was keen and said he would be happy to come to the Colombian-Panamanian border. Instinctively I guessed that I had a very good man; Don Pablo endorsed my sentiments. Don Lubin was to play a major roll in our fortunes, acting as my Sancho Panza, Solomon and Cicerone. He never let me down, never asked for payment until I pressed some dollars into his hand just before the frontier. He also acted as my watch-dog, and valet de chambre. He was my liaison officer.

Whenever a difficult decision had to be made I invariably deferred to him, with his cautious, canny wisdom and his great knowledge of local customs.

During this day (18th June) I had a minor accident. I gripped a sapling palm tightly to steady myself from falling flat on my face. Unluckily the sapling palm is covered with very sharp needle-like two-inch black spikes called *espina de palma*. A dozen or so of these bayonet like spines drove deep into the upper part of the palm of my left hand. A real agony, I found I had absolutely no movement in my hand for twenty-four hours, in spite of penicillin tablets from our medicine chest. Only gradually did the pain and the lack of feeling and movement subside. Don Pablo extracted the spikes from my hand with a machete. These *espinas de palma* are used by the Yanomano Indians who dwell in various parts of Colombia and Venezuela. The Indians (Yanomano means Fierce People) have an intriguing technique of shinning up these prickly palms to pick off the palm fruit that lodges in the uppermost branches. With two sets of two long poles the tree is scaled by alternating the different sets in leapfrog fashion. The palm fruit is extremely nutritious.

An hour later, after conscripting Don Lubin to the colours, Don Pablo and I fetched up at Campamento Doria, hard by the River Leon. This was Kilometre 40 and Wade and the baggage had arrived hours before. Don Lubin came in just before dark.

We were very kindly given the run of an almost brand new hut with beds and mosquito nets. When we reached it, Campamento Doria had only been established twenty days. It is right on the line of the future Pan-American Highway but I was told that the Gap would probably not be closed for another eight to ten years yet. Indeed this camp was the only evidence of any activity that I saw on the Colombian side of the frontier so I was not surprised it was going to take so long.

Fifteen technicians were working on the study of subsoil. The Campamento had five drills that bored down forty to fifty metres below the surface. At this temporary Camp I was told which plants were used by locals against lethal snake bites in lieu of serum. The plants were called Contra de Culebral and Papallula and employed in the following manner. First, grab the nearest Heath Robinson tourniquet, a vine, a rag or anything equally handy, remembering to tie it above the wound. Second, cut the stricken part with a razor blade. Third, put as many plants as possible in a basin or pot of hot water and soak the injury for a protracted period, until boiled lobster pink. I was not informed where one found the plants or where one found the pot.

After dark the boss of Campamento Doria entered the hut he so generously had given us for the night. He was very drunk on *aguadiente*. He sat on a bed and kept on repeating like a worn out gramophone with a worn out record and a worn out needle in a worn out groove, the following monologue:

'They're f . . . g Nixon now; very, very, very bastard; one-time may be I join the guerillas. I hate f . . . g Gringos, I hate f . . . g Gringos, I hate f . . . g Gringos.'

After this drunken diatribe had gone on for some time, although I was his guest and therefore beholden to him, I decided to get rid of him. I had no intention of having our North American cousins disparaged, especially as they were not there to defend themselves. I had been silent, bristling and boiling with suppressed rage; I suddenly spoke in crisp no-nonsense definitive tones, 'Could I have a cup of tea. I always have one at four-thirty p.m. sharp, but I missed it today as I was up to my neck in water at the time.'

This statement knocked the drunken guts out of him. It put him off key as it was meant to do. Immediately he made a comic volte-face and said, 'Oh! you English and your cups of tea. I will get you one, but surely you English have it at five o'clock?'

'No – four thirty.'

'No – five.'

'No – four thirty.'

'No – five.'

'No – four thirty, and I am thirsty, very thirsty. . . .'

He left the hut and did not come back, but a cup full of Lipton's tea bag did. I prefer China.

Come the morning he was exceptionally charming and exceptionally oily, obviously suffering from creepy contrition. He pleaded with me to write to him.

I was glad to quit the camp and chivvied my party to hurry and get the hell out as soon as they had demolished their gargantuan breakfasts of countless cups of coffee, mounds of toast, porridge, bacon and egg.

To our horror we now found that the banks on either side of the River Atrato were totally impassable. Tall trees stuck out of the banks which in reality were very deep swamps; and I couldn't swim. Even in the dry season it would have been a very considerable undertaking.

Wade Davis who was a very strong swimmer did not even consider the possibility of swimming through this tree bestrewn swamp with its wild animals, currents and underlying obstacles. But like me he was a purist and an idealist and would never dream of cheating. We had said we would walk through the Darien Gap and walk we would, but clearly we would have to return south first by boat and then start again along another route. Instead therefore of proceeding *down* the Atrato by canoe, which would have been cheating, we travelled with Don Pablo in a long dug out canoe *up* the Atrato to Puerto Libre without a pang of conscience because we were going due south and so backtracking. There was no alternative. In the dry season, we would have had a go but in the wet, when the rivers in these inhospitable regions rise and fall with extraordinary rapidity after rain, we had no chance or choice, however well-equipped and organised, but to zig-zag back south and try to break through on foot elsewhere.

When forced to take to the water, except across the Straits of Magellan which I was unable to swim or ford, I always asked which way the water flowed before I embarked up it, so that no one could ever accuse me of travelling north by water. Wade too was adamant. So having discovered that the Atrato flowed south to Puerto Libre, we set off.

When we arrived at Puerto Libre, I endeavoured to pay off the estimable Don Pablo with extreme furtiveness. 'Never show money,' I had been warned again and again until the phrase had almost become an act of faith. So I took Don Pablo clandestinely behind the local general store and fished for my money from the bowels of my rucksack. When I had succeeded in collecting the relevant amount of notes, the wind suddenly arose and they fluttered all over the place like confetti. I should have known the entire populace of Puerto Libre was looking from the back window with alarming avidity, goggle-eyed with greed. In my experience it is not true that Colombians are robbers. They are no worse and no better than other South American countries I had passed through, though perhaps they are just better at it.

Don Pablo then departed after a mandatory shoulder to shoulder photograph. His parting words were: 'I hope you return soon, so I can have friends of your calibre.'

Puerto Libre was founded about forty years ago. It consisted of a dozen wooden shanties built on stilts three or four feet high against flooding standing in one long line. Its entire length and breadth was no more than a couple of football pitches before petering out into the Monte jungle. It had three badly built latrines that hung ponderously over the Atrato, punctuating the bank. The excrement was devoured by scores of fish in an instant. Lem Putt, hero of *The Specialist,* would never have approved their construction. I preferred the wide open spaces, myslf.

Ten people got drowned last year by the floods. The rain made the climate both hot and fetid. Zancudos or nocturnal mosquitos attacked with all the viciousness and whine of strafing Stukas at exactly six forty-five p.m. just before night-fall; it seemed a planned attack. One could set one's watch by the arrival of Zancudos; wave after wave.

Here the Atrato was approximately 300 yards wide, ochre coloured and looking as calm as a millpond, but in fact it was deceptively fast flowing. Across the other side, on the left bank, there was a finca called Sautata which had been established by Turcos 100 years ago. Turco is a very loose word in South America; it applies to all peoples of Middle Eastern origin, be they Christians, Muslems, Sufi or anything in between. But what I did not know is that it also applied to Germans. Germans had built Sautata, with the lush green hills behind, from nothing except jungle. Soon huge sugar cane fields flourished, with a concomitant large liquor factory. There was also a hospital and later a runway.

At the outbreak of Hitler's war the Germans had returned to the Fatherland to fight and had never come back. Some sixteen years ago Sautata was purchased by a certain local tyrant, who, according to the inhabitants of Puerto Libre, immediately kicked all the former workers off the land in an arbitrary manner. The farm now carried 2,000 head of cattle, 100 mules and five employees.

No one at Puerto Libre seemed to know how big it was either in hectares or acres, but estimated it to be four thousand metres by three thousand metres which seemed a bizarre way of measuring or pacing land.

The owner of the one and only store was Don Rodrigo to whom I had an introduction from Dr. Hector Anaya, Professor of Logging at the Universidad Nacional in Medellin. Don Rodrigo was up river when we arrived but according to his plump and comely wife, he was expected back hourly. She owned one of the biggest bottoms I've seen.

Don Rodrigo's wife gave us some floor space to sleep on until Don Rodrigo arrived nearly forty-eight hours later. We sorted out our gear and food supplies which included porridge, canned meat, sugar, salt (very important), biscuits, dried soups, and coffee. We had a mountain of food, for we did not know what lay ahead.

I stationed faithful Don Lubin in the room to keep watch over our possessions until he became a permanent fixture like the table and chairs, the only furniture.

Don Rodrigo eventually arrived in a heavy rainstorm. He had come hurtling down the Atrato at incredible speed, in his new light boat with its puissant Japanese outboard motor.

My first impressions of Don Rodrigo were not good and they stayed that way. A tall, very fat man of elephantine proportions with a florid, aquiline nose that appeared to drip into his mouth. I felt he could almost nibble his nose if starving for a quick snack. His eyes were beady, porcine and set far too close together, as if in competition to get as near to the bridge of his nose as possible. He gave the impression of physical power, and at the age of only thirty-eight was unhealthily obese and unwieldy and like his spouse, big bottomed.

Don Rodrigo did not appear pleased to see us, even after perusing my introductory letter, but eyed us shrewdly in a malevolent kind of way. I looked at him bang between the eyes for a very long moment, for our lives might well depend upon him. He did not meet my steady gaze, his beady eyes flickered everywhere, except on me. I decided he was a slippery customer and never changed my opinion.

Wade informed me that Don Rodrigo traded in pot, tiger skins, barilla skins, crocodile skins and probably anybody's skin for a price. One thing was certain, I would not make a good lampshade.

I persuaded Don Rodrigo, at a price, to ferry us and

our baggage a few minutes' journey in a southerly direction to the first viable trail which would lead to the Panamanian border and Darien. This very muddy trail emanated from the little riverain hamlet of La Loma situated on the right bank of the Atrato at right angles to the stream. I counted nine shanties constructed of long planks of Ceiba wood, roofed with rusty corrugated aluminium. The inhabitants were all pure black. Had they been brought over from West Africa by the Spanish or Sir John Hawkins four centuries ago? It is interesting that enclaves of pure African stock are still preserved to the present, unadulterated, except by adultery! All whom I met were extremely courteous, generous and good humoured.

At La Loma a couple of small packmules were available plus a reliable-looking young guide and muleteer called Don Leo who was asked to ride an additional mule and lead the two baggage mules behind him. But first I had Don Lubin carefully cross-examine and vet Don Leo who was only about twenty-two. He was passed as suitable and given an unwritten contract to guide and transport our baggage to the Panamanian frontier at Palo de Letras, a ficticious place-name marking a fictitious frontier. The words Palo de Letras were, and are, purely symbolic. A long time ago someone carved his initials in a big Ceiba tree. These initials, after the passage of time, looked like 'M' and 'W' hence the Tree of Letters. The actual Colombian-Panamanian frontier was not delineated until 1948 and it took four years to mark it out from the Pacific to the Atlantic with the United States of America acting as the arbitrating power.

Before leaving La Loma, with Don Leo riding in front leading his two pack-mules and Wade, Don Lubin and I taking up the rear, Don Rodrigo suddenly beckoned me apart, solemnly and soberly warning me that there were many bandits, robbers and rustlers on, or along, our route; that they were very dangerous and that I must at all times, night and day, keep a sharp lookout; nevertheless, his beady, porcine eyes flickered over me with blank, although canny, disinterest. This disinterestedness gave me food for thought. I suddenly realised our lives were at stake and the burden of this responsibility weighed heavily upon my shoulders. Don Rodrigo was not, repeat not, of the histrionic type; he was cool and calculating, especially when he knew where there was money.

However, the above admonition in no way dismayed me, being thoroughly well grounded and hardened to this sort of talk. In fact, the five people our caravan passed were the acme of graciousness, doffing their sombreros and wishing us a *'Feliz Viaje'*. All five were mounted and well caparisoned. The going was very muddy, cloying and squelching, especially in the multifarious shallow ravines we had to negotiate.

One of Don Leo's pack-mules had a couple of 'wedding bands' welded together to protect its vagina from the incursions of its virile brethren. Although, of course, mules are sterile they can still carry on, with brio, an exercise which renders them apathetic, lethargic and useless for work. This form of chastity belt was novel and amusing, but probably not for the mule, poor soul. The 'wedding bands' were of brass and brightly burnished . . . a brace of Bravingtons.

En route, during that six hour mid-summer day of 21st June, Wade the enthusiastic ethno-botanist pointed out papaya shrubs, breadfruit used as a starchy vegetable, yucca, a bread substitute, banana, platan trees, and balsa with its soft buoyant wood. The vast ceiba, a tree of gigantic girth and height, was few and far between; from it long wooden planks are fashioned and it is the source for kapok used in sleeping bags and life jackets.

This initial six-hour excursion took us over rough-and-tumble hurlyburly country, made infinitely worse by the rains.

We made slow, but steady progress often ploughing through ravines and rivers up to our bellies, and beyond. Don Leo had told me at La Loma that we would probably have to camp in the jungle that night. We would be miserable if it rained, which it nearly always did.

However, we had a stroke of luck, we hit upon a human habitation. This was a finca of thirty-seven hectares (ninety-one acres) owned by Don Ramon and his chain-smoking wife and kids. On arrival Don Ramon was away from home and his wife was naturally loath to let us in and take shelter; but after a time, kind soul, she handed delicious bunches of huge and succulent bananas over the high fence that encased the finca in a square like a P.O.W. cage.

When her husband returned he immediately said we could stay the night under some thatch roofing supported by four poles, inside the P.O.W. fence. There was a small, very hybrid Dobermann pinscher who barked at us in a rather unfriendly manner, baring its sharp yellow teeth and affording us very mean looks. One of our party, not me, actually, asked the Senora if it was safe to enter the gate. 'Yes,' she replied. 'He is not hungry at the moment, but you never know, he may take a liking to you.' We understood exactly what she implied. We entered with some trepidation.

Don Ramon approached me and whispered in my ear loudly and sonorously. 'There are many, many bandidos and *ladrones* (robbers) about – but do not worry I have The Gun.' The Gun was an incredibly ancient twenty-bore 'hammer' shot gun, its breach tied up with frayed pieces of string and elastic bands. The Gun was an encouraging sight, giving one a sense of security, the sort of security I had never known before and was unlikely to know again. 'The Gun,' continued Don Ramon, for some reason thoroughly excited as he cradled it with loving hands as if fondling an infant in swaddling clothes, 'shoots too.'

This piece of news horrified me, whereupon Don Ramon seeing my perturbation let off a fusillade; the report was deafening, the recoil pure slapstick, of the custard pie variety. Clearly, we were in good hands despite the Dobermann that eyed me, balefully.

We were literally caked with mud, so went to have a wholesome wash in the nearby little river but only got muddier still slithering up the slope to Don Ramon's finca and falling back into the river again.

Innumerable pigs were rootling around but luckily they were fenced off and did not sleep hugger-mugger with the family. The walls of the finca were constructed of balsa wood and heavily thatched with palm leaves. Don Ramon grew a little of everything, such as: platanes, yucca, maize, caria sugar cane, cacao, beans, avocado, papaya, oranges and rice.

The next day we left hopefully for Paya, the first Panamanian frontier post, but after two hours stopped at a 100 hectare (247 acre) finca belonging to some Choco Indians. We asked if we had a chance of reaching Paya that day, to which the headman of the Chocos said 'No'. If we tried we would have to sleep in the jungle with the rain cascading down. So we stayed with the hospitable Indians. We were given a house which we had to climb up to by a special kind of ladder fashioned out of a long pole and Wade remarked to me in jocular fashion, 'Sebastian, keep your hands off the women, the men don't like it.' 'Don't worry,' I replied. 'I won't even look at them.' But with so many succulent bosoms, very young and very ripe, rippling and nippling under our noses, one would have to be a eunuch or a saint not to have stolen a furtive glance just now and then. Soon after arrival our blood pressure came back to normal for the headman told the Choco girls to cover their breasts, bursting for freedom, in front of the Gringos.

On the way to this Choco finca, Wade had told me some facts about the Datura plant. The seeds of Datura are apparently psycho-active and put people in a complete alteration of consciousness. One of the by-products of this is amnesia. Some Indians use it as the essential element of puberty; whereby the boys are put in a hut with a strictly limited amount of food and water and given Datura seeds; this sends them into another world so they forget what it is to be Boy and learn what it is to be Man.

Whilst we waited at the Choco finca, Don Leo, the owner of our mules, told me his mules were currently worth respectively 9,000 Colombian pesos (approximately one hundred and fifty pounds), 6,000 pesos (approximately one hundred pounds) and 5,000 pesos (approximately eighty-five pounds) whereas horses were only worth 1,500 pesos (approximately twenty-five pounds). The reason is that horses can't climb, have no balance or resistance and less strength. The reason why mules are so valuable and preferable is not only because they have more balance and more resistance, but they can carry heavier loads for far longer periods. Also a horse when hungry or thirsty does not possess the wisdom to stop eating and drinking when sufficiently replenished. For instance, a horse will drink and eat itself to death without compunction.

A male horse and a female donkey (currently worth about eight pounds), because of the latter's small womb, produce smaller progeny. This is preferred as a smaller mule can walk faster and has more resistance than its larger confrères.

A female horse and a male donkey produce a bigger mule which has more force, but with much less resistance and less speed.

At the Choco finca, I lost my watch, which was more precious to me than the Koh-I-Noor. I shouted loudly, forcing my party to hunt high and low. After scattering in all directions of the compass within the Choco compound, I suddenly noted it was on my wrist. I also lost my irreplaceable cigarette lighter (matches are useless in the jungle); again my party scattered in all directions until I noted it was in my right trouser pocket, where I always keep it.

We left the finca at six forty-five a.m. while the Monte was comparatively fresh next day, 23rd June – with every intention of reaching Paya, the first Panamanian border post, that day. It promised to be a longish day and Don Lubin and Don Leo and his mules who had no passports undertook to take us to the actual yet fictitious frontier line at Palo de Letras. There would be no path and neither of the Dons used a compass. Instead they would try to walk as near as the jungle allowed to the line their bumps of locality told them was in the right direction. From Palo de Letras to Paya is a comparatively short walk, but I had to have three Chocos to carry the baggage. Three agreed to come provided they were paid before completion of the day's march, pleading that they feared bandits and robbers on their return journey. I said 'no' categorically. The Chocos started to whine in chorus, and repeated that they feared bandits and robbers. I still said 'No' – with a touch more vehemence. I was not going to take the chance of the Chocos leaving Wade and me stranded in the jungle with mountains of luggage. They came at last, reluctantly. Incidentally the Choco Indians are allowed to cross the Colombian-Panamanian frontier to and fro at will. That day the jungle was often completely silent except for the cacophony, curiously well cadenced, of the electronic buzz of cicadas and crickets. I kept humming the ditty as I squelched through the appalling mud – 'Mud! Mud! Glorious Mud, There is Nothing Quite Like it For Cooling the Blood' as I slithered, slipped and fell on my rump every few minutes; a very exhausting acrobatic exercise.

We forded four fast flowing rivers which were not very deep and about the breadth of a cricket pitch, café au lait in colour. At the fifth river Don Leo turned to me and stated – unequivocally – that it was impassable, much too dangerous for men and mules, and that because of the superabundance of rain, it was in spate. I said nothing but grabbed a stout stick cut for me by my butler, Don Lubin, plunged in and waded across with impunity. The river was perfectly viable and I ordered the reluctant Don Leo and mule-train across. However, by eleven a.m.

the mules really could not go further, because of a vast tangle of large trees which blocked the track and its periphery.

With real regret I bade faithful Don Lubin 'Adios'. Never over optimistic, Don Lubin's last lugubrious valedictory words to me were, 'The Panamanians are sure to kill you.' He then waved a hand as did Don Leo: good men both. After untying the baggage from the mules, the three Chocos took over. Throughout the Darien Gap country, undergrowth was dense and big trees were few. It was not as difficult to traverse as Amazonian jungle for there the trees and creepers are closer together. I'd known worse terrain.

At noon, exactly, we reached the Panamanian border. There was nothing there, except a clearing, in the centre of which was a mouldy, broken plinth, surrounded by tall, hewn trees scattered around. Wade and I had ourselves photographed, shoulder to shoulder, by one of the Chocos wielding a Pentax. It was 'A Big Moment'.

CHAPTER ELEVEN

PANAMA

We reached the first Panamanian frontier post three and a half hours later, and met our first Panamanian policeman who manned the *puesto* single handed; he was extremely helpful.

No sooner had we arrived than he invited us to stay at the *puesto* of the Guardia Civil. The first thing he did, however, was to have one of his civilian minions disinfect all our leather goods which we carried in our rucksacks or about our persons; even my belt holding up my filthy trousers did not escape his eagle eye. I sat down to avoid embarrassment and humiliation. 'All things leather' were disinfected by law because of Foot and Mouth emanating from Colombia. I mourned my poor old portfolio which I thought would never be the same again, but it stood up well.

The young policeman, who was only about twenty-one, then thoroughly examined our passports and my letters-of-credence from the British Embassy and Colombian Embassy in Quito plus a letter from the Panamanian Consul in Medellin, all of which I had had photostated. The kind policeman appeared perfectly content, especially when his alert eyes alighted on three of my buff envelopes headed 'ON HER BRITANNIC MAJESTY'S SERVICE', which had been given to me by our Consul in Medellin. She thought they might smooth my path; they did. The policeman neither frisked nor searched me. Wade, the gentle giant, had 150 dollars stashed away in a thin plastic container at the bottom of his shaving cream tube: a clever ruse.

Business over, Wade rode down to the nearby Kuna Indian hamlet on a mule, I do not remember what for, probably food, for he was always hungry. Meanwhile, I was given cup upon cup of yerba tea which was simply delicious; in this instance brewed up from lemon leaves.

The policeman then cordially invited me into the post and indicated a very comfortable bed. Delighted, I returned for more tea; and on the way, I fell down the slippery mud covered steps of the *puesto,* and sprained and bruised my left ankle very badly indeed. This little accident made me virtually hors-de-combat. I could scarcely hobble. I felt very stupid and very foolish, but such is life.

From now on until I reached Panama City three weeks later every bloody step I took became an individual act of will. The ankle swelled up alarmingly quickly and became strangely discoloured. Clearly, total disaster was close at hand. If this accident had happened say, in Bolivia or Peru, I would probably have given up. But nothing, absolutely nothing short of fracture or fatality would stop me crossing The Gap. I knew I would be, figuratively speaking, the slowest ship in the convoy but my flotilla would have to bear with me. They did. Wade was wonderful about it all; his courage and patience were a joy to behold, especially as it was the wet season. From Paya to Panama City, in the jungle, I spent much of my time on my back or front, which, I suppose, made a change.

Next day Wade and I set forth for Darien. It was the 24th June and we had conscripted three Kuna Indian guides as carriers, intending to make the little village of Pucro that night where there was a police *puesto.* However, after about four hours of jungle bashing, we emerged like Nunez Balböa on that Peak in Darien and beheld a large clearing below us.

'Look,' said Wade, 'there is a house, a civilised house and a man in a T-shirt. He must be an American, possibly a missionary.'

'Well,' I replied, 'let's go and see.'

The man in the T-shirt was neither an American nor

a missionary. He was a Panamanian. He greeted us warmly in beautiful Bostonian English and immediately proffered refreshment, which we accepted. I was glad to sit down and take the weight off my legs, as my dear old Nanny used to say, and no doubt still does.

Clearly, Don Luis was no ordinary person. About sixty, he wore glasses, a T-shirt, khaki trousers and a slight limp. His manner, his *savoir-vivre,* told me he was a man of influence and education. A cosmopolitan man, possibly a man of power, an *Eminence Grise,* perhaps.

Why was he here in this God-forsaken spot in the epicentre of wildest Darien? Ostensibly he cultivated his own back garden, the ultimate fate of Voltaire's Candide, owning three plantations of some two hundred and fifty acres each; not contiguous. He produced coffee, corn, rice and beans. He told us that to cultivate coffee it is necessary first to plant orange trees to provide shade, then to sow the ground with coffee beans. When the sapling bushes are about one foot high they are transplanted to a permanent place.

All this was interesting, but why, why was he here with two Choco Indians and two Colombian blacks as employees? He told me his wife was in Panama City sewing and sewing. He gave me a telephone number to ring when I reached the capital. 'Just say I'm well,' he said laconically. Or was it dramatically?

During later conversations he told me he was an intimate friend of Senor Don Roberto Emilio Arias Rosano Guardia de Arias, husband of prima-ballerina Dame Margot Fonteyn and that he had supported Arias financially in the elections of the early fifties. A friend of Arias called Jinya Jimenez had thought that Arias was going to betray him, so motivated by hearsay and gossip, he had chased Don Roberto in a car through the streets of Panama City. When Arias stopped at some traffic lights at the intersection of Via Brazil and 50 Street, Jimenez got out of his car and shot Arias six times with an automatic. As all the world knows Arias is paralysed from the waist downwards and can scarcely speak except in whispers.

Sometime back Don Luis was exiled to Spain for political reasons but he had come back to his farm in Darien and subsequently gone into hiding in Panama City. He had spent one year hidden in one room. Eventually after many petitions, Don Luis had regained his full Panamanian citizenship. He was, and is, a free man. Nevertheless, he was thinking of moving as he was afraid the government might think he was planning a counter coup, which, categorically, he was not. He also distrusted the local policeman who lived at Pucro – three-quarters of an hour through the Monte, who had no regard for human life.

While we were with Don Luis there was a police report that three Colombians, including one, one-eyed white, had murdered seven Choco Indians very nearby. The police caught the assassins and shot them with the rough hand of jungle justice. They were not even buried, but left to the scavengers, the buzzards and vultures, to pick out their eyes and intestines piecemeal.

While I put my feet up, endeavouring to take the pressure off my blasted ankle which gave me the most awful twinges of pain when I walked on it, Wade went over to the village of Pucro and found an Evangelist missionary who gave him a Bible beating, which Wade, quite rightly, resented.

Finding that Wade had not returned by five o'clock in the afternoon, after his Bible beating, Don Luis and one of his employees set out to find and escort him back through the jungle. A very dangerous black tiger had been lurking in the immediate forest through which Wade's path lay. The black tiger always attacks from behind with his left paw like an all-in wrestler in a clinch. Don Luis carried a Beretta, but he returned just before nightfall without Wade. I was not worried as I knew Wade was very sensible, had a healthy respect for the jungle and would not commit himself to it without a guide. Undoubtedly he was staying with the Evangelist and enduring further Bible beatings over a good dinner. He returned safely next day.

That night Don Luis warned me against vampire bats that often pay a visit to the finca. They have one very sharp, rather nasty tooth which makes the incision: and the lapping, licking motion of their tongues consumes the victim's blood from fingers, toes or other extremities, that happen to be around at the time. The saliva has some chemical substance that prevents the blood from clotting and their chosen victim can (and does) wake up in the morning still bleeding; and what's more, these monsters, as big as medium-size birds with a wing-span of at least a foot, return again to the same place. They are notorious for transmitting rabies . . . I expect I got it, because I got bitten through the fine mesh of my khaki mosquito net. The bite didn't hurt at all, although subsequently I felt drained of energy. The vampires hover and flap their wings very quietly and rapidly above where they are going to make the incision; lulling their unwitting victims into a hypnotic, trance-like state of mind.

Don Luis also warned me against the ordinary tiger when I sallied out of the finca to try and find a place to defecate. I was very constipated at the time and treated myself to long sojourns well hidden in the Selva jungle.

Upon my return Don Luis scolded me, saying not only would the black tiger catch me with my trousers down but so would the ordinary tiger. Although the ordinary tiger is less aggressive than its black brother it will attack when hungry, and often is . . . like Wade.

I was also warned about the puma, the Latin American lion. Its colour ranges from red-fawn to pale-fawn; it is pacific, except when hungry, at bay or with cubs. The puma is not frightened of man or beast, unlike the tiger, who attacks out of fear; the puma is really a big cat, five to seven feet long, and fears nothing.

I was also admonished about the Puerco de Monte or wild boar, which is by far the most dangerous animal in

Latin America. It hunts in packs from fifteen to three hundred strong and has four fearsome very sharp teeth/tusks, two up and two down, of approximately two inches in length. It is, perhaps, fortunate that man can get wind of its smell before it reaches him.

Don Luis told me when wild boars are shot, the hunters cut off the feet and head and remove the intestines on the spot, before carrying them home. Back home the hunters cut them into strips and smoke them to preserve the meat. It is customary for the hunters to kill five or more at a time; depending, of course, on how many they can carry. Each wild boar weighs between fifty and sixty pounds, just the carcass alone. One hunter, Don Luis claimed, can carry up to one hundred and twenty pounds, of pig.

The local policeman, stationed at Pucro, came over for a chat with Don Luis. As the policeman sauntered off, his rifle across and behind his neck and shoulders, Don Luis said to me, 'I distrust that man, he has killed many human beings.'

That afternoon – 25th June – there was a very heavy obliterating rainstorm; literally cascades of warm rain, profoundly refreshing after the heavy towering pregnant weather we had been having for the past twenty-four hours.

Next day we regretfully left Don Luis. His last words to me after I had asked him when he was coming to Panama City where his wife was 'sewing' were, 'Who knows, you make me feel I want to come now.'

We left with three Kuna Indians, whose boss was a particularly patient and reliable person called Caesar. He was always giving me a hand in the many difficult places, while Wade excelled in towing me across swollen rivers as my bloody ankle was giving frightful pain in an unremitting sort of way.

We left Don Luis at seven a.m. and reached the Choco village of Capete at three p.m. Our baggage and rucksacks had spent considerable time underwater, for the previous day's heavy rain had caused the various rivers we forded to swell and flood.

The Choco jefe at Capete was charming, gave us a house to ourselves, ascended into by an impromptu ladder, for like all the others it was on high stilts. I noticed that the children had the biggest pot-bellies I had ever seen and I have seen some. I suppose the reason was worms, but no pigs were visible. Perhaps I would get a pot belly too?

As at the first Choco finca before the Panamanian frontier, we were surrounded by very young but very ripe bosoms. I tried, really I did, to stare fixedly at the roof which was just like any other Choco roof, not particularly interesting . . . intrinsically so to speak.

'Wade has severe diarrhoea, poor boy, hope he won't crack,' noted my diary.

At Capete there was a great deal of talk about the most recent murders which was rather boring really as they appear to be such a pitiless plethora. I am ashamed to admit I went to sleep staring, I hope, at the roof during this highly animated rendition of atrocities, doubtless very real; but somehow I could not be induced to take them seriously. I should have taken them seriously. They were serious people. Wade and I could very easily be the next victims if anyone chanced to see the very large number of dollar green-backs I had about my person. Throughout our traverse I never pretended to be poor. I was what I was – a millionaire, compared to everyone else in this vicinity, and I made not the slightest bones to hide the fact. It was as if I really wanted to be cut up, shot, bumped off and thrown to the vultures. I do not think Wade was quite in accord with this totally selfish disregard for danger. However, I had no intention of making concessions. If I was a millionaire, I would, I reasoned, paradoxically, get better service and I did, most of the time. I have always believed, figuratively speaking, in plenty of armour without protecting my flanks, as it were, in potentially dangerous situations or tight corners. Ironically, speed saves money . . . and gets results. *Pronto; presto.*

We left Capete early next day for Yape, which was another small Indian settlement. The walk only took three hours and it was easy going too. Wade had dysentery than which there is nothing more debilitating; I admired his courage, he never complained of his lot! Otherwise, jungle as before. I had no physical strength left, but I still had my will – and that said *Go on, Go on.*

On 28th June we reached Yaviza, the biggest little town in the province of Darien, at least three thousand souls of one kind or another.

No sooner had we fetched up at the police station, than we were literally pounced upon, vulpine-like. Everything, but everything, we possessed in our rucksacks was ripped out and strewn across the floor of the post, without the semblance of ceremony, civility or courtesy. Even my numerous dollar bills were laid out in piles across a desk for the encircling throng to view and see. Soon, very soon, the entire township knew by sinister but highly effective bush telegraphy, that there was a millionaire in their midst. Alas a live millionaire, a millionaire still alive.

Apparently a report had just come through from Paya, the first frontier post, that we had a haul of marijuana on, or about us. Even our hands were carefully, thoroughly smelt. The minimum sentence for peddling or smuggling marijuana is eight months in the cooler with no remission for good behaviour.

Why was my money so brazenly prostituted around, very, very slowly put into relevant denominations and finally very, very slowly counted? Did the police think I rolled marijuana into a hundred dollar green-back for a quick puff? 'No,' Wade interpreted, 'the police can't understand how an Englishman can have so many dollars on him when an Englishman's currency is sterling.' Wade explained that I had bought them quite legally at the Banco de Londres in Medellin, Colombia and gently chided them – as if talking to children – that the only currency valid in the Republic of Panama was the dollar. They seemed to have forgotten this. Strange for a Republic so dollar conscious.

It was stifling in the police station; it was like the Black Hole of Calcutta and potentially as dangerous in a different kind of way and I got very angry indeed with this cavalier treatment. I faced a plain clothes detective or pimp, wearing a horrid yellow shirt and operatic dark glasses, with my hands, or rather fists, on my hips, my nails digging deep into the palm of my right hand, the flesh almost bleeding to give this venal creature one helluva of a haymaker. I probably would have, if Wade had not looked at me in the nick of time with an eloquence that defies speech, as much as to say, 'For God's sake, watch out, they all have automatics and they are all loaded and they will all shoot without the remotest compunction.'

However, my blood was up. I ordered, in loud clear English, this plain clothes pimp to: 'Pick Them Up, to Pick Everything Up.' He looked shaken, but did nothing, until dear kind Wade set an example by getting down on his hands and knees and slowly start to sort out our possessions and put them back in their relevant places. I followed suit and soon all the police, to their credit, did the same. The sergeant, a tall man with kind eyes, suddenly shook hands with me, his grip was firm and friendly and spontaneous. I fully sympathised and fully realised the police had their duty to perform, but it was the way they performed it that bugged me. Wade was so alarmed by my vehemence that he went off to buy packets of cigarettes 'for Sebastian's temper' and even opened his tube of shaving cream to find his 150 dollars the police had overlooked.

The atmosphere then cooled and I asked the pimp with the horrid yellow shirt to take us to the 'best restaurant in this f . . . g place'. He did, and asked me for a dollar for this little service. It was only about a block, not a stone's throw away, and I nearly throttled him en route, keeping behind him, fingers and fist itching like the paw of a black tiger.

After lunch we returned to the police station and I asked if porters and guides could be rustled up to take us through The Gap to Santa Fé. Two coloured gentlemen were produced. Neither was very young and both appeared to me to have coldblooded, calculating venality creeping over their countenances. Both Wade and I agreed that if they were to guide us we would undoubtedly soon be lying dead somewhere in the jungle with our throats cut or stomachs gutted, our flesh being gradually eaten away by echelons of well-drilled soldier ants and our eyes picked out by the predatory vultures that wheeled overhead, ever on the alert.

Immediately and instinctively I swung on my heel, turned my back and made off to the neat house of an Australian missionary who was part of the New Tribes Mission to the Choco Indians. The two coloured gents followed hot foot, demanding money for their services, although they had rendered none. I bristled and fumed but paid up a token amount to rid myself of them.

At the mission I found a gigantic kindly Australian on top of the roof of his house, putting a piece of corrugated aluminium into place.

'Down in a minute,' he said.

I waited, helping a young New Zealander to hold the ladder. I told them both what had taken place at the police station and asked if they could find me three Choco Indians. They replied in the affirmative after long careful consideration.

Wade and I dined with Dave Scoble, the Australian, and I told an unparliamentary joke by mistake and Dave's wife left the table for a while. Dave, a very broad-minded man, gave me a hint of a twinkle. I liked him immensely. Wade and I learnt quite a lot about the Chocos from these two magnificent men.

The unchristianised Chocos employ witchcraft. They

have diviners who prescribe what herb or vine will cure which malady, and provide antidotes for poisoning. Healing is done by blowing on a witchdoctor's stick, and singing to the deities who need propitiating, who also have a cider-like brew called *chicha* made for them. But this all stops when the Chocos accept Christianity and they burn their sticks – something on the lines of the vagabond Jews and exorcists who burnt their books for St. Paul at Ephesus.

The missionaries, most hospitably, gave us beds for the night in a clean, well-built little one-roomed bungalow.

While Wade remained deep in conversation with Dave, I went to bed and sleep, only to be awakened by the loudest whiplash of thunder I have ever heard in my life. It was just one single whiplash, seemingly dead overhead and like an explosion.

Not long afterwards Wade came into the bungalow and settled himself on a trestle camp bed. In the dark he confided to me, 'Sebastian, I have never been so frightened in my life.' He was referring to the police interview.

'Don't worry,' I replied as compassionately as I could, 'we still have a sporting chance of getting through.' (A damn silly thing to say.)

But this did not alleviate or mitigate Wade's fears; fears well founded apropos my money and all the township knowing about it, plus those frightening guides they offered us.

'Aren't you frightened?' he persisted.

'Yes, of course, but I am sure a good night's sleep does wonders. You'll feel completely differently in the morning light, you'll feel a completely different man; believe me, Wade.

'I guess that's how the British won the War,' Wade said in all sincerity.

Tears rolled down my face in the darkness. I was intensely proud of my country, although too young to fight for it. Crying is alien to my nature, but cry I did. I was grateful to the darkness that hid my tears from Wade, on the other side of the room.

Wade was, indeed, back to his indomitable, resilient self at first light, for, as he afterwards wrote in his journal:

> Come the beauty of the morning, the light is so welcome after the darkness. The darkness makes every scare and fright that much worse and the darkness plays tricks with your mind. Nevertheless, the Big Missionary is really worried about us.

The Big Missionary was, indeed, worried not only for our lives, but for our salvation. He provided a twelve bore and .22 rook rifle for the former and two Bibles for the latter. He also provided us with a big breakfast, and afterwards, as we thanked him, I took the opportunity to fall down the steps, three steps, and badly bruised and sprained my right ankle. How stupid could I be? Especially as I refused a support Band-Aid the New Zealander had kindly offered, thinking it would do no good, mad fool that I was.

I could foresee that I was in for a nightmare journey to Sante Fé. How in the hell was I going to make it? Santa Fé was a large cantonment where North American construction engineers were working on building the long talked about Pan-American Highway. Our lives depended on speed through the jungle, especially initially away from Yaviza, where as I mentioned before the entire township must have got wind that an English millionaire had fallen into their heinous hands. And then there was the distinct possibility that the two venal coloured gents might track us down, by some foul means and kill us. There was no doubt that we were in a tight corner, about as tight as they come.

On disappearing into the jungle we almost immediately happened upon a poor starving skeletal little mongrel. It was crying piteously having been abandoned by its cruel and unfeeling master. Covered in sores, it alternately scratched and cried. It attached itself to us, crying all the time. I wanted to carry it, but carry it where for God's sake? I love dogs and tried to block my ears. Its plight pained me so. In front of my men I christened it Perdido, hoping the word meant The Lost One. Perdido it was called from then on, until its plaintive bleats faded forever as it fell back further and further behind us. Its frail legs could not climb the long, very slippery, very rocky water course we followed, all that day. It was only afterwards that it struck Wade and me that the dog was a plant to indicate our direction to would-be followers. The more we thought about this, the more we were convinced. Why else did our three Chocos insist on following this absolutely unnecessary slippery and rocky water course which to me was akin to martyrdom rather than plunge direct through the bush? Clearly the Chocos wanted to shuck off any and all pursuers, with evil intent, by obliterating our line of march. Very wise.

I went very badly and very slowly over these high, treacherous rock falls over which streams lapped and serpentined, terrified that I would fall, which I did on numerous occasions, and fracture a leg, which I did not. This contingency would spell curtains for me. I knew all about leg fractures for at the age of sixteen I had broken my left thigh rather badly in three places while playing a three-a-side game of scratch rugger. Initially it was thought that I would never walk again without a calliper or crutches; and even after the subsequent operation it was thought my left leg might be much shortened. In a word I would be a cripple. But the military surgeon who operated did a splendid job, leaving it only one and a half centimetres short. Because my legs were not of equal length I was failed for the Army. Today, the broken leg is stronger, but over rough rocky terrain it definitely unbalances and slows me; and now in addition I had two badly sprained ankles, so my position was unenviable, to put it mildly.

We camped that night beside a rocky rock-garden-like stream. Wade and the three Chocos slept dormitory fashion, line abreast under a long green piece of allegedly waterproof sheeting, hoisted on poles cut from the all surrounding selva with Heath Robinson improvisation. Only Wade and I had mosquito nets. I cocooned myself nearby in my 'waterproof' hammock-mosquito net combination. I could only just get my Li-Lo inside. Then the rains came, and how they came. Undoubtedly the poor little dog did not survive the night. All of us were totally inundated, none of us slept. Rain poured through my waterproof hammock as if the roof had not existed. A river very soon flowed beneath my Li-Lo which was on the ground. I reached for my portfolio in the darkness, lightened only by fireflies, and a torch that wouldn't work. I deflated the Li-Lo, doubled it up and placed it over my stomach and thighs. Between my stomach and thighs I hugged my portfolio containing diaries, passport and money (in that order of preference). I hugged it all night in one position, without daring to turn over or move in case I disturbed my very large embryonic baby – while the rain cascaded and a river flowed and swirled underneath and around my body literally. Sleep was out of the question. I tried to concentrate all my thoughts on keeping my precious portfolio dry. Everything I possessed was inside, everything of value; intrinsic and sentimental. Around doom watch – about two o'clock – my thoughts involuntarily strayed back to a horror story that missionary Dave Scoble had told. A true horror story of how some Colombians had tied a Choco husband and wife to a tree and cut off the husband's penis and shoved it down his wife's throat before killing them both.

At eight twenty a.m. after lighting a fire which was difficult after the deluge and cooking up porridge and rice, we decamped and staggered off into the Monte, bleary-eyed, 'drawn' and distraught. Ironically, we went well, although the going was arduous and much cutting with machetes had to be done to open up the way ahead. While one or other of the Chocos did the 'cutting' we hung around pestered by mosquitos. I was only conscious of my ankles; for me mosquitos did not exist, not even the constant slappings of my party as the mosquitos bit.

That night we camped again in the jungle, careful this time not to pitch on sloping ground. We camped early at three p.m. We were all dog tired and pillaged our food store mercilessly, canned meat, canned cocktail sausages (a great favourite of mine), canned sardines, rice and biscuits. We ate well and slept well.

Next day, 1st July, was Dominion Day, Wade reminded me. One of the Chocos shot a macaw – which delighted all except me who loathes game birds in general, chickens in particular. Much tedious cutting, although these constant halts were balm for my ankles, relieving the pressure.

Wade's clothes, I noted, were visibly rotting on his body, as were mine, because of mildew and fungus mould. That night I estimated conservatively that I had covered over nine thousand kilometres, although mere distance had now become purely academic. I registered no excitement, no sense of achievement. I just jotted it down. Bathos if anything.

Second of July, more exacting cutting. Wade and I were plagued by aching gums: 'Lack of vitamin C,' said 'Doctor' Davis.

Hell, I thought, I suppose I shall have more molars out if this aching persists.

'Doctor' Wade Davis added that lack of vital Vitamin C can be the harbinger of scurvy. For some zany reason this thought tickled me pink: I wanted to go down with scurvy in a masochistic kind of way; it seemed to suit our historical and topographical ambience. It seemed right and proper as we neared the Spanish Main. Names like Nombre de Dios (still extant), that Peak in Darien,

El Draque, ('Fran' Drake as he always signed himself) haunted me . . . and the bullion of course.

While these dotty thoughts tumbled through my mind, I suddenly realised we had got lost. The Chocos' bump for locality had failed. With no compass, 'mislaid' in mysterious circumstances in Paya at the first frontier post, we had no guide line. Occasionally an aeroplane came over, glimpsed fleetingly through small pockets of blue and azure strato-cumulus high above the tree tops of our green hell.

Lost, we endeavoured, in pairs, to follow the 'planes' tenuous trajectories. For all I knew they might be travelling to Tahiti or Timbuktu. Our course did not depend on vision, but on the throb of the aircraft's motors, the kind of throb that gives some indication of the plane's size, number of engines and thus its direction and range. Lost. We again camped in jungle beside a stream. The Chocos solemnly forecast *sotto voce*, 'No Rain Tonight. Full Moon. Change of Moon'. Of course it rained like hell. All non-precious possessions swamped – routine as before – deflate Li-Lo, double it up over stomach and thighs and place fortfolio between body and Li-Lo and keep still. Got away with it except for another sleepless night. Hell! You just have to lie there and take it; and 'think of England'.

Fourth of July, American Independence Day. Hummed the Star Spangled Banner in homage and salute to that great nation, while the Chocos proclaimed, categorically, that we would reach Santa Fé today. Lost they were, but I did not know they were out of their minds too.

Dangerously short of food and bullets, but sufficient for game. Wandering around in apparent circles was, indeed, demoralising (I mean, you don't seem to get anywhere do you?).

Suddenly there was a staccato shout ahead. One of my scouting Chocos had made a landfall in the form of a seemingly abandoned finca or ranchito. Another shout, a rusty old bin a quarter full of beautiful bananas found.

Signs of civilisation . . . perhaps. Again the Chocos proclaimed that we would reach Santa Fé. This time in two hours. Next day we were up early after a very good night's rest. God we needed it. Excited. Very soon we picked up a wide, almost motorable dirt road. The projected Pan-American Highway? The Highway to Santa Fé? We were virtually through The Gap. Entirely fortuitously too. Everyone except myself, who was in very considerable pain from ankles, was excited and expectant. I was not.

After exactly two hours along the Highway-to-the-Sun, we encountered a party of men marching, slowly and deliberately, Indian file, in the opposite direction, the direction from which we had come. I noted that they were all armed. I was not surprised. One of the Chocos asked if Santa Fé was close.

'Santa Fé,' they replied in a sullen surly way, 'is at least a week if not two, away.' They passed on.

We practically passed out. Morale at lowest ebb, well below zero. Without the least false piety I uttered involuntarily, 'God works in mysterious ways.' This remark, for some reason, struck Wade forcibly – later I was to repeat it in similar circumstances.

Without retracing our steps, demoralising enough, we endeavoured to fight and fight our way to freedom. To find the freedom of the open road. To cut and cut and cut our way out of this all encompassing, all embracing, claustrophobic, catastrophic, clammy hell. To try and find the unfindable survey stakes that marked and pegged out *La Linea* – the line, the over-grown line of the projected artery that will one day close – The Gap. To carry on until we dropped . . . until we dropped again and again. . . .

I was very proud of my party; they went to work with an unquenchable, undying spirit and will. It was their finest hour. I shall always remember it – remember it with pride.

Suddenly out front there was a terrific war whoop

from Wade. 'Sebastian, Sebastian, Sebastian, we are through . . . we are through . . . through the Darien Gap; here's the road! The road!'

Stunned, I simply did not register until I broke out of the foliage and found myself standing on a wide stretch of dirt, uneven unmotorable road that could only lead to Santa Fé. How far we did not know but did that matter now? Photographs were taken; I could scarcely stand as I held Dave Scoble's rook rifle, naked to the waist. The weight of that very light .22 was practically unbearable, so thin and lax were my arms. They might have been made of matchsticks, they looked like matchsticks and perhaps they were matchsticks.

Some two hundred yards down The Road we found a crystalline, limpid, pellucid creek, an idyllic spot to camp, except for the mosquitos. The last of the rice was consumed on banana leaves with a wild and plump turkey shot that day. We were all very hungry, but I still eschewed game. Poor Wade was so ravenous he ate the bones of the bird – while I gobbled up the last grain of rice, carefully 'portioned' (horrid word) out on big long banana leaves. The same big long banana leaves the Chocos slept on.

Two days later we marched into Santa Fé. It was July 7th.

At Santa Fé our remarkably courageous, redoubtable, stalwart Chocos departed for Yaviza by river, a journey of some nine hours.

Wade and I spent three days in the most hospitable hands of Morrison & Knudsen, a North American construction company, operating in thirty-eight different countries around the globe. We spent three restful days licking our many wounds, regaining a little physical strength, re-charging our mental batteries.

These really wonderful people, both North American and Panamanian, gave us the run of a well appointed adjoining double-room and as much food as we could guzzle in the dining room – all gratis – and by God how we guzzled! especially Wade who was more ravenous, the more he ate. Food kept him good. Although highly intelligent, all his drive emanated from the body, in a word the physical. Without plenty of food he was very unhappy, but by the end he, like me, was marching on the will.

These marvellous people mothered and smothered us with kindness. My ankles were treated by the Cantonment doctor with a shot of penicillin in the rump plus a bottle of penicillin tablets for free.

Ironically, I managed quite successfully to get bitten by a small 'rogue' scorpion which crept up on me in my bedroom at night. The ensuing pain on the tip of my longest finger on my left hand really was excruciating and remained so for far too long. 'A big scorpion's bite,' said Wade, 'is lethal.' True or not I was not prepared to put his statement to the test. Penicillin was of no avail; nothing mitigated the pain. Curiously enough my finger did none of the things that I expected of it; it did not swell up; it did not become discoloured; it just hurt . . . it hurt like hell. It did not even drop off or anything vaguely interesting like that.

There is an airstrip at Santa Fé and a small aeroplane takes forty-five minutes to fly over the intervening 120 kilometres to the capital, in a straight line. There is also the river on whose waters the heavy construction equipment and the bulldozers are brought to Santa Fé, otherwise Santa Fé is entirely isolated from the world outside.

Three Negroes, not attached to Morrison & Knudsen, were conscripted to guide and carry for us. I liked the look of all of them from the start. They and Wade were given a ride in the back of a truck from Santa Fé as far as Kilometre 13, while I walked. My ankles felt very, very, very much better and I skimmed along the dirt track road like a hovercraft; with the same sort of motion, that is. A great sense of freedom possessed me, coupled with the thought that from now it would be a cake walk to Panama City. How wrong I was.

Nevertheless, I covered the thirteen kilometres in just over two hours, highly delighted that at last I had got my old rhythm back. The surface of the road was flat, soft and even, making walking a real joy. I felt emancipated, a disenfranchised slave ridden of his ball and chain. Even Wade was amazed that I caught up my party so soon.

'We expected you around noon,' he said, 'and it is only ten-thirty.'

While marching, a North American driving a truck pulled up beside me and leant out of the window. 'Watch out,' he solemnly adjured, straight-faced, 'I have just seen a big black panther cross the road and he is heading in your direction.' I laughed uproariously and he drove on.

The road beyond Kilometre 13 is not motorable although Morrison & Knudsen have bulldozed it as far as Kilometre 35.

As soon as I arrived at Kilometre 13 we started. Within three hours one of the Negroes went lame; he had pulled a tendon in his right leg – badly. There was nothing for it but to find shelter and rest him.

Fortunately we had only just passed an un-manned palm thatched Campamento refuge for men working on the highway. With two, opposite, lines of slatted beds in rows, dormitory fashion, and a cooking appendage, we had nothing to mope about except our fervent desire to push on at all costs. Frankly, it was maddening to be held up, hell bent as we were.

The injured one was made comfortable and lay supine, inert, seemingly dead; perhaps he was, he didn't say.

There was some cause for concern: I had an awkward and frustrating situation on my hands, but I was used to it. My first thought was to send all our guides back to Santa Fé, lock, stock and barrel and muddle through with Wade, alone. There was only about seventy odd kilometres of jungle from Kilometre 35 onwards and then the track emerged onto a hard, beaten earth shingled road; which in its turn merged into asphalt. At least that was what I had been told. The asphalt was then said to lead direct to Panama City.

Wade did not fancy the idea. He had a healthy respect for the jungle which I hadn't. I argued that when we had cut and pruned everything down to the bare necessities of life, we could rush it now that my ankles were much improved. He still did not fancy it and I didn't really blame him, especially as neither of us knew in what condition the seventy kilometre trail was likely to be at the height of the rains. And, of course, neither of us knew the way.

I then made up my mind to take one Negro with me and complete the job. I picked on the oldest and the most reliable looking. His name was Don Hortensio and he was forty, but looked older. He had big white mule-like teeth with a big set mule-like white smile. His eyes were set wide apart, slightly protruding and slightly bovine. He said he was honest: he was.

I sustained a restless night as poor Wade was constantly getting up from his bed. A naked white figure squatting in the moonlight, he seemed to squat and squit all night through. My heart bled for him. Was it dysentery or diarrhoea? I trusted it was not the former; although the latter is equally debilitating.

Come the morning he very unselfishly escorted the two remaining Negroes back to Santa Fé. As we said goodbye, his face looked drained but his handshake was firm. It was very sad to see him go, he had been my right arm for nearly a month. He had been out in all weathers, he had never given up, he was not that sort. All he worried about was, 'Have I really been through The Gap, Sebastian?'

'Yes, Wade, you have been through The Gap.'

'Are you sure?' he reiterated.

'Yes, Wade, I am sure; remember you were told so by the Construction Engineers. From now on it's all downhill, free wheeling,' I said. He looked relieved – rejuvenated. Wade Davis's last words to me were, 'What an adventure crossing the Darien Gap without maps or compass and in the rainy season too. The greatest adventure of my life.'

Shouldering his pack, head held high, he left. He was a great credit to his country. I hope we meet again one day, somewhere, sometime, soon. If all men had his courage, character and humanity, the world, our world, would be greatly enriched.

(From Santa Fé, Wade flew to Panama City, went to the British Embassy and left me a letter and his film and then flew back to Colombia.)

After he left, Don Hortensio and I walked up to Kilometre 35, the furthest point of the road, before disappearing once more into the bush. It started to rain heavily as we picked our way along a muddy track; the mud became slippery and I again turned an ankle, the right one. This slowed us. That night we slept at a Campamento of Panamanians. They fed us and bedded us, gratis. They were charming and did everything for our comfort.

As I have said, this stretch of jungle was about seventy kilometres; only seventy kilometres, but we took five days to get through.

I was hobbled by my damned ankle and Don Hortensio managed to get us lost on several occasions for *La Linea,* The Line, was overgrown in numerous places. Heavy rain further slowed our advance. We had to tread delicately like Agag across impromptu bridges made of long, narrow hewn trunks precariously balanced over swollen rivers. This was a dangerous undertaking as our basketball boots were as slippery as the impromptu bridges. Neither of us were acrobats, but we were then; we had to be.

Wild boar were prevalent in this region. We were constantly stopping to take a sharp lookout. Don Hortensio stiffened and sniffed like a pointer. He told me the wild boars surround one and when they do that one must shin up the nearest tree fast. If a tree is unavailable strike a match, snap a lighter or light a cigarette. For some instinctive reason the most dangerous animal in Latin America cannot bear the smell of fire and bolts as fast as it can. Don Hortensio kept on reiterating that they were especially dangerous in this particular neck of the woods. I never saw any or even smelt them. I felt let down. Paradoxically, I would have liked a brief encounter, but it was not to be, even though I took the elementary precaution of undoing the strap of my rucksack that circumnavigated my middle in readiness for instant action, on a signal from Don Hortensio. None of the trees looked scaleable and my matches and lighter were carefully cloistered in the depths of my sack.

After five long days, we emerged onto the road that led to Panama City. We were not excited, we had been through too much to register emotion; one way or another.

At the little town of Chepo nearly sixty kilometres south of the Capital, Don Hortensio could go no further. His whole being pained him. Boarded a bus for the city.

I walked into Panama City alone. Alone, once more.

The finale belongs to a dog – my poodle. My mother wrote:

> About three weeks ago, each evening for about a week she became very restless, wouldn't lie down, looked at the door, the window etc. for two or three hours at a time. Suddenly the day before your message came that you had arrived she settled down peacefully as usual. We are convinced that she knew you were in danger and difficulties and then knew you were safe.

CHAPTER TWELVE

PANAMA CANAL

Well, I had made it. I'd traversed the continent of South America on foot and crossed the Darien Gap. The end was hazardous, ghastly, a gruelling nightmare where Death stalked. Only willpower kept me going. Underweight by about five stone, two sprained ankles, both swollen and discoloured, my feet and ankles covered with gore, blood and bites, a mass of suppurating sores, stung by a hornet on the neck, bitten by a scorpion, nipped by a vampire bat, ticks under the skin, I looked in the mirror and saw what days in the jungle could do.

I beheld my shrivelled, emaciated body, spotted chicken-pox red with insect bites. I knew I needed to pick off all the ticks and leeches that the dirt hid. I looked down at my feet, scaly, infected, skin just peeling off from lack of vitamins and foot rot. It hurt to try on a size fourteen shirt that someone gave me charitably and to find it fitted after years of size sixteen. But worst of all is to look in someone's face and see: 'My God, we have to help this kid', and you wondered who they were talking about and you looked at them from your rotting clothes, stiff, dismal grey from days of sweat and mud. Nobody could understand why I had come all that way through the jungle. Who knows . . . but I believed in God.

A most hospitable couple called Vaughan, (he is our British Airways representative in Panama City), let me stay with them in their apartment on the seventeenth floor of a high rise block. From the window I could look down on a mini plot of land of less than a quarter of an acre, hardly room for a dog to cock its leg on, which I was assured was to be sold for one million dollars. Inflation seemed to be galloping here, all right. I thought

I'd better not stay long but had to decide whether to return to England to recuperate or whether to continue my walk up through North America to Alaska. Or should I walk across to Washington?

But could I go on? I wanted to go on, to accomplish the longest walk in the world and indeed I knew I could. My legs would keep going, my brain would accept it but what about the rest of me? They told me that I was in bad shape and that if I continued I would become a wizened old crock, toothless, bald, emaciated, permanently broken in health. All my teeth would fall out and maybe my liver would pack up. Did I want to live the rest of my life on soup?

Evidently I had lost too many vitamins, too many chemicals to be able to replace them by a few injections. The whole chemical balance of my body was temporarily upset.

The problem was, how long would it take me to get fit and could I afford to sit around in this incredibly expensive place waiting? Return to England to recuperate, they said, and maybe for once they were right. The U.S. would of course be full of vitamins but where would I get them in sufficient quantities in Costa Rica, in Guatemala or in the Mexican Desert? Had I contracted the dreaded Chaga disease perhaps on my journey? This was evidently something peculiar to South America and said to be carried by the armadillo. The prospect of imminent relapsing fever setting in on top of everything else made me feel that maybe a return to England would be a good idea after all.

First, however, I walked to the Panama Canal and marched across it so that I had indeed covered the continent of South America in every respect and had clearly set foot in North America too, to prove it. I'd made it, despite all those Cassandras who had cried impossible, despite all those who had feared that I would be murdered, run over or hit by typhoid. As I made this last lap, I thought back over all that had happened to me since

Tierra del Fuego and decided that the Peruvian Desert had been the worst section of all: that burning asphalt, so hard on the feet. The Gap had only taken about a month, which had been less than I had expected: of course, we had zig-zagged about so much, we must have covered about one and a half times the actual straight distance across.

Wade had left a note for me with the film and it formed a fitting epilogue to our successful traverse:

> The luxuries of jungle life: the smoke of the fire that chases away the bugs, a banana almost gone bad sitting in a bin, a thatch hut found in the wood, a rainless night, a fresh kill, whatever it may be, water deep enough to bathe in, a hint of solid shit, a full night's sleep, a lemon tree found in the jungle . . .

It had been a good walk. But should I have done it the other way round, beginning with the hot jungle and progressing slowly towards the Antarctic cool?

Ideally I would like in the future to do it all over again, but next time downhill all the way from Alaska to Tierra del Fuego.

Niki Lauda and the Grand Prix Gladiators

RONNIE MUTCH

Winner of the Formula 1 World Motor Racing Championship in 1975, Niki Lauda was poised to repeat his triumph the following year when tragedy struck. The world was stunned by news of his near-fatal crash at the Nurburgring circuit – it seemed this great driver's career was finished for ever. Yet in a death-defying show of courage and tenacity, Niki Lauda was back on the track within six weeks, powering his way to the top.

Here at last is the full and incredible story behind the great gladiator's return!

0 7221 6287 1 Biography

Margaret Powell Down Under

MARGARET POWELL

'Margaret,' said one of Margaret Powell's new Australian friends. 'You have been paid the greatest compliment a woman could be paid in this country. We have accepted you as a man.'

That, for Margaret Powell, just about summed up Australia. In the land of wide-open spaces, koalas and beer, she soon found that being a woman – and a Pommie woman at that – was a decided disadvantage!

Undaunted, however, Margaret sets out to recount in her own inimitable style her adventures Down Under. With tremendous gusto – and sometimes with tongue firmly in cheek – she tackles Australia on its own terms. And the result is a provoking, often hilarious piece of wit and wisdom that does more than justice to one of our most irrepressible ladies.

'Any Britons still thinking of making the Great Trek from here to there might do worse than read along with Mrs. Powell' –*Sunday Telegraph*

0 7221 0421 9 Autobiography/Travel 95p

Rudolph Valentino

ALEXANDER WALKER

Rudolph Valentino is one of the most enigmatic personalities that the movie industry has ever projected. His short career, lasting barely seven years, induced a state of sexual frenzy among his female fans, and his name has become virtually a synonym for tireless ardour in the pursuit and capture of women. Yet, in reality, Valentino was attracted only to women who were stronger-willed than himself, and, indeed, he has been regularly alleged to have been homosexual. The popular memory of him as an impulsive and barbaric 'sheik' has likewise obscured his talents as an actor whose artistry was of uncommon range and sensitivity.

Alexander Walker has seen all Valentino's films, talked to those who knew him, and researched unpublished material to gain insight into this controversial figure. The result is a detailed, evocative study which considers Valentino's own sexuality, amorous reputation and screen technique – a brilliant examination of the screen's most legendary lover.

'Alexander Walker has done an expert job, to emerge with a succint, balanced and highly readable record of the career and appreciation of Valentino's undeniable talent' –*The Times*

'Excellent' –*Evening Standard*

0 7221 8868 4 Biography 95p